The Publican's Handbook

The Publican Newspaper

THE LEADING WEEKLY TITLE FOR THE PUB TRADE

YOUR CHANCE TO RECEIVE FREE COPIES!

The Publican Newspaper is written for professionals working in, or entering the licensed trade. Regular features include:

- The latest industry news
- Industry law update
- Property & recruitment pages
- New brands coverage
- Special reports
- City & management news

In addition to *The Publican Newspaper*, you will also receive the following titles absolutely FREE:

Pub Food Magazine

Community Pub Magazine

Town & City Pub Magazine

Rural & Village Pub Magazine

WITH ALL OF THESE TITLES IN ONE PACKAGE, HOW CAN YOU AFFORD TO MISS OUT!

To obtain your copy of *The Publican* call Reader Services on
0181 424 2467

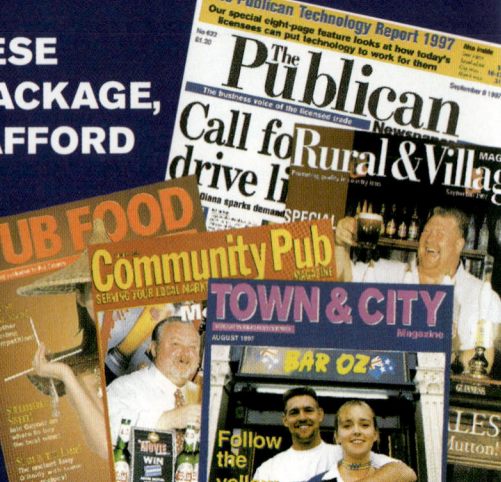

The Publican's Handbook

**Consultant Editor:
Ted Bruning**

KOGAN PAGE

in association with
The Publican
Newspaper

The rules and regulations governing business practice in public houses and other associated topics covered in this book, including national and international legislation are subject to change. Kogan Page Limited and the editors cannot assume legal responsibility for the accuracy of any particular statement in this work. No responsibility for loss or damage occasioned to any person acting or refraining from action as a result of the material in this publication can be accepted by the editor or publishers.

Published in 1997

Apart from any fair dealing for the purposes of research or private study, or criticism or review, as permitted under the Copyright, Designs and patents Act, 1988, this publication may only be reproduced, stored or transmitted, in any form, or by any means, with the prior permission in writing of the publishers, or in the case or reprographic reproduction in accordance with the terms of licences issued by the Copyright Licensing Agency. Enquiries concerning reproduction outside those terms should be sent to the publishers at the undermentioned address:

Kogan Page Ltd
120 Pentonville Road
London N1 9JN
kpinfo@kogan-page.co.uk

© Kogan Page 1997

British Library Cataloguing in Publication Data

ISBN 0 7491 2296 3

Typeset by BookEns Ltd, Royston, Herts.
Printed and bound in Great Britain by The Thanet Press Ltd.

WE WOULD LIKE TO THANK ALL OUR ADVERTISERS AND IN PARTICULAR OUR SPONSORS:

90% OF MALES ARE HAPPILY MARRIED.

TO ELEVEN MEN.

NO ORDINARY LAGER — CARLING F.A. PREMIERSHIP — NO ORDINARY LEAGUE

CONTENTS

Foreword — ix

Introduction — xi
Ted Bruning

List of Contributors — xiii

1 Choosing your Pub — 1
Barry Gillham

2 Bar Design and Merchandising — 25
Paul Cooper

3 Training for Licensees — 60
Andrew Palmer

4 Hiring and Firing — 76
Christine Bradley

5 Publicising your Pub — 91
Danny Blyth

6 Beer and Cider — 101
Ted Bruning

7 Wines and Spirits — 133
Ted Bruning

8 Catering — 155
Tony O'Reilly

Contents

9   Stock and Financial Control   182
Paul Adams

10 Maximising Machine Income   189
Ian Chuter

11 Security in Licensed Outlets   198
Brian Taylor

12 Fire Safety   211
Glen Gorman

13 The Family Trade   219
Ted Bruning

14 Adding Value   229
Paul Cooper

15 Television, Music, Sports and Entertainment   245
Paul Cooper

Health and Safety Notes   48, 87, 99, 121, 170, 227, 242
Teresa Miller

Legal Notes   22, 52, 90, 99, 128, 154,
Tony Lyons   181, 188, 197, 209, 227, 242

Appendix I Licensing Justices   259

Appendix II Disability Discrimination   261

Appendix III Useful Phone Numbers & Addresses   263

Appendix IV Checklist of Essential Contacts   266

Index   267

Index of Advertisers   274

FOREWORD

Running a pub is still seen by many people as their dream job. Although it can be a rewarding experience, many enter the trade as naive dreamers who find that the reality of being unprepared can be a financial and emotional nightmare. Being a publican is, in fact, extremely hard work and requires total dedication and commitment, as well as being prepared to work a 70-hour week.

As with any investment, those who wish to enter the pub trade should research the market thoroughly. There is finance to raise, stock to purchase, laws to meet and staff to train. And in an ever-competitive world, today's publican also has to be a master in marketing.

Having been editor of *The Publican Newspaper* since September 1996, and having worked on the title for the three years before that, I have heard hundreds of stories - good and bad. I also know a lot about the trials and tribulations of the hospitality industry, having grown up in a pub and as someone who ran their own restaurant.

But I don't want to put people off. This is a vibrant industry and one which, if handled correctly, can be a lot of fun.

The Publican's Handbook is an essential tool for anyone who wants to own or manage a pub. It covers everything from licensing law to promotions, and stock control to insurance. And just in case you come unstuck, there is a list of useful addresses too. It is not a manual, and reading it will not guarantee your success. But it will arm you with some sound practical advice and ideas to help you in your venture.

So, to sum up, my advice is if you want to be a licensee, be prepared first. That way you should be able to reap the rewards of working in this exciting marketplace, and ensure you are financially successful too.

Lorna Harrison
Editor, *The Publican Newspaper*

Sarina

SaarGummi

Sarina Rubber Floor Covering, Environmentally from SaarGummi: Versatile, Acceptable and Simply Beautiful.

rapid reply 61

JAYMART RUBBER & PLASTICS LTD
Woodlands Trading Estate, Eden Vale Road, WESTBURY, Wilts BA13 3QS
Tel: 0373-864926 Telex: 449776 JBUNNY G Fax: 0985 217417

JAYMART

INTRODUCTION

Ted Bruning

The pub trade has always been a lot more complicated than people imagined. Even in those far-off days when police officers and servicemen could dream of retiring to a pub with roses round the door, there were all the complications of licensing law and book-keeping to deal with, as well as less technical but equally daunting problems such as under-age drinking and brewery relations.

But the changes of the last 15-20 years have made the whole business even more complicated than that. The virtual collapse of the traditional short-term low-rent tied-on-everything brewery tenancy has left publicans with a bewildering array of long leases, discount agreements, quasi-franchises and heaven knows what else to cope with!

The market-place, too, is much harder than it was. Country pubs and town tenancies alike are going bust at an alarming rate, and no publican can simply assume that when he opens his door there'll be customers waiting to come in. They have to be found and fought for.

There's been an amazing explosion in the range of beers licensees need to know about, too. Few publicans are entirely tied, and even those who are have a much wider range of tied products to choose from than their predecessors. Food service, increasingly an essential contributor to turnover, brings its own complications: you don't just have to be able to cook, you also have to be able to operate within one of the most regulated business environments on the planet.

And then there's crime. From drug-dealing to extortion, today's pubs are a magnet for criminals. They're places where people can meet and do business in relative anonymity, and where cash is available. Both facts attract criminals like moths to a candle.

This book does not, could not, answer every day-to-day query a publican might have arising from these and other issues, although I hope it can answer most of them. It has a more important function: to let the self-employed publican share the experience of people who have been involved

Introduction

in the licensed trade – some of them as hands-on doers, others as intimate observers – for many years, and to help him focus on the issues that really matter in establishing a profitable and enjoyable business.

In journalism we have a precept that, while we can't be expected to know all the right answers, we should be expected to ask all the right questions. I hope this book helps you to ask all the right questions.

LIST OF CONTRIBUTORS

Paul Adams is a chartered accountant of 25 years' standing. His first experience in the leisure industry was with Ladbrokes in their casino division. Having moved to Ladbrokes head office he was in charge of corporate planning and involved in projects such as the expansion of the chain of Hilton Hotels.

In 1984 he joined David Bruce as Financial Director of the Firkin pubs. His first taste of the pub business – within a week of joining – was the bank's bouncing the VAT cheque. Once the finances were sorted out he played a major part in expanding the chain to 11 pubs, taking responsibility for all operational matters in the pubs.

When the Firkins were sold in 1988 he converted the old buffet at Kew Gardens Station to create the Pig and Parrot – still a highly successful pub now trading as a Firkin.

Having been involved with a further three pubs with David Bruce, he decided to purchase a third share of the Wychwood Brewery in 1992 with the specific intention of starting a pub chain. In November 1992 the first Hobgoblin opened in Staines and since then the chain has grown to 27 pubs spread throughout the south of England.

Danny Blyth is a journalist and publicist specialising in the licensed retail, leisure and travel industries. He regularly contributes to trade publications such as the *Licensee & Morning Advertiser*, *The Publican Newspaper* and has his own column in *Free House*. He also contributes regular features to in-house publications of companies such as Inntrepreneur, Whitbread and Bass Leisure.

List of Contributors

Danny also presents leisure features on London News radio and is regularly published in a range of other publications from *Fish Restaurant International* to *Travel Trade Gazette Europa* and *Garden Answers*.

In addition he has acted as a publicity consultant on specific campaigns and product launches to firms like Allied Domecq, Scottish Courage and Hop Back Brewery. He has recently published his own guide-book to outside bar and function business, sponsored by Wadworth 6X.

Christine Bradley a partner with Pannone & Partners since 1985 specialises in employment law (all aspects, contentious and non-contentious). Christine heads the Employment Unit which regularly presents work-shops and seminars designed to provide a practical approach to current employment law problems.

The range of clients for whom Christine acts is broad, from the very large Plcs with nationally recognisable names down to the smaller high street or corner shop type business.

Ted Bruning is a freelance journalist who worked for seven years on the *Morning Advertiser* – then the licensed trade's daily newspaper – before becoming a contributing feature-writer for *Brewers' Guardian* and *Caterer & Hotelkeeper*. He is also deputy editor of the Campaign for Real Ale's monthly newspaper, *What's Brewing*. Books include *Historic English Inns*, the CAMRA *Guide to Real Cider*, and *Historic Inns of London*.

Ian Chuter is Rank Leisure Machine Services' National Accounts Director, responsible for key accounts including national retailers, regional brewers, motor-way service stations and licensed betting offices. With more than 16 years experience in the amusement machine industry, part of his brief is to develop existing business, as well as exploring opportunities for potential new business in what is a dynamic sector of the leisure industry. A company within the Rank Organisation Plc, Rank Leisure Machine Services is one of the UK's leading operators of amusement machines and electronic leisure products.

List of Contributors

Paul Cooper commenced his career in the catering industry working part-time in a pub for Unicorn Inns plc. He worked his way up through the company and spent two-and-a-half years as Assistant to the Operations Director. After graduating from Sheffield Hallam University, he held the position of Commercial Development Manager at Unicorn Inns. During his time with Unicorn Inns he was responsible for developing their two highly successful retail brands (Newt and Cucumber and Wig and Pen) and launching thirteen units. He also developed a comprehensive training and development programme, moving the company towards achieving Investors In People accreditation.

Unicorn Inns was bought by Morland's in 1995, and Paul took up a position with Wolverhampton & Dudley Breweries, as Specialist Retail Brand Manager.

He is now a consultant to the Licensed Retail Industry. He works with both independent retailers and brewers, offering services in training, marketing, food development, brand development, purchasing, trouble shooting, desk top publishing and new unit openings.

Barry Gillham, FRICS FSVA PPAVLP ACIArb, joined Fleurets in 1964 at the age of 16, passing his chartered surveyor's exams by the age of 19. At just 21 he was made an Associate Partner, becoming a full partner in 1974 and senior partner in 1979. He became Chairman of Fleurets in 1995.

In 1975 Barry led the team that valued all the 7500 pubs belonging to Watneys, Trumans and Berni Inns.

In 1976 he became Secretary of the Association of Valuers of Licensed Property, a role he performed for 13 years before becoming President from 1989 to 1994 (its centenary year).

Fleurets is the oldest firm of Chartered Surveyors to specialise nationally and exclusively in the sale and valuation of hotels and licensed property. Founded in the 1820s, it had only one office, in Bloomsbury, until 1979. Since then it has opened offices in Birmingham, Brighton, Bristol, Leeds, Manchester, and Suffolk to cover the country.

Barry continues to be involved actively in the sale, letting and valuation of public houses on a nationwide basis.

List of Contributors

Glen Gorman started his fire service in Lancashire in 1984. During his ten-year service he completed a four-week fire safety course to enable him to carry out inspections of pubs, hotels, and other businesses under the 1971 Fire Prevention Act. Soon after winning promotion to sub-officer he completed the nine-week Watch Commander's Course at the Fire Service College at Moreton-in-Marsh.

In 1994 a transfer to the London Fire Brigade brought further promotion to the rank of station officer and a position as Inspecting Officer in what must be one of the country's busiest Fire Safety Departments, City of Westminster. A large proportion of the premises in the area are high risk, from small privately owned backpackers' hostels to five-star international hotels – any of which have benefited from the advice the author has provided over the past three years.

Glen has also completed a 12-week Specialist Fire Safety Course at Moreton-in-Marsh – one of the highest national qualifications available in this field.

Anthony Lyons is the specialist licensing partner in Manchester law firm Pannone & Partners. He previously ran his own firm, Copeland Lyons – one of only two in Britain to specialise in liquor and entertainment law. His client list includes major names such as Cafe Inns and Peter Stringfellow, and he is legal adviser to the Federation of Licensed Victuallers Associations.

Teresa Miller BSc MA MCIEH qualified as an environmental health officer in 1987 and has specialised for the most part in the areas of food hygiene and workplace health and safety. She currently works for a local authority in the Home Counties and is primarily concerned with food businesses and associated environmental health issues.

List of Contributors

Andrew Palmer is an award-winning business journalist who edits *New Innkeeper*, the monthly business journal for career licensees and staff and the official magazine of the British Institute of Innkeeping.

A judge of the prestigious National Innkeeping Training awards and the *Publican* awards, Andrew was the award-winning editor of the *Publican* newspaper after its relaunch as a weekly title. He is also a director of the Publican Conference. As well as editing *New Innkeeper*, he runs a communications and copywriting agency operating in the licensed trade.

Tony O'Reilly was born in Dublin and trained in most aspects of catering and food handling. He is a well-known lecturer and writer on catering, having published articles in most trade titles and contributed to four books. He is also a consultant and development chef to the Meat and Livestock Commission and a consultant to the Restaurant and Hotel Industries.

Brian Taylor is group security adviser at Scottish & Newcastle. A geordie by birth, Brian joined Newcastle City Police as a cadet and became a constable in 1959. In the early 1960s, he graduated to the Northumbria Police CID, serving in the City Division, the Regional Crime Squad, and the Club & Vice Squad.

As a Detective Inspector he served in the Fraud Squad, and was promoted to detective chief inspector in the Newcastle City West Division.

He was then appointed to help launch the 'Community Approach to Policing' before becoming superintendent in charge of crime prevention at police headquarters. He returned to operational duties as sub-divisional commander, deputy commander, then chief superintendent divisional commander of South Tyneside Division, retiring in May 1991 after 32 years' service.

He joined Newcastle Breweries as security manager before being appointed to his present position in the group.

PUB FLOORCOVERINGS

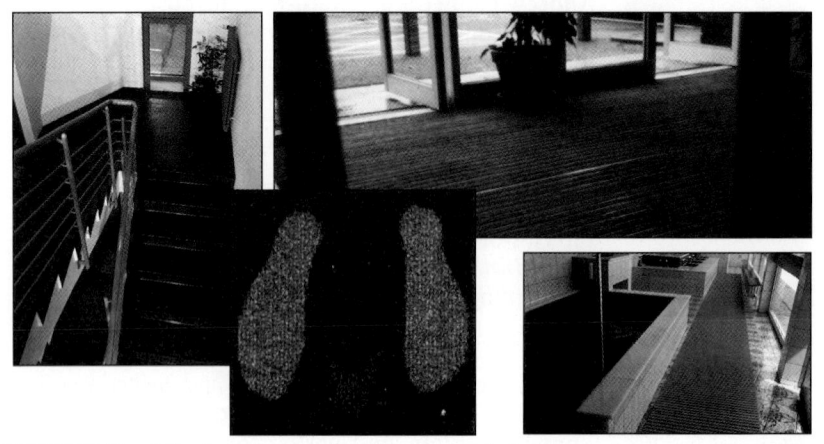

JAYMART Rubber & Plastics Ltd., of Westbury, Wiltshire, celebrate 30 years of supplying specialist floorcoverings and entrance matting systems for public houses. Pub floorcovering are subject to constant attack from dirt, grit, mud, food and drink spillages, burning cigarettes, chewing gum, digging shoe heels, chair and furniture legs and castor's, etc., so can be quickly ruined if nit intelligently selected, protected and maintained.

As a vital first step, JAYMART probably stock the world's most comprehensive collection of scientific entrance matting systems for pub entrances. Their own manufacture prestigious aluminium matting (and matwell) ranges boost that important first impression appearance of the pub, but also quickly pay for themselves not only prolonging the life of internal floorcoverings, but also improving safety and cutting maintenance time and costs. Recommended aluminium entrance mats for pubs are "INTERCEPTOR", "STREET-KING" and "STREET-BEATER", all of which are extremely hardwearing and even able to withstand extra heavy beer keg etc, traffic, if necessary. Even more competitively priced aluminium mats are available for conventional foot traffic only entrances e.g. "STREET-FIGHTER" Coir/Aluminium, "INTER-ZONE" Ribbed Polypropylene / Aluminium, "FOREFRONT" Synthetic Brush / Aluminium etc. All these mats are tailor made. "WELLMAID" Aluminium and Brass Matwell frames, as well as "BEVALU" surface mounted frames with anti-trip bevelled edges are also supplied.

JAYMART also offer a very wide choice of other lower proceed entrance matting types. "IN-GENIUS" synthetic Brush-on-vinyl Barrier Matting is incredibly effective, very hardwearing, colourful, suitable for outdoor as well as indoor use, and available in lettered or monogrammed format if required. "BRUSH-OFF" p.v.c. backed coir matting is extremely popular for pub use, but it must be borne in mind that its dyed colours are not u.v. resistant. Recently introduced environmentally friendly "FLEX-TUFT" rubber tyre tiles make an excellent dirt barrier system. Made from recycled rubber bus and truck tyres, "FLEX-TUFT" tiles have a buffed absorbent nylon pile surface in a choice of four delighted designer selected mottled colours. Fully adhered, "FLEX-TUFT" tiles are exceptionally hardwearing and guaranteed 5 years against premature wear. They also make a superb spiked footwear resistant floorcovering in many problem areas e.g. golf clubs, cricket clubs, etc. and in weight training areas.

A range of all-rubber scraper entrance matting is also offered. These are not moisture absorbent, but are very hardwearing. The best are "SAFE-T-GUARD" and "PICADOR" rubber ring mats, which are of open cavity design with good built-in drainage facility. "BRUSH-KLEEN" flexi-fingered matting is a very effective dirt catcher.

The foregoing entrance mats are usually installed in matwells or within wall-to-wall confines, but JAYMART also offer an extensive selection of very attractive and effective looselaid freestanding surface mounted entrance mats with anti-trip bevelled edges e.g. "ABSORBAMAT" square studded polypropylene-on-rubber mats, "SUPERTUFF" olefin-on-vinyl mats, "WAR-ZONE" olefin-on-vinyl mats, "BRUSH'N'DRY" polypropylene-on-vinyl mats, "SAFE-T-LINK" rubber ring link mats, etc.

A welcome trend in many pubs is now to cover their main entrance hall or lobby areas completely with dirt and moisture trapping barrier carpeting. Jaymart offer heavy duty polypropylene and nylon types. In the former, "ZIGAZAGA" has an eye-catching chevron ribbed surface and "POLYRIB" has bold linear ribbing. In the latter, "Vebe TRAFFIC" in an exciting new development, cleverly combining beauty and brilliant dirt trapping ability.

For the main customer floor areas of the pub, JAYMART offer a comprehensive collection of eye-catching studded and texture anti-slip rubber safety floorings, which also have the priceless assets of cigarette burn resistance, flame resistance, remarkable durability (25 years is not unusual!), colour choice and superb sound deadening properties. Their sophisticated "SARINA" range is also supplied in special qualities e.g. oil resistant, golf spike and ice skate resistant, electrically conductive and a special extra flame resistant / low smoke emission quality for emergency exits etc. "EUROSTUD SYSTEM 30" is an ever increasing popular very low priced studded rubber tile flooring of slightly lesser overall quality than "SARINA". Even more competitively priced will be three new as yet unnamed roll studded floorings, which are due for introduction at the end of June / early July. Both "SARINA" and "EUROSTUD SYSTEM 30" have complementary stair treads within their system.

JAYMART also supply specialist anti-slip, anti-breakage and anti-fatigue standing mats for those wet and / or greasy areas behind and in front of bars, counters, sinks, cookers etc., e.g. "TOPDEK", "PICADOR", "SAFE-T-ZONE", TREADLOCK", etc. rubber ring mats with built-in drainage. "SAFE-T-ZONE, "PICADOR" and "TREADLOCK" have an interlocking connector system facilitating large area or length coverage. These products are also suitable for external use and in pub cellar, for which Jaymart's "MAT-LOCKER" and "SUPERIFLOR" extra heavy duty solid textured surface rubber floorings are also recommended due to their ability to withstand barrel dumping.

Jayamrt also, incidentally, stock "BULL" rubber mats with regulation white stance lines. For protecting areas by drink vending machines, they recommend new "THE CATCHER" rubber mats or their "ABSORBAMAT" or "GATEKEEPER" carpet-on-rubber mats, all with raised anti-trip bevelled edges, for preventing spillages from ruining adjacent floorcoverings and for reducing slip and fall accidents. For external areas, they offer a choice of "TUFTURF EXTRA", GREEN-KEEPER", "GRASSHOPPER" OR "ASTROTURF" simulated artificial grass carpets. For children's play areas, they also offer a wide choice of suitable products, and are hoping to shortly introduce a specialist flooring for placement by swings, climbing frames etc., for cushioning the impact and reducing the dangers of falling accidents. For those very vulnerable wear areas by pool tables, billiard tables, skittle alleys, etc. JAYMART stock an extensive selection of rubber mattings e.g. "RIDGEWAY" and "PACEMAKER" fine fluted, "AZTEC" pyramid, "FISH-FACE" herringbone ribbed etc. These products are also popular for kickplate purpose on kitchen doors, vending machines etc. For bathrooms, a choice of interior rubber safety bath and shower mats is offered. A wide range of anti-slip studded and textured floorings are also available for bathroom floors, but it should be borne in mind that whilst these should reduce slip and fall accidents, they will probably not eliminate them entirely. "VERSATILE" tiles are also, popular as giant chess or draught boards.

Jaymart's excellent new "SCAN-LOCK" and "PLASTIFLOR" interlocking solid vinyl flooring tile ranges are available in various surface finishes, i.e. studded, textured, smooth etc., and are ideally suited for pub use, particularly for areas where subfloor conditions or financial reasons make suitable adhered floorings prohibitive, or where the area is only to be covered or protected temporarily e.g. for dances, conferences, exhibitions, etc. Both these elegant tile floorings can be easily uplifted or stored or moved to another area when not required. Special bevelled edging is also supplied.

Free samples, literature, prices etc., are available upon request from Jaymart Rubber & Plastics Ltd., Woodland Estate, Eden Vale Road, Westbury, Wiltshire BA13 3QS - Telephone No. (01373) 864926 - Fax No. (01373) 858454 Contact: Chris Emberson, Sales Dept.

xix

MAYFAIR TAVERNS IN RECRUITMENT DRIVE

Mayfair Taverns, the Banbury based national pub company, is offering openings for potential new tenants, along with top quality training, as it looks to add to its growing reputation across the country.

The company has a progressive ethos and is justifiably proud of it's commitment to becoming the best pub company in the business.

Managing director, Tony Wilkinson, is convinced that tenants respond best when given the appropriate level of support, and is quick to stress that at Mayfair Taverns, the door is always open to the people on the front line. He commented; "It is important that the tenants feel that they can come to us with any grievances or better still, suggestions for the development of their business they may have.

"At Mayfair Taverns, we want to be the best pub company in the country, and to achieve that aim we have to be accessible and supportive. Any new Mayfair Taverns tenants will find us open, progressive and keen to work with them towards improving their business. It has to be a two way thing."

First time tenants and experienced pub people alike are encouraged to come on board at Mayfair Taverns, and with B.I.I. recognised training schemes available, the company can promise to give everybody the opportunity to prove themselves in a demanding but rewarding profession.

The training courses will put new tenants in touch with past masters of the trade and in just five days, a wide range of subjects will be covered, ranging from cellar management to food hygiene and from licensing laws to customer service.

Courses are run three times a year, and can be attended by individuals or partners, with both residential and non-residential options available. Prices will be modified accordingly, with there also being a chance to attend separate modules on a daily rate.

Wilkinson continues: "It is all very well saying that we want to have the best possible tenants. Every pub company wants that. The Mayfair way is to make it clear to interested parties that our standards are high, but that the support and our rewards are equally impressive."

Mayfair Taverns offers both a three year lease and a twenty year commitment, giving an opportunity to both experienced licensees and those entering the trade for the first time. A Mayfair Taverns business development manager will take time to learn more about individual's strengths and help them turn their attributes into tangible success.

With an experienced team working towards one common goal of establishing Mayfair Taverns as the best pub company, long term goals are very much attainable.

For further information on becoming a Mayfair Taverns tenant, or alternatively, on any aspect of the training courses, please contact Lisa McCormick on 01295 275012.

MAYFAIR TAVERNS

We're open.

Tenancies for big personalities.

Mayfair Taverns is a fast-growing pub company with big ideas. We strongly believe that independence guarantees success and we care about building up close relationships with our tenants. We now have a number of exciting opportunities around the country for enthusiastic people with the drive and commitment to make a success of themselves in the pub business.

If you already have some experience of the business, either pubs or restaurants, and are interested in taking up a tenancy with us, we'd love to hear from you. But even if you are a beginner, there's not too much to worry about. Bring plenty of enthusiasm and character – and let our training do the rest.

To find out more - or get in your application - please contact **Lisa McCormick at Mayfair Taverns** on **01295 275012**.

CHAPTER ONE

CHOOSING YOUR PUB

Barry Gillham

WHAT DO YOU EXPECT FROM PUB LIFE?

So you have decided you would like to run a pub. Why? I have been over 30 years in the pub business, buying, selling and valuing. I think I have visited, in a professional capacity, perhaps one-third of the 65,000 pubs in the country. Yet I have never had the urge to run one.

You can see from my picture that I am big and fat and cheerful - your archetypal publican if ever there was one - but there's a serious stumbling block: when I'm in a pub I like to drink - and if I drank too much, I'd be a lousy publican. But if I remain sober, I can't stand drunks. They forget the punchlines to jokes, they spill drinks, sometimes they are sick in the toilets. So if I were sober, I'd still be a lousy publican.

That's why I shouldn't run a pub. How about you?

You really need to analyse the reasons why you would like to run a pub and make sure you aren't wearing rose-tinted spectacles. I find that 80 per cent of the people who enter the licensed trade leave within three years, never to touch the pub business again. The other 20 per cent love the life and stay in it until they retire - sometimes at the same pub, sometimes moving two or three times, sometimes even building up a small chain.

There is virtually nothing in between. You either love the job or hate it. Very few people stay seven or eight years and then change career.

The trick, therefore, is to make sure you are one of the 20 per cent before you make the mistake of entering a trade to which you are not suited - or perhaps going into the wrong branch of a trade in which you might have been successful had you received the right advice and training.

I always advise people to work in the trade in a part-time capacity first. Before the days of comprehensive training courses, this was the only way to gain entry. I believe it is still the best way, although I accept that a training course today is a must.

The Publican's Handbook

The benefit of working evenings and weekends, in addition to a full-time job and spending any spare moments traipsing the country to look at potential pubs of your own, is that you will be working a 100-hour week. This is the best training for entering the licensed trade because it will prove you have the stamina. Your legs and feet will take the strain of standing for hours on end. You can survive on six hours' sleep and, most important, you can work with your spouse for long periods of time and resist the twin temptations of alcohol and the opposite sex. Many of the 80 per cent who fall by the wayside do so either because they drink too much or because sex rears its ugly head. There are many combinations of husband falling for barmaid or wife running off with captain of the darts team. Sometimes jealousy alone is enough to break a marriage under pressure.

So although the fact that you have worked part-time at the Dog and Duck for six months may not be something for you to put on an application form it is, I believe, an essential test. If you are still keen to take a pub after six months' work at your local, in addition to a full-time job, including a holiday relief and two or three long weekends on your own, you are more likely to succeed in this trade.

The demands of the lifestyle will, of course, vary from pub to pub. Often the smallest pubs (or those with the lowest turnover) are the hardest work because the licencees have to do it all themselves. Don't be fooled by the number of staff you see in the Rovers Return, Coronation Street, or the Queen Victoria, Albert Square - it may only be on the busiest two or three nights plus a night off that staff are employed in a typical Rovers Return-type local.

In most backstreet locals the day begins with the licencees doing the cleaning, glass washing and bottling up from the previous night. During the day one partner will run the bar while the other does the cooking. Any spare time is taken up with the books, the VAT, the ordering and the cellar.

If you have children, time must be devoted to them (not to mention the domestic housework). Most licencees of low volume businesses are also odd job persons dealing with unblocking toilets, unsticking window frames, cleaning leaves from gutters and replacing the odd tile or slate (most pubs are over 100 years old - some of the best are 500 years old - and need constant doses of tender loving care).

Many pubs now open all day, and the days of an afternoon nap have long gone. Trade may be quiet, but it will still require one person in the bar between 3pm and 8pm, so at best each partner will get two or three hours away from serving.

Usually, the busier a pub is the more staff it can afford and, hopefully, the shorter the licensee's working week. One of the major chains operating the biggest and best town centre pubs, has recently announced that its managers will only be required to work a 50-hour week, four days on and three days off. In this sort of pub the manager will be required to 'manage' - ie interview staff, compile working rotas, go to company training days and implement the trade-boosting ideas they are given. They won't have to clean the toilets, cook or even pull pints. They may have very little time to talk to customers. This may not be your idea of how you would like to run a pub. There are many different lifestyles between these two extremes. Possibly the most successful (and I would say enjoyable) is where one partner is a chef who is also good at paperwork and the other partner is a front-of-house manager good at chatting up customers and motivating staff.

If this describes you to a T, you need to find the right pub, on the right terms.

HOW DO I BECOME A PUBLICAN?

What sort of pub would best suit your means and ambitions? There are many ways into the pub trade, and many types of pub: are you aware of the distinctions?

Managed houses

Breweries and other pub-operating companies tend to run the biggest and best of their pubs directly, employing managers and staff on salaries and bonuses and keeping all the profit themselves. Most managed houses (a little over one-third of the country's pubs) have a turnover topping £6000 a week. Some, such as steak bars and theme pubs, have turnovers of well over £1m a year.

Most managed house companies have their own training schemes. Prospective managers will be expected to work first as trainee managers, then as relief managers, before they are given their own pub. Managers receive a wage, often augmented by bonuses related to turnover and/or profits.

However, there are also many small companies running marginal pubs under management. Often these offer the worst of all worlds. Training is scarce or non-existent, there is tight control of costs because there is insufficient profit really to warrant management, and promised bonuses never materialise because unrealistic targets have been set.

This sort of job is often the first step on the ladder for many entrants to the trade. Sadly, it produces a high proportion of the dropouts. There are many good small managed house companies but there are probably more poor ones.

Traditional tenancies

Traditionally, brewery-owned pubs with insufficient trade to warrant management, ie turning over £2000–4000 a week, were let on tied tenancy.

At its simplest, a tied tenancy is a short-term agreement (usually three years, but sometimes less and occasionally more) whereby the tenant rents the pub and buys beer from the brewery. The tenant is responsible for all the expenses of running the pub, ie staff wages, gas and electricity, business rates, and some repairs and decoration. If the business makes a profit, the tenant keeps it. If the business makes a loss, the tenant bears it.

The Publican's Handbook

With more than 1,500 pubs spread across the country **PUBMASTER LIMITED** is one of the best known names in the industry and yet in many respects it is also one of the newest. For in November 1996 the company became independent from the Brent Walker Group making it a completely autonomous company whose only business interests are in pubs.

That focus is on running tenanted pubs........creating partnerships with landlords to develop businesses to mutual benefit.

Pubmaster is introducing a totally new strategy to ensure that its business competes against the increasing pressures from the rest of the leisure industry and the cheap imports of beer. Chief Executive John Sands says:"We now have freedom to develop our business and we are quite clear that we have to work more with our tenants to help them attract and keep customers. We are equally aware that to get the best out of the business we have to offer opportunities to tenants so that their hard work and loyalty is rewarded." In its first year of independence Pubmaster is investing £15m in its estate and will continue to invest both in its existing pubs and in acquiring new pubs. The company is also pioneering franchising which will appeal to many experienced landlords as well as providing a new route into the business for many people. Pubmaster is developing several "brands" which will give it the opportunity to offer packages which include providing training, full business support including help with marketing and advertising and accountancy and business management support. John Sands says: "Franchising offers a number of major benefits such as a longer lease and the opportunity for the franchisee to work within a proven business framework. It is totally new kind of opportunity which will appeal to many people especially as they will be investing in a tried and tested formula and befitting from our purchasing power and our years of experience."

Pubmaster is now actively looking for the two most vital things in its business......licensees and pubs.

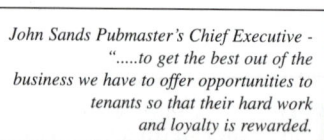

John Sands Pubmaster's Chief Executive - ".....to get the best out of the business we have to offer opportunities to tenants so that their hard work and loyalty is rewarded.

A unique occasion for Pubmaster - the official handover of The Crown Inn at Addingham near Ilkley which is the first pub bought by the company after it became independent. Regional Operations Director Stephen Howe marks the occasion by presenting a landscape painting to retiring owner Barbara Harrison watched by new tenant Maureen Milner.

Choosing your Pub

We've got a lot to offer the right partner.

Pub Tenancy

support — *teamwork* — *flexibility* — *choice*

If you're thinking of taking on a pub tenancy you'll be looking for the right partnership to make the most of your talents.

Pubmaster is Britain's leading Independent Pub Retailer and we're currently looking for tenants to join our business partnerships throughout England and Wales.

We have a huge variety of pubs and locations from bustling city centre houses to quaint country locals. Our approach promotes teamwork and creativity in our tenants, whilst offering all the flexible support that comes from being part of a major retail concern.

So, if you can bring to the marriage social skills, business sense & organisational ability, together with drive and enthusiasm to run your own business and an investment of 10K or more we should be talking.

Take the first steps towards a perfect partnership by ringing Carol Reed at Pubmaster on 01527 577222

PUBMASTER

Pubmaster Ltd., 72 Sherwood Road, Aston Fields, Bromsgrove, Worcs. B603DR

The degree of tie, ie whether it is on all beers, whether a guest beer is allowed, whether the tenant is tied on certain wines and spirits or has to share takings from gaming machines or juke boxes, varies from company to company. Generally tenants are required to pay the full list price for products on which they are tied. Naturally the price at which tenants buy in supplies will affect the profitability of the business and needs to be carefully assessed.

When the government investigated the licensed trade in 1988 it made various recommendations. This resulted in most of the national brewers giving up traditional tenancies, but the majority of regional and local breweries still have large numbers of pubs run on tied tenancy.

A number of new companies were set up following the Beer Orders mentioned above to buy the large numbers of pubs that the national brewers were obliged to sell. In the main, they also run their pubs under tied tenancy. They are not brewers but have trading agreements with one or more brewers and their tenants are given a list of products that they must buy via the 'PubCo' in a virtually identical manner to the traditional brewer's tied tenancy.

Modern long leases

The Beer Orders required that national brewers should let their pubs 'at arm's length', which was taken to mean that they could no longer retain responsibility for repair of the building. It followed that if tenants were to be required to take responsibility for repairs, they wanted longer, assignable, leases which would have a capital value.

The national brewers therefore followed the trail blazed by the Inntrepreneur Pub Company some years earlier in granting 10- to 20-year full repairing leases. These vary from traditional tenancies in a number of important ways.

The tie is generally only for beer (with provision for a guest ale), although some are totally free of tie. The lessee is free to buy wines and spirits where he wishes, and there is no tie in respect of gaming and other machines.

The most important difference, however, is that the lessee, as well as being responsible for the profits or losses of the business, is able to sell the business for what it is worth – good news for the successful licencee, but bad news for the unsuccessful lessee who has to find someone to take a loss-making business off his hands. (With a traditional tenancy it is the landlord's job to find your successor when you decide to go.)

The average leasehold pub turns over £3000–5000 a week, and leases sell for an average of a little over £50,000, although the majority sell for £20/30,000 and a very small number for over £100,000.

Free houses

A little under one-third of the country's pubs are owned by the operator on a freehold basis, creating the stereotype of the thatched country pub with roses round the

Choosing your Pub

door. However, there are now many urban free houses as well – remember, the Rovers Return used to be owned by Newton & Ridley until Jack and Vera bought the freehold. Similarly, those evil Mitchells bought the freehold of the Queen Vic in 1993. The scriptwriters are sometimes confused, but I believe the Woolpack in Emmerdale is also a free house.

Free houses are generally, but not always, the lowest-trading pubs because their barrelage does not warrant their being owned by a brewer or a PubCo. Average free house turnover is between £2000 and £4000 a week.

HOW DO I GO ABOUT FINDING THE MOST SUITABLE KIND OF PUB?

Managed

There are many avenues to try. The two licensed newspapers, *Publican* (weekly) and *The Licencee* (Mondays and Thursdays) carry recruitment advertising; they can both be ordered through your newsagent. The bigger companies run their own training schemes; their addresses are published in the *Brewery* manual, published by Hampton Publishing and available through your local library. Or you could approach local pub managers, who will be able to give you the name and address of their head offices.

Tenancies, free houses and leases

Again, the two main publications carry advertisements, as do *Dalton's Weekly* and *Caterer & Hotelkeeper*. Most of the advertisements, however, will not have been placed by brewers and PubCos but by agents, sometimes known as brokers.

Tenancy brokers

Tenancy brokers have been around for over 150 years. Brewers and PubCos generally give letting information to around half-a-dozen brokers, who disseminate it to interested parties. Applicants for pub tenancies generally first attend an interview with one or more brokers. As well as completing an application form they will be given basic information as to how the system works, how to draft a business plan, and how to present their ideas and personality to the brewer or PubCo when they find a pub they like. The broker will also act for the tenant on his 'ingoing' to the pub.

Brokers generally take their fee from the ingoing tenant.

Freehold agents

Agents who deal with the sale of freehold pubs are generally different firms (Fleurets is one of the few that deal with freeholds, tenancies and leases). Agents generally act for the vendor, preparing details in much the same way as an estate agent but in addition supplying information on the accounts of the business, licencing, planning etc.

Most free houses are sold by a relatively few well-known agents who specialise in the trade. They therefore have a wide variety of pubs on offer and can supply good advice to the uninitiated. You are recommended to visit the offices of two or three agents, by appointment,

The Publican's Handbook

SAVILLS LICENSED RETAIL
The Comprehensive Solution

Demand for licensed retail premises is continuing at very encouraging levels with many different styles of operations being sought after. The demand is, similarly, coming from a wide range of organisations including, individual and multiple operators as well as larger pub operating companies.

Savills Licensed Retail offices have ben active across all sectors of the market, advising individual operators, multiple pub companies, private investors and investment funds who are all seeking to secure their position in this dynamic market place.

Our principal northern office in Manchester is run by Derek Griffin who reports strong interest from a variety of operators for both existing licensed operations as well as new developments and the conversion to licensed use of existing buildings. A variety of pub and restaurant users have taken space in two of the most recently available licensed retail schemes at Swinegate Court, York and the Speciality Shops development at Crown Court, Leeds. Savills Licensed Retail is the retained advisor to the developers of both of these schemes.

In addition to town centre developments such as these, there continues to be a high level of interest in traditional pubs which remain one of the most enduring of all leisure pursuits. This has been demonstrated by the very high level of demand that we have seen for pub businesses as diverse as The Kingstown Arms at Hedon, near Hull, which we sold on behalf of a private client to Mill House Inns Limited and the variety of community locals that we have let on free of tie leases on behalf of Phoenix Inns.

This experience has been mirrored across the South and South West of England and Wales where Chris Irving heads up the licensed retail activity at our Oxford office. Amongst notable recent transactions completed by the office are acquisition of new premises in Cardiff for Grosvenor Inns and the sale of a substantial freehold freehouse in Clevedon for a private client.

In addition to the variety of licensed retail business opportunities available through our Oxford office we are also advising Bristol City Council and St John's College, Oxford in respect of rent review and estate management cases. This highlights another aspect of the services that are available from Savills Licensed Retail as we offer full professional services support to owners and operators of licensed retail businesses to deal with all property related matters.

The full range of services provided by Savills Licensed Retail is available across London and South East through our West End office where the principal contact is Nick Bennett. Recent examples of instructions undertaken from this office include the provision of strategic consultancy advice to a Local Authority in Greater London concerning a major redevelopment site and valuation and consultancy advice to a private client to effect the purchase of a licensed retail investment. Such activity is in addition to the agency work we conduct for a variety of clients in dealing with sales, purchases and lettings.

The agency and professional services provided by Savills Licensed Retail are supplemented by the funding and financing services we offer. In this area we provide funding solutions to new and existing licensed retail operators to either assit initial establishment or facilitate expansion. As an example, we arranged the funding package through which Scorpio Inns purchased their portfolio of 110 public houses from Whitbread. We are continually working with a variety of organisations in this arena and, with current levels of activity in the licensed retail industry, we can expect to see considerably more transactions in this area.

Savills Licensed Retail with its national network of offices and dedicated licensed retail expertise is uniquely positioned to assist and advise licensed retail operators in the establishment and existing licensed retail operators to either assist initial establishment or facilitate expansion of their businesses. We look forward to helping you.

Choosing your Pub

SAVILLS

INTERNATIONAL PROPERTY CONSULTANTS

SAVILLS' PROPERTY CONSULTING EXPERTISE EXTENDS TO ALL ASPECTS OF LICENSED RETAIL PROPERTY

Based throughout the country, our fully experienced team provides a comprehensive service to individual and mulitple owners and occupiers. Backed by our extensive market and industry knowledge our services include:

- *Valuations*
- *Lettings*
- *Sales*
- *Funding*

- *Consultancy*
- *Rent reviews*
- *Acquisitions*
- *Portfolio Management*

For further details please call us on:

Fountain Court
68 Fountain Street
MANCHESTER M2 2FB
Tel: 0161 236 8644
Fax: 0161 228 0544

1 Berkeley Street
LONDON W1X 5AA
Tel: 0171 647 1840
Fax: 0171 491 0505

Buxton Court
3 West Way, Botley
OXFORD OX2 OJB
Tel: 01865 726000
Fax: 01865 726262

Savills Galbreath Offices & Associations Worldwide

to take advantage of this 'free' advice.

Sale of leases

The sale of leases is handled both by tenancy brokers and free house agents, although increasingly it is seen as a marketing job to be given to the larger specialist agents.

HOW CAN I TELL I'VE FOUND THE RIGHT PUB?

Management

You will be an employee. Your main income will be paid as wages. It will be up to you to obtain as much trading information as you can so that you can decide whether your bonus is likely to amount to something or nothing.

Tenancy

When you take a tenancy your only relationship is with the owner of the pub. You do not 'buy the business' from the previous tenants, so you have no right to see their books, accounts or VAT records. Often the only information you will be given will be in the form of 'barrels' of beer supplied by the owner of the pub to the previous tenants. These supply figures may be up to 12 months out of date (and most businesses drop off once the tenant has decided to go). They may not include guest beers, wines and spirits, food or machine take.

A prospective tenant will need to construct a shadow profit and loss account and would do well to take advice at this stage. His broker will be able to give basic advice such as how to calculate the conversion of a barrel of beer into takings. But with many pubs now doing as much as 50 per cent food trade, guesstimates could be way out.

Prospective tenants should therefore take advice (at the appropriate fee) from a professional licensed property valuer, accountant or stocktaker. At the very least he should be guided by an experienced publican or compare the pub on busy and quiet nights to two or three others where trading figures are available and which might provide reliable guidance.

Free houses and leases

Where these are being sold by a publican you will generally be asked to pay a price which includes goodwill – you are buying a business as well as a building: the better the business, the more you will be asked to pay.

If you are paying more than the building (or lease) and the trade furniture is worth then you have a right to be provided with up-to-date proven accounts. However, it is up to you to ask for them and to have them vetted carefully by an accountant or valuer. If you are borrowing money the lender will generally commission a business appraisal report. The valuer preparing this will look at existing accounts and make a judgement as to whether the business ought to have been making more or less money than shown in the accounts. (The seller may be an alcoholic widow or a famous TV personality.) The lender will only be concerned to know that the business is worth more than it is lending, but even if you are borrow-

Choosing your Pub

ing little or nothing you should consider having your own business appraisal report carried out (Fleurets does these for a fee starting at £600 + VAT. This could prove a very wise investment).

If the accounts are out of date you should consider carefully whether business is likely to have fallen since they were completed, and by how much. You may consider asking to see recent VAT returns, or insist that later accounts are prepared and audited before you commit yourself.

Some pubs are sold or leased by breweries or Pubcos without the benefit of accounts (often because the pubs were previously let to tied tenants and no accounts are available). These will generally be cheaper because you are not paying for goodwill. They may look like a bargain, but remember that it may take a while to build up the business during which you may make losses which must be weighed against the savings in capital cost.

WHAT TRADING INFORMATION DO I NEED?

The most important figure is turnover. Everything stems from how much is put into the till to begin with.

Accounts are always shown with VAT excluded. Weekly takings are often shown inclusive of VAT as the amount paid into the till. This is a most important point to remember. If you are shown accounts a year out of date with a turnover of £100,000, and then takings for the last 12 months showing a weekly turnover of £2200 you may think that turnover has risen (52 x £2200 = £114,400), whereas in fact it will have fallen to a net-of-VAT figure of £97,362.

You need to consider if the accounts show the full turnover. Catering is often a separate business run by a spouse. Sometimes staff or a window cleaner is paid out of the till. Sometimes, heaven forbid, a licencee may even pay for his gambling, holidays or new shoes out of the till. The gross profit margin often gives a hint as to how much should be shown on the takings line, as most operators are keen to claim all their 'inputs' against tax even if they don't always show all the takings.

Beware the seller who has more than one business and who may artificially inflate the takings figures of the business he is selling with money from one he is retaining. An astute adviser will be able to give you pointers on the amounts spent on major outgoings such as wages, light, heat, rent, and rates compared to what he would expect to see for an average business.

This could direct you to the consideration of a business which has an excellent turnover but poor profits due to a 'pile it high, sell it cheap' policy or perhaps rent, rates, and other costs which impinge on profitability.

Accounts may be prepared with the main aim of depressing profits and thereby saving tax. Quite legitimate expenses such as depreciation, private use of car, wages and pension payments made to the owners can be added back. Unusual levels of outgoings for major repairs may need to be averaged over several years. Out-of-date accounts may show a rent which has since been increased. A valuer will produce what is known as an 'adjusted net profit' to reflect what the purchaser is likely to achieve as opposed to what the audited accounts actually show.

HOW CAN I TELL IF THE PRICE IS RIGHT - AND WHO CAN ADVISE ME?

Managed houses

Other than possibly a security bond, you should not expect to have to make any investment.

Tenancies

You buy furniture and stock at valuation, and you pay a security deposit which earns interest and is refundable (subject to your having paid all your bills) at the end of your tenancy. The tenancy details you are given will also have an 'estimated ingoing' figure which may include fees or working capital. Once you are accepted as the 'ingoing tenant' your broker will act on your behalf in negotiating the best price for the furniture and stock.

Leases and free houses

Before you rush into anything you are best advised to look around. After four to six weeks looking at three or four properties each weekend, you will establish a 'feel for the market' - ie, what you will be expected to pay for the sort of pub you wish to buy.

Essentially, price is determined by demand. A pretty pub with good living accommodation in a sought-after area will command a high multiplier of the adjusted net profit.

But don't be fooled by asking prices. Different agents have different policies. Agencies which ask the vendor to contribute to the cost of advertising can afford to have large numbers of properties on their books at prices dictated by the vendors, however unrealistic. But the vendor is committed because he has spent his own money, and eventually the pub will sell for a price the market will bear. Others, including my own company, charge on an all-inclusive no sale/no fee basis. Since these agents pay for the advertising, they are keen to get properties on to the market at or very close to a price they believe will be achievable.

Your mortgage broker is often a good source of advice in that he will tell you whether you can afford to buy the pub of your dreams. This is not the same as telling you what the pub is worth, but it will save you wasting time.

A valuer acting for your lender, for you or both, is the only person who can really tell you if the price is right. Some agents, including Fleurets, have separate valuation departments which can advise you in respect of pubs being bought through other agents (although do beware of conflicts of interest).

If you intend raising a mortgage be sure that your valuer is approved by your chosen lender or lenders, or you could end up paying for two valuations, and be sure your chosen valuer really specialises in pubs in the area.

Remember, a valuation is not a building survey and you will prob-

Choosing your Pub

ably need a report on the building from a building surveyor as well (both the surveyor and the valuer are likely to be members of the Royal Institute of Chartered Surveyors (RICS) but it is unlikely that one person will have the necessary expertise to do both jobs properly).

There are other rules of thumb to remember. Free houses traditionally sold for around seven times profit or 1 times turnover, and 20-year leases sold for three times profit. Prices are currently much lower than this, with free houses selling for around five times profit or 0.9-1.4 times turnover, and leaseholds selling for only one or two times profit.

However, averages are a dangerous thing. Even as I write, we are, hopefully, ending a six-year recession. Since pub valuations are a product of profit multiplied by a 'feelgood factor', they are more than usually volatile. In good times, both figures rise; in bad times they both fall. There is no substitute for an up-to-date valuation produced by an experienced and qualified valuer with local and specialist knowledge.

HOW DO I KNOW IF MY CHOSEN PUB IS APPROPRIATE TO MY AMBITIONS AND THE NEEDS OF THE LOCAL MARKET?

If we think back to our 80:20 success ratio, there is another big mistake to be avoided: trying to turn a successful pub into something it is not.

If you buy a pub that is the hub of the village's sporting life, you will have paid a price or a rent that reflects the trade enjoyed. It is very high risk to try to create a food trade either in addition to or instead of beer-bashing laddish trade.

Pubs have changed over the years, and these changes have all been made by licencees who have taken risks. However, those risks are minimised if you either take a pub which is run-down (with an accordingly low price or rent) or seek to develop a theme which is still in its infancy.

If the pub you are looking at has not already been operated in the way you have in mind, you should consider carefully whether you will be able to make a successful transition. It may be just too well known in its existing incarnation for you to be able to change it. Would you be better off seeking an alternative pub more to your liking?

Look at what is already being provided in the area. Every area needs a variety of pubs. Some young people's music venues, some older folk's venues for food or games, some for gays, some for bikers, maybe even some for gay bikers. But the narrower the market you want to target, the better you must be. You also need to be very good to provide 'yet another pub specialising in XYZ' in an area already overloaded with similar outlets.

I have always found assessing the local market to be one of the most enjoyable parts of my job, involving as it does sitting on many barstools chatting up many barmaids (politically incorrect as this may be!). A 'market' can vary according to the type of pub and its location. For a quality food house it can be some dozens of

The Publican's Handbook

Dalton's Weekly is unique. It is the only publication in the country specifically dedicated to advertising businesses, holidays and property for sale. Each week Dalton's Weekly publishes the largest selection of shops and businesses for sale of any paper or magazine in the country. The choice can range from a small fish and chip shop to a 50 bedroomed hotel with full leisure facilities. All areas are featured throughout the UK together with a regular selection of bars and restaurants for sale overseas in sunnier climes!

Dalton's Weekly has a specific section for pubs for sale that each week carries an extensive choice of businesses being sold by specialist pub agents together with a range of individual pubs being sold privately. As an all advertising publication the essence of Dalton's Weekly is to provide the widest possible range of opportunities presented in a no-nonsense format without any alluring editorial, though the specialist agents that advertise each week are always on hand to offer advice on the pro's and con's of buying what could be your first pub. Some agents offer specific pub finance deals and a number run their own landlord training courses.

A recent edition of Dalton's Weekly featured a corner pub in the vibrant area of Ladbroke Grove, London with a freehold asking price of £750,000. In the same edition a detached village freehouse in Shropshire with 1 acre of grounds was available for the freehold price of just £150,000. Leasehold Pubs can be obtained from around £15,000 and the leading brewers offer tenancies on a franchised or partnership basis for a similar investment. Overseas you can buy a busy bar in Mallorca with its own living accomodation for £50,000-though you may of course choose to look in the property abroad section of Dalton's Weekly to find a home away from the noise of your popular bar!

Dalton's Weekly is readily available nationwide from all newsagents every Thursday, £1. Or you can take out a subscription by contacting the subscriptions department on **0181 949 6199**. If you have access to the internet you can visit Dalton's web site on www.dalton's.co.uk and view a selection of businesses for sale that may not as yet have appeared in the paper.

If you're considering selling a business of any description, Dalton's Weekly's advertising rates offer excellent value for money for national coverage. The paper is regularly promoted on Television & Radio and we exhibits at all pertinent trade and consumer shows. So whether you're buying or selling a pub or other licensed business, one essential name rolls off the press every week- Dalton's Weekly, your perfect partner for buying or selling.

Choosing your Pub

Looking for a Pub?
We've got DAL*tons* of them!

tons of pubs in *tons* of places...*tons* of choice in *tons* of locations...at *tons* of different prices...

It all adds up to...

DAL*tons* Weekly
Britain's best bet for licensed businesses for sale - *bar none*.

Available from all newsagents, nationwide every Thursday.

Daltons Weekly plc, C.I. Tower,
St George's Square, New Malden,
Surrey. KT3 4JA.
Tel: 0181 949 6199 Fax: 0181 949 2718

JEFFREY GREEN RUSSELL
SPECIALIST LICENSING SOLICITORS

Contact Julian Skeens

HEAD OF LICENSING

Apollo House

56 New Bond Street, London W1Y 0SX

Tel: 0171 499 7020   Fax: 0171 499 2449

DX: 4462Y MAYFAIR

URL: http://jgrweb.com/.   INTERNET: JMS@jgrlaw.co.uk

The Publican's Handbook

Shipley & Overturning Marsden

Julian M Skeens - Jeffrey Green Russell

As I sit down to dictate this article upon my return from the Court of Appeal which was considering the case of R -v- Stafford Crown Court ex parte Shipley designed to overturn the damaging decision of Marsden.

The hearing took place on Tuesday and Wednesday the 29th and 30th July 1997 and is of such importance to the licensed trade that the whole of the argument as well as the judgment has been, or will be, recorded for posterity.

The opening words were uttered by Lord Justice Simon Brown "I am told there is to be a record. We shall try and inject such life into this not immediately, obviously and enthralling day as we can". There is plenty of life "but not as we know it Jim!"

For those of you in the licensed trade who have been star trekking on Mars for the last few years perhaps I should very briefly re-cap. The case of "Marsden" decided that the Magistrates Court could limit the start as well as the end time of premises with a Special Hours Certificate and it raised an important question as to whether or not the sale of intoxicating liquor had to be ancillary to the provision of music and dancing and substantial refreshment throughout the trading day.

Special Hours Certificates were first introduced in 1949 for hotels and restaurants in London that could demonstrate by way of a certificate from the Inland Revenue that the lions share of their trade came from the provision of food and accommodation.

They were then given additional but different Permitted Hours in which to trade. It was not until April 1961 that the additional hours were allowed outside of London and in 1964 that Special Hours Certificates were permitted in all On Licensed premises ie. not confined to restaurants and hotels.

The underlying problem is that just one sort of licence i.e. a Justices on Licence has to cover the full gambit of premises that have late hours from restaurants, pubs, a Palais de danse to a Ritzy disco where each Licensee has to establish that the sale of alcohol is ancillary to the provision of food and dancing but of course they are providing very different facilities within that category. Unfortunately as the diversity of styles of premises have increased by the ingenuity of man and woman the law has not been able to keep pace and so operators and their lawyers are for ever trying to force their concept into the straight jacket provided by the law.

In the Court of Appeal it was accepted on all sides that there was no power to impose a commencement time before 1988 the crucial question is whether the 1988 Licensing Act introduced that power.

You may recall that the Licensing Act 1988 was the Act which did away with the dead afternoon etc. Coincidentally it changed the wording of Section 76 of the Licensing Act so that the Permitted Hours for premises with a Special Hours Certificate are now defined as the ordinary Permitted Hours on weekdays which shall "extend until 2.00am in the morning following"

The Licensing Act 1988 also introduced and gave an unlimited discretion to the Magistrates not only whether or not to grant the certificate but also whether or not to impose a limitation on the Permitted Hours.

Now if one looks again at Section 76 of the Licensing Act 1964 we see that the Permitted Hours are doing. The premises have a Justices on Licence and the permitted hours are 11.00am to 11.00pm, the Licensee is applying for an extension of those Permitted Hours until say 2.00am in the morning the power to impose the Limitation only arises at that time.

The Marsden camp has come up with what the Shipley camp would say is a ludicrous proposition that a Licensee can apply for additional hours and actually be granted less hours than he already had and yet for that privilege he would then have to sell his alcohol as ancillary to substantial refreshment and music and dancing.

In the Shipley case itself the Licensing Justice imposed a 7.00pm start time and a 12.00 midnight closing time. Therefore instead of being able to trade for 12 hours the Licensee was then only allowed to trade for five hours an in a busy market town it was a commercial nonsense to accept the Special Hours Certificate.

To bring the Special Hours Certificate into

Choosing your Pub

force not only do the Magistrates have to grant the Special Hours Certificate but the Licensee than has to give notice to the Police to bring those permitted Hours into effect and therefore the Licensee in Cannock did not give that notice and could continue to trade from 11.00am to 11.00pm.

The second question that the Lords of Appeal had to consider was whether, if a premises had the benefit of a Special Hours Certificate, the Licenseee would have to prove that the supply of intoxicating liquor would be ancillary throughout the trading day.

Prior to 1988 if one had a Special Hours Certificate the earliest time that one's Permitted Hours could cease was midnight and the Permitted Hours would be extended until such time as the music and dancing stopped.

It will be appreciated that there were three elements to the additional Permitted Hours. First of all the granting of the Certificate; second the notice to the Police activating the Certificate and third the way one used the premises. The Act was contemplating that music and dancing need not be provided up to midnight and therefore could not be insisting that the Permitted Hours were ancillary before midnight.

However the Marsden camp pointed out that one of the grounds for revoking a Special Hours Certificate was that "on the whole the persons resorting to premises or part are there, at times when the sale or supply of intoxicating liquor there is lawful by virtue only of the Certificate for the purpose of obtaining intoxicating liquor rather than for the purpose of dancing or of obtaining refreshments other than intoxicating liquor".

Clearly then there is a conflict, on the one hand the Law was saying you don't have to provide music and dancing and on the other hand was saying if you don't provide music and dancing and substantial refreshment your Special Hours Certificate could be taken away but it should be remembered that this is a discretionary ground and that there are other mandatory grounds.

The Marsden camp than extended the argument to say that you have to provide substantial refreshment and music and dancing throughout the day but had difficulty with the words underlined above "by virtue only of the Certificate". These words are clearly not verbiage and to be given any meaning must suggest that there are duplicated Permitted Hours which are lawful by the Justices on Licence and there are other Permitted Hours which are lawful by the Justices on Licence (ie 11.00am to 11.00pm) and there are other permitted hours which are lawful by Special Hours Certificate (see also s.83) the Shipley camp suggest that those hours authorised solely by the Special Hours Certificate are from 11.00pm onwards and that it is only during those hours that one has to comply with the requirement to make alcohol an ancillary to music and dancing and substantial refreshment.

These arguments took up three days in the Divisional Court and two days in the Court of Appeal where three of the finest legal brains in the country sought to unravel the complexities which have been drawn in to Licensing Law over the years by piecemeal amendments.

I had hoped to been the happy position of announcing the result or at least able to give an indication of what the result will be, unfortunately I cannot. Lord Justice Simon Brown concluded the proceedings with the words "I think it goes without saying that it is a case where we shall take time: indeed, it may be alas some considerable time. No doubt parties would like an answer as soon as possible but it is peculiarly difficult questions you ask and it is a particularly difficult time of year at which to ask them. So we will do the best we can but it will not be this side of October and it could be substantially the other side".

Certainly I would never wish to play Poker with these Lords of appeal and can not begin to try and guess what the outcome will be. The Shipley camp is still convinced that it had the right answer but then so is the Marsden camp.

I did say that it had taken two full days in the Court of Appeal and clearly there were many more arguments than mentioned above. For the really curious or should I say masochistic there is a full transcript available.

villages over a 15-mile radius, the whole of a market town, or a number of backstreets in a large city.

When 'assessing' you are checking on a number of factors: what is being provided well locally and where are the gaps in the market; which pubs are 'over-trading', from which you could expect to take trade; which pubs are currently poorly run or decorated or furnished but which may provide stronger competition in the near future; what prices can be sustained by the local economy?

You will also be looking at your target market. How many potential customers are there? Is potential custom growing or shrinking? Are local employers taking on staff or rumoured to be closing down?

This is a job you may share with professional advisers. You may have access to invaluable local knowledge. A professional valuer may have access to trade figures at local competitor outlets which could assist in your estimation of the potential of the pub you are interested in. An expert valuer could also use publicly available figures from the rating authority to provide an estimate of recent trade at all the pubs round and about.

HOW DO I SET ABOUT FINANCING THE COST OF MY PUB?

Tenancy ingoings

Most brewers and PubCos expect the ingoings for a tenancy to be financed from unborrowed cash. You are only buying furniture and stock, not acquiring a business that can be sold and will have no previous accounts to go on, so a bank is unlikely to lend money in any event. The average ingoing is £10,000-20,000 - not much more than the cost of the average new car, yet it will provide both a home and a business.

There was a vast amount of chaos following the Beer Orders in 1990 which meant that many pubs were occupied by temporary tenants. These problems are in the main over and done with, but some companies still have vacancies where they are prepared to take applicants with less cash than they need and buy the inventory and/or build up a security deposit over a period of time. Potential tenants should have a minimum of £5000 cash.

Lease premium

New-issue leases direct from brewers or PubCos work just like tenancies in that the lessee buys inventory and stock and sometimes pays a deposit. Leases coming up for assignment are sold at prices which are negotiated by the incoming and outgoing lessees. It is difficult but not impossible to raise a bank loan against a pub lease. It is more usual to put up some form of security (perhaps a second charge against a private house) while using the accounts of the pub business as proof to the bank that the borrower can afford to repay the loan. Brewers of course will not be interested in lending against tied leases, although there are some free-

Choosing your Pub

of-tie leases which could provide security for a free trade loan.

Then there are loan sharks. I would strongly advise using only a broker who has been personally recommended to you. High-street banks are generally only good for top-up loans or overdrafts. They regard pub leases as fairly low on their list of preferred loans and seek only the best security.

Leases can be had for very little money. Most sell for £20,000-30,000; a few fetch over £100,000 but these are likely to show a potential income of £50,000-100,000 a year.

Free house purchase

As I mentioned before freeholds have traditionally sold at one-and-a-half times turnover. This is because, depending on interest rates, a business can generally support a loan of around one to one-and-a-quarter times turnover. Banks have aimed to loan only around two-thirds of the purchase price, with the balance coming from the purchaser's own resources.

At the time of writing, prices are generally lower than this range, but banks are still looking to lend to a maximum of only 70 per cent of purchase price. In addition to funding the other 30 per cent, the purchaser will need money for stock cashflow and possible improvements. It does not pay to be underfunded when starting a business.

Let us consider two alternatives.

(a) An immaculate, well-maintained, furnished and decorated free house with a cur-rent proven turnover of £200,000 and a net profit of £50,000.

purchase price 5½ times net profit	= £275,000
bank loan of 70%	= £192,500
cash required by buyer	= £82,500
plus stock	= £5,000
plus fees for solicitor, survey	= £8,250
plus cash in hand	= £10,000
purchaser's total requirement	= **£105,750**

In this case, the buyer needed cash resources amounting to 38.5 per cent of the purchase price.

(b) A run-down pub being bought from a brewery. Needs £30,000 spent on structure, £20,000 on new inventory, £10,000 on decorations. Likely to take £150,000, but will take 12 months to reach this level.

purchase price	= £100,000
bank loan of 60%	= £60,000
cash required by buyer	= £40,000
plus stock	= £2,000
plus fees	= £5,000
improvements as above	= £60,000
six months' losses	= £30,000
living expenses for a year	= £10,000
purchaser's total requirement	= **£147,000**

Thus it can be seen that, on paper at least, the buyer of a run-down pub needs more cash than the buyer of an existing success. In practice such pubs are often bought by people who are able to do much of the renovation themselves and will be funded over a period of time, perhaps taking a second loan from a brewery. I have made no allowance for the VAT payable as this is refundable to the business; although it has to be found on day one it can be re-used as working or development capital when it is reclaimed.

Finance for buying a free house comes mainly from banks, which require a business viability study as well as a building survey. Brewers still provide free trade loans, but increasingly these are used to 'top up' bank loans or for development capital when the owner wishes to build an extension. Brewery loans for the purchase of free houses are most prevalent in the north of England where a higher proportion of sales will come from beer.

WOULD A LOAN TIE BE APPROPRIATE FOR A FREE HOUSE?

With interest rates currently low and available discounts on beer high, it is unusual for a free trade loan to be the best source of finance for the purchase of a free house. There are exceptions, but brewery finance is more usually used in small doses over short periods.

In our first example above, the prospective purchaser may only have £90,000 cash. To enable him to buy he would borrow £16,000 on second charge from a brewery but would aim to pay this off as soon as possible because he will be better off claiming discounts on beer supplies. However, without the brewery loan he would either have been unable to buy or would have commenced business in such a tight financial position that he may have got off on the wrong foot.

BUSINESS PLANS, CASHFLOW FORECASTS, AND INDEPENDENT FINANCIAL ADVICE

All lenders will require business plans and cashflow forecasts. Even if you are fortunate enough not to need other people's money or are taking a tenancy or a low-priced lease, you would be well advised to prepare these plans for your own use.

In any event, landlords are likely to want to see them from applicants for tenancies and leases. Remember our 80:20 rule. Those who fail are philanderers, dipsomaniacs and the financially challenged. (Den Watts of EastEnders fame was all three.)

There are professional firms that will produce business plans and cashflows for you, but many are 'off the peg' financial models which you will have to adapt to the business you intend to run. It is also important that you understand what has been produced for you and what to do to turn paper into profits. Training courses will tell you the basics so that you can work with the professionals to achieve results.

A good mortgage broker will usually work through a business plan with a potential buyer as it

Choosing your Pub

PUB TENANCIES

small big or Do **you** know the difference?

YOUR OWN SMALL BUSINESS
Take business for instance. Whilst the opportunity to run a big business is probably beyond the reach of most of us, you may often have thought about the challenge and enjoyment of running your own small business. The problem is, you don't know where to begin of how to make the best use of your limited capital.

EXCELLENT REWARDS
There is an exciting small business opportunity which offers a low cost of entry and where your energy, personality and business acumen can bring you excellent rewards, as well as providing an enjoyable, if demanding lifestyle.

WE'LL APPRECIATE YOUR NEEDS
We're talking about the chance for you to take on a traditional pub tenancy – but a tenancy with a difference. Unlike many companies that have become just too big to understand or appreciate your needs in running a small business, we are still proud to be small.

YOU'LL DISCOVER YOUR FULL POTENTIAL
We are also an independent family brewery, with a high quality estate and five generations of experience in running pubs. As a result, we are sensitive enough to be able to treat people as individuals, to match your skills and personality to the right type of pub and to provide you with specific help and support to allow you to discover your full potential.

TAKE CARE OF CUSTOMERS
We operate a traditional three year agreement, with sensible rents, where we take care of the repairs and leave you secure, to take care of the customers.

SUPPORT & HELP TO GET STARTED
You'll enjoy excellent support and the benefit of our experience to help you get started. We'll supply you with a superb range of top beers and lagers including our own award-winning traditional ales and you're likely to have the opportunity to develop a good food trade.

TAKE THE BIG STEP
If all this sounds interesting and captures your imagination and enthusiasm, why not take the big step of contacting us for an informal and confidential discussion about your future in the pub trade. We'll arrange a full and frank discussion, with seasoned managers, about your suitability and the opportunities we can currently offer.

YOU'LL LOVE THE FREEDOM
People who join us as pub tenants love the freedom to make their own business decisions but appreciate the back-up from a team of cheerful, friendly professionals. They usually wish they had taken the step years earlier.

If you're interested in an Everards pub tenancy, call Janet Sheppard today on 0116 201 4225 to make an appointment, or write to her at:

Everards Brewery Limited, Castle Acres, Narborough, Leicestershire, LE9 5BY.

EVERARDS ESTABLISHED 1849

LET'S TALK ABOUT OUR FUTURE TOGETHER...

will form part of the application for the loan. Otherwise you will do well to get a recommendation on a stocktaker and/or accountant who specialises in the licensed trade. Your agent, mortgage broker or even a friendly local licencee should be in a position to recommend one.

Accountants often specialise: you want one who already handles a large number of public house accounts. Similarly a good stocktaker can be a provider of good, relatively cheap advice both before you buy and, most importantly, in the first few months of running your business.

WHAT SOLICITORS TO USE?

I think you've got the message by now: use specialists. You need specialist valuers, agents/brokers, accountants, mortgage brokers and stocktakers. Similarly, the solicitor who was jolly good for your mum's divorce or your brother's fraud case is unlikely to be much use when you're buying your pub.

Solicitors charge by the hour. One who doesn't know what he's doing is likely to take twice as long - and charge twice as much. Solicitors need to know how to tie in the dates of the transfer of the licence with exchange and completion of the sale. Regular dealings with those providing mortgage funds will also smooth the path.

At Fleurets we have two or three solicitors in each region that we are able to recommend on the basis of a combination of speed, efficiency and cost. Agents are probably in the best position to judge these factors.

CONCLUSION

I trust I have given you food for thought. Most of what I've said may sound off-putting. If you still want to run a pub you should be much better equipped to do so once you have read this book. But don't forget, it is no use just seeking advice. You must act on it. Good luck. I hope you buy your first pub through Fleurets.

Legal Notes

Without doubt anyone interested in acquiring a pub should seek guidance from professional advisers experienced in the area of licensed premises.

You should consult:

♦ a surveyor who will check out the property;
♦ an accountant to assess the viability of the figures and prepare cashflow forecasts and a business plan;
♦ a solicitor to handle the lease/conveyancing formalities and the transfer of the Liquor Licence.

You must also ask questions of your own. Ask as many questions

Choosing your Pub

of the seller as possible and if your questions are not answered to your satisfaction, then walk away.

Ask locals for their views. Ask the police if they are aware of any problems. Consult representatives of the local authority to establish whether there are any outstanding noise complaints or concerns of a similar nature.

If you are applying for a **new licence**, the recommended approach is to consult a solicitor with liquor licensing experience. Be careful, as this is very much a specialist field. Seek out the licensing specialists in your area for the best advice.

To apply for the **Transfer of a Licence**, application must be given in prescribed form to the Clerk to the Licensing Justices, the police, the local authority and any parish or district council (Schedule 1 Licensing Act 1964). You will have to satisfy the police and court that you are a fit and proper person to hold a Justices' Licence. Typically this will involve a meeting with the local licensing officer who will check for any criminal convictions and carry out an interview with a view to establishing whether you are sufficiently familiar with the licensing laws. Criminal convictions may or may not be a bar to obtaining a licence depending on when and in what circumstances the conviction arose, the severity of the matters involved, and the attitude of the local police and justices. Failure to immediately disclose any conviction, no matter how irrelevant you may consider it to be, is, however, fatal to any licence application. The police will expect you to be frank and truthful.

If, for any reason, your application is opposed, then you present your application to the magistrates who will listen to the arguments both for and against. They will then decide whether or not to grant a transfer. There is a right of appeal against refusal to the Crown Court within 21 days of the date of the decision.

Town and Country Planning legislation may affect your public house, so it is important to ensure that appropriate enquiries are made at your local council before making any commitment.

Planning restrictions can take many different forms. For example, they may limit trading hours, impose parking restrictions, or restrict the way in which the premises may operate.

Ignoring planning considerations is inviting trouble: local authority planning inspectors can and will take costly enforcement action.

Find out in particular whether your pub is in a conservation area and, if your building is of a historic nature, whether listed building controls apply.

Remember to ensure that, if you are considering altering licensed premises, you obtain the prior consent of the Licensing Justices. **Alterations** which give increased facilities for drinking in a public or common part of the premises or conceal from observation a public or common part of the premises where intoxicating liquor is sold and the remainder of the premises or any street or other public way require the prior consent of the Licensing Justices. Courts do not have the power to grant back-dated consent.

If in doubt, seek advice.

CHAPTER TWO

BAR DESIGN AND MERCHANDISING

Paul Cooper

This chapter deals with the servery itself:

- design;
- layout;
- equipment;
- how to make it work for you.

This is probably your most dramatic personal statement in the pub and is certainly your greatest sales aid. It can send many messages to customers about you and your pub. The question that must be considered is: is it saying what you want it to say?

WHAT TO STOCK

In the first instance, you need to establish the range of goods you are going to sell. You should consider the full spread of products available: beers, ciders, minerals, spirits, wines, snacks, tobacco, confectionery. Determining your drinks is dealt with in Chapters 6 and 7 but I will deal with the other products here.

There are three options available when considering tobacco products:

- not to stock the products;
- to sell them from behind the bar;
- to sell them from a cigarette machine.

The first option is not one that should be considered seriously unless your pub is to be completely non-smoking. Although the margins are small, tobacco sales can provide additional income and incremental profit with no extra effort on your part. Selling tobacco products also provides an additional service to an average 30 per cent of your customers.

If you decide to stock cigarettes behind the bar, you must consider security – cigarettes tend to be the most pilfered stock lines in a pub.

The remaining choice is whether to have a cigarette machine or not. Cigarette machines can be purchased outright, rented or supplied and maintained by a company who pay you commission based on sales. If you purchase a machine, you will have to pay for any maintenance that is required. A machine provided by a company who pay you commission is usually maintained as part of the service. The choice is based on personal preference, but most people opt for the latter as it creates fewer problems for them.

Depending on your customer profile, additional tobacco products such as rolling tobacco and papers, cigars and pipe tobacco should be considered. If there are potential sales to be made you should stock the products; they provide both additional income and a service to your customers. However, there are some publicans who prefer not to stock rolling papers as they feel it encourages drug use.

It is more or less essential that you stock matches. Providing them on the counter top in the frog of a brick on which to strike them could be a nice touch.

Most pubs stock bag snacks, and some stock confectionery. You must decide whether or not these products will appeal to your customer profile. If you run a family pub, you will probably have a demand for confectionery and standard bag snacks. A town centre young persons' pub will probably have little demand for sweets, but stocking an adult premium range of bag snacks, eg tortilla chips, Brannigan's crisps etc (and of course charging premium prices), will generate sales.

Other impulse lines may be worth stocking, eg hot nuts, jellybean machines, pepperami, etc, but you should consider whether they will generate sales. There are always new products on the market that may work in your pub.

DESIGN

Although the bar has to be essentially functional, it should still be considered within the overall design of the pub. When designing the bar, ensure that it will match the pub and does not clash with the rest of the decor. It must appear to be an integral part of the premises and not look as though it were plonked in as an afterthought. If you are running a trendy wine bar, you may want to have your bar built in black with chrome fittings – which would look somewhat out of place in a thatched 15th-century inn.

Similarly, what is there already may not suit your needs or the character of the outlet. In the 1960s many beautiful traditional pubs were lovingly refurbished and fitted with the then obligatory melamine-topped bar. I have yet to see one of these design wonders of a bygone age that still looks as trendy and tasteful as when it was fitted. Depending on the money you have available, though, it may not be necessary to rip out your bar and start again. It may be simply a case of replacing or re-covering the top and front.

The position of the servery within the pub is equally as important. You must ensure that it is prominent and easily accessible from all areas of the bar and that it does not create bottlenecks.

BAR

Bar Equipment and Refrigeration Company Limited

A Complete Refrigeration & Air Conditioning Service to the Brewery Industry

Telephone 01767 317444

Adleigh House, Shortmead Street, Biggleswade, Bedfordshire SG18 0BB   Facsimile 01767 318844

The Publican's Handbook

PUB TALK

There are times when customers need to use the phone - perhaps to call a taxi or arrange to meet friends. This is why, for a public house, a payphone is an essential feature. Without one customers would become restless while publicans may find their own phone bills soaring sharply.

One of BT's latest payphones, the Contour 100, is compact, coin-operated and small enough to work well in any semi-supervised public location such as a pub or bar. Also available is the Contour 200, suitable for publicans as it's tough metal casing is resistant to vandal attacks which is ideal for unsupervised areas. However, it's the technological features of the Contour range which makes them especially popular.

Call rate setting is one of a number of these useful features. Owners can also simply activate a secure private owner mode, and their personal calls are charged to their own phone bill at the normal rate. This flexibility is crucial for some publicans.

Other features on the Contour are designed to make calling easier for customers. The memory button permit users to press one digit instead of looking up numbers or having to remember them by heart. For example customers would only need to press one number to get straight through to a local taxi service.

Of course the Contour has many more

A payphone is vital for public houses - A customer denied the chance to make a call is an unhappy customer. Thankfully payphones are becoming more sophisticated and now offer a range of time and money saving features

benefits which could be invaluable to public houses. A liquid crystal display in six languages, volume control and a raised pip on the middle key to cater for the hearing and visually impaired.

And there'll be no need to change the payphone when new coins are introduced, like the new 50p, later this year. Contour is "futureproofed" and can be easily programmed to accept new coins.

Meanwhile, the Contour also has important features common to domestic phones such as last number redial. Also, a next call option facility allows users to move straight from one call to the next without putting down the receiver.

The Contour 100 is available on a BT fixed price rental or as an outright purchase of £249 (exc VAT). Other BT Private Payphones include the Contour 50 and Contour Cardpay which accept BT Phonecards.

For further information or to place an order call Freefone 0800 44 22 55.

Bar Design and Merchandising

Customers standing at the bar will be in the way if it is positioned next to toilets, entrances, etc. The size of the bar also needs consideration. If the bar is too small it will be impossible to serve customers within an acceptable time, if it is too large you are wasting drinking space and reducing the number of customers you can fit into the pub. In either instance the outcome will be the same: lost sales.

The amount of space behind the bar should be considered in the same light: too little and staff cannot work efficiently, too much and you are wasting space.

It is a personal choice whether you have bar trays, beer mats, bar towels, serviettes or nothing on the counter to stand drinks on. The most important thing is to ensure that it remains clean, dry and free from spills. Wet or dirty items should be replaced as often as required and not left until they are sodden and disintegrating, and ashtrays should be emptied into a metal receptacle and cleaned regularly.

THE BAR BACK AND COUNTER TOP

The bar back or back fitting is the greatest sales aid you have; it is where your customers look to find out what range of products you sell. Yet few pubs maximise the potential of the back fitting to ensure that customers know exactly what products they provide.

The design and layout of the back fitting should be determined by the products, your sales mix and the type of pub. But before examining the back fitting in detail, we will look at the counter top and how best to display your products.

Draught products form the majority of items displayed on any counter top, and although generally declining in sales still account for well over 50 per cent of sales. Considering the huge proportion of sales they generate it is amazing how little time is put into planning their positioning on the counter.

You will soon find that customers tend to head for a particular part of the bar when they enter the pub. This position has the greatest selling potential and will usually be the busiest point. Place your best-selling products at this point and don't clutter it with items that detract, eg a glasswasher or glass collection point.

Also consider the most convenient positioning of products in relation to each other – that is, store the tonic near the gin! Minimise the distance that staff need to walk from any one part of the bar to a particular product; it may help to divide a large bar into several stations, with the whole product range available at each one. Tills should be positioned with care, because ease of access to them will affect service speed.

The golden rule is to group all products of a similar kind together, enabling customers to see the full range all at once. Cask ale drinkers will head straight for the handpulls, so lining up all the handpulls side by side allows them to choose from your full range. If you have a couple of handpulls at one end of the bar and a couple at the other end with different ales on them, the customer may think you only stock two ales when in fact you stock four. In addition, a bank of four handpulls has a much greater visual impact than two sets of twins.

If you have more than one bar, make sure you have the full range on display in each bar. If volumes do not warrant having more than one pump for each product line, use the pumps on one bar as dummies so the customer knows what is available, even though it may mean staff occasionally having to slip into the other bar to complete an order.

The same principles apply to keg products: position products of the same kind next to each other. There are two ways of displaying keg products:

- ◆ *T-bars*: these enable the full range of products to be displayed next to each other but may not be in keeping with your type of outlet;
- ◆ *branded fonts*: these may be more suitable but they can look cramped and cluttered.

The choice is purely personal.

Another item that warrants consideration in the layout of the counter is glass collection. Designated collection points are essential in a busy pub to ensure you don't run out of glasses, and thus jeopardise the speed of service, but don't clutter up the counter top either. Collection points should be positioned to avoid key selling points but they should also be easily accessible from all areas of the pub.

Displaying drink

Premium bottled drinks

Premium packaged lagers have seen a huge growth in popularity over the past 10 years. Starting from a very low base, they now account for 10 per cent or more of liquor sales in pubs that offer a full range of products and for a much higher proportion of sales where the product range does not include cask or keg products.

Flavoured alcoholic beverages (alcopops) and ready-to-drink spirit mixes have recently grown in consumption and are becoming more and more popular.

These would traditionally have been displayed in fridges below the back bar counter. But if they are big sellers in your pub – and generally they are now the second biggest selling product group – they warrant more prominent display. The best way to exhibit them is to install eye-level chillers, a fancy name for high-level glass-fronted fridges. They display the products how customers want to drink them: cold. To be effective, though, they have to be designed into the back fitting. A bar cooler plonked on the back bar counter top looks exactly that and has a negative effect on the display you are trying to enhance.

If you don't have the money to invest in eye-level chillers or they are not in line with the decor and style of the pub, an alternative is to create displays of bottled products. These should be neat, clean, uncluttered and make use of any point of sale material you can get.

Once you have created a display, it is important to keep it neat, clean

Bar Design and Merchandising

SOLUTIONS FOR SOFT DRINKS DISPENSE

BOC Sureflow which was established in 1987 is now the leading dispense gas supplier in the UK and part of the world famous BOC Group. The company has lead the way in providing not only the best and most reliable services but also a range of quality products tailored to each customer's needs - be it a traditional pub or club, restaurant or even fast food outlet.

The growth in post mix soft drinks dispense has increased the number of outlets requiring CO_2. BOC Sureflow has been at the forefront of developing links with major soft drinks companies and leisure outlets with companies such as Britvic, KFC and soft drinks producer Ben Shaws all relying on BOC Sureflow.

"BOC Sureflow supply all our managed outlets with dispense gas and around 95% of the franchise operations" explained Kevin Higgins, Director Pepsico Restaurant Services.

"One of the key elements in our decision to work with BOC Sureflow was the level of service they provided for our outlets. With KFC restaurants across the whole country it was important that we could rely on prompt and efficient deliveries of gas cylinders at agreed times and with minimal disruption for the staff of the restaurants."

Soft drinks manufacturers, Ben Shaws, who supply over 5,000 customers with tailor-made dispense facilities and offer the largest dispense product portfolio in the country have no doubt BOC Sureflow is the best in the business. "We always recommend BOC Sureflow to our customers, such as garage forecourts, independent grocers and shopping groups who have little experience of dispense gas" said John Bairstow, Ben Shaw's Dispense Products Manager. "I know I can rely on BOC Sureflow to keep our customers happy with excellent service, a high priority on safety and competitive prices".

All customers are issued with a Service Charter detailing the standards they can expect from BOC Sureflow. Should the company fall below any of these specifications then it will investigate the reasons. The Service Charter covers all aspects from prompt and reliable deliveries at specified times and (if requested) cylinders connected at the point of use; to full technical support; and safety advice. If, through any fault of BOC Sureflow a customer runs out of gas then £20 worth of gas is provided free of charge.

– and intact. Staff have a tendency to sell bottles from displays, which leaves them looking tatty; and a dusty display tells the customer that the product doesn't sell. Displays must be backed up with a stock of cold bottles in your under-counter fridges.

There is a tendency to fill fridges with a single row of each product sold. The most effective use of fridge space is to have blocks of product, with a maximum of two products per shelf. The appearance and sales impact can be further enhanced by vertical stacking, ie having the same product on two or more shelves in a vertical line.

If you are unable to achieve this presentation due to lack of fridge space you should examine your product range and establish whether you really need to stock all the products, whether they all need to be in the fridges (it is preferable to serve chilled soft drinks but not essential as ice can be added), or whether there is space for additional refrigeration.

Point of sale (PoS) merits a quick note. PoS kits usually contain enough material to re-decorate your entire pub. But use it sparingly. A small amount, well-placed and well-selected, will look much more effective than plastering the pub with PoS until it looks like a discount store. Keep the leftovers, though: it's important to replace your displays every four weeks at least, or they'll lose all impact. Another point: those Christmas tree lights that many publicans feel necessary to drape around the over-counter shelf all year round. I was once told that they use these lights when they are serving after time – being less bright than the normal lighting, they're less likely to attract police attention. Don't use them: they're tacky.

Minerals and soft drinks

Consumption of minerals is increasing for three reasons:

- ◆ public intolerance of drink-driving;
- ◆ increasing awareness of the health risks of alcohol;
- ◆ a growing number of teetotallers.

With this increase in consumption comes a demand for more exciting adult-oriented soft drinks such as flavoured mineral waters.

There is little to be gained from displaying standard soft drinks prominently, as everyone expects them to be there. But adult-oriented soft drinks are not available in many pubs, and therefore can create a point of difference. To make your customers aware of these products and promote them they should be displayed in the same way as premium packaged lagers.

The same could also be said of the many branded soft drinks such as Tango, Lilt, Fanta and so on which have hitherto been more the province of the CTN trade than the pub trade.

With the growth in family dining out, it makes sense to be able to offer under-14s the same brands of soft drinks they drink at home – and if you do, make sure they're aware of it.

Spirits

The normal way of displaying spirits is on Optic, and a traditional

Bar Design and Merchandising

BOC GASES
SUREFLOW

SAFETY

It goes without saying that buying from BOC Sureflow also guarantees peace of mind. All Sales Servicepersonnel are fully trained in safety procedures and are able to offer advice and guidance on gas dispensing.

All the necessary safety information on products is provided free of charge. Free leak tests can be carried out to ensure that a system is operating efficiently and without wastage while Carbon Dioxide monitoring can be provided as an additional safety precaution.

FLEXIBILITY

For large outdoor leisure facilities such as Alton Towers where there are numerous restaurants and snack food bars all around the grounds as well as mobile carts with soft drinks for visitors to purchase, BOC Sureflow's large cylinder packages as well as the traditional cylinders provide the ideal answer. They are flexible, easy to use and cost-efficient. BOC Sureflow deliver to no fewer than 52 separate points around the grounds which solves management headaches of cylinders not being in the correct place at the correct time.

COSTS

The BOC Sureflow price promise also means customers can rest easy, secure in the knowledge that not only can they rely on the quality of the product but also that it will be very competitively priced.

FOR FURTHER INFORMATION ON BOC SUREFLOW PRODUCTS OR SERVICES CALL 0345 302302

The Publican's Handbook

The very best in gas dispense

BOC Sureflow offers an unrivalled service nationwide in the supply of both carbon dioxide and mixed gas for dispensing beer and soft drinks.

Mixed gas is a combination of carbon dioxide and nitrogen in three different proportions – 30% carbon dioxide for ales and stouts, 50% carbon dioxide for ales and lagers and 60% carbon dioxide for highly carbonated lagers and ciders.

Mixed gas offers a number of benefits over traditional carbon dioxide:

■ Beer wastage through fobbing can be significantly reduced

■ Beer is dispensed faster with mixed gas which enables more customers to be served in a given time period

■ The pint's presentation can be consistently improved with a longer lasting, tighter, creamier head

■ Slower moving draught beers can be kept in good condition for longer

■ Mixed gas avoids the need for unnecessary and complex electric pumps

The sort of dispense equipment required is largely dependent on the level of throughput. For those outlets dispensing under eight barrels a week the traditional 14lb cylinder is popular and cost effective.

For pubs using more than eight standard 14lb cylinders a month BOC Sureflow offers three further options:

The Large Cylinder Package

The large pre-mixed cylinder has a capacity five times greater than standard 14lb cylinders. Gas is piped into the ring mains. Up to two or four cylinders of any mixed gas or carbon dioxide can be connected together via a manifold providing the equivalent of up to 20 traditional cylinders.

As the cylinder empties a simple switch changes from empty to full. BOC Sureflow will deliver the new cylinders to the point of use and connect them up. The Large Cylinder Package will save time. For customers using more than eight standard cylinders per month the Large Cylinder Package saves between 20-30% in gas costs.

Gasgen 2000

An air separation unit is an on-site nitrogen generation and carbon dioxide gas blending system for mixed gas dispense. Gasgen 2000 can generate up to four mixtures of gas thereby enabling the dispense of a wider range of drinks from a single gas source. In addition the wall mounted unit is ideally suited to the cellar environment and has the added advantage of using free nitrogen to dispense wines and fruit drinks as well as blanketing for cask conditioned ales. Carbon dioxide can also be used for post mix. For larger users the Gasgen 2000 offers an average saving of up to 10%.

BOC GASES
SUREFLOW

Bar Design and Merchandising

BOC GASES
SUREFLOW
The guaranteed dispensing gas service

Bulk Liquid Carbon Dioxide Tank

The liquid tank provides the equivalent to 32 traditional 14lb carbon dioxide cylinders. It is an ideal solution for high volume soft drink or beer dispensing. It is particularly convenient and cost effective if the usage is greater than eighteen 14lb cylinders per month.

THE BOC SUREFLOW PROMISE FOR EQUIPMENT

- We will not require customers to commit to a contract.
- BOC Sureflow will carry out a free site and safety survey.
- Installation and maintenance are usually free of charge.
- We have an emergency call out service should your BOC installed equipment break down where service engineers will arrive within four normal working hours.
- Full training on the use and operation of the systems is provided by BOC Staff.

AND A SPECIAL GUARANTEE OF RELIABILITY

If through any fault of **BOC Sureflow**, you run out of gas, we will provide you with £20 worth of free gas.

FOR MORE INFORMATION ON BOC SUREFLOW

call **0345 302 302** quoting ref: **ADV64**

SERVICE CHARTER

The BOC Sureflow Service Charter

■ Free emergency service seven days a week to supply extra gas within 24 hours

■ Reliability – we will deliver the quantities required on the days it is needed so that gas supply does not run short

■ Cylinders are delivered to the point of use and connected as part of the service

■ Collection – to ensure a safe and clutter free area, we will remove our empty cylinder promptly

■ Free leak tests – if you wish, we will ensure that gas is not being wasted by undertaking leak tests on your dispensing equipment

■ Free replacement – our cylinders are well maintained, and filled with the highest quality food grade gas. Any cylinder that proves to be faulty will be replaced free of charge

back fitting would have an Optic rail running its full length at eye level.

But in the context of declining spirit sales, you need to think about whether this is right for your pub. The eye level of any back fitting is the best sales area available. Is it advisable to devote the whole of this area to products that are in decline? You may gain a greater advantage from turning part of this area over to displaying higher volume products, growing products or new products on display shelves or eye-level fridges.

On the other hand, Optics provide a quick and easy method of dispensing spirits and reducing their numbers can lead to a reduced speed of service.

One alternative is to have two Optic rails in the same place one slightly lower and behind the other. Or you may decide that your style of operation is better suited to free-pour spirits and thimble measures.

Whichever method of dispense you choose, there are a number of details to take into account when deciding the layout of your spirits:

- group spirits into white spirits and dark, with sub-groups of like products, eg whiskies, vodkas, etc;
- place two or more bottles of the same brand together.

These techniques enhance presentation and can increase sales.

Wine

Wine is probably the most difficult product to display effectively. A combination of ice buckets, wine racking and display shelves will send your customers the message that you stock a range of wines.

This should be backed up with a wine list, either on paper, card or blackboard, giving information about the wine to assist customers in their choice - country of origin, percentage alcohol by volume, taste style, etc. If, due to your customer profile, you stock only a basic range of wine, it may be enough to display it in an ice bucket or fridge and train staff to provide other information should anyone ask.

Impulse purchases

Some products, including bag snacks and hot beverages, are impulse purchases. Customers do not come to your pub to buy a packet of crisps but may purchase them to accompany other products.

You can increase sales of impulse products by ensuring they are displayed prominently. Customers are more likely to make a purchase if they have seen them. The ideal ways to display impulse products are at eye level or by means of a blackboard advertisement. You could put crisps in baskets on the back bar or have special shelves built to display them. Hot beverages can be promoted by positioning a coffee machine behind the bar in full view of the customers.

New products

New products need prominent positioning. Place your displays and point of sale in the hotspots of the bar - the places that catch customers' eyes. These are different in every outlet but are typically

Bar Design and Merchandising

prominent corners and above till positions.

Making space

A number of other considerations should be taken into account when analysing a back fitting. Tills are often put here but it may be a good idea, where possible, to move them to the counter front. This reduces the number of times staff turn their backs on the customers and also frees space on the back fitting for displaying products – you are not in business to sell tills. Nor do you sell glasses, so don't use the back fitting to display them. There is no advantage or sales building potential in doing this – it just wastes valuable space.

Gravity dispense

Serving real ales direct from the cask, as well as making a feature out of the casks on the back fitting creates the image of the traditional pub serving traditional products.

There are disadvantages, though. In order to maintain the beer in peak condition you need to provide some kind of cooling system, which is ugly and takes up space. As it is not easy to get a head on beer drawn straight from the cask you risk impairing the presentation of the beer. And unless there is a large amount of space it is not practical to rack barrels to allow them to condition.

However, if you wish to display one or two guest beers in this way the problems are somewhat reduced.

Blackboards

Blackboards are often part of the bar area or back fitting, and it is important to use them to their best advantage. They can convey innumerable messages to customers:

- promotions;
- forthcoming events;
- food specials;
- menu;
- new products;
- wine list;
- cask ale list, etc.

But blackboards will only work as a sales aid if they are well written. This is a skill not everyone possesses. A badly written or incorrectly spelled board will give a negative message to customers. If you are not good at writing blackboards, it is worth trying to find a good blackboarder among your staff and delegating the job – be honest with yourself about your ability. In some areas there are professional blackboarders who will create wonderful boards that really do the job of communication well.

Bar stools

Bar stools are a feature common to nearly all pubs, and in many outlets they are beneficial. People like to stand or sit at the bar, particularly if they are on their own, and bar stools give out the friendly message that it is all right to stand or sit around the servery and maybe chat to the staff.

Busy outlets, however, need to encourage customers to move away from the bar once they have bought their drinks. If you have to keep the

The Publican's Handbook

New cellar lifting and storage system

A new system that will lift and position casks and kegs in cellars, in many cases more than doubling the cellars capacity, has been introduced by brewery engineers Chadburns Ltd.

The system comprises a overhead hoist, which doesn't use any valuable floor space, and a stillage system that will enable casks to be stored in two tiers. Also incorporated is an automatic tilt that will gradually tilt the cask as it is emptied.

The introduction follows the publication of the Health and Safety at Work guidelines which does not allow even a 9 gall cask to be fitted manually. This means that in due course all cellars will have to be fitted with a mechanical lifting device, which is far from easy in most cellars with restricted floor space and head room.

The new system lifts and positions casks of various sizes on a two tier stillage systems. The control is by a simple to operate push button which enables the casks to be positioned accurately in the stillage. The optional automatic tilt mechanism ensures that the minimum amount of ullage is wasted, increasing the beer output by around two pints per cask.

Details of the cellar system is available from Chadburns Ltd, Park Lane Bootle, Merseyside L30 4UP. Telephone 0151 525 4155.

Bar Design and Merchandising

Getting a Quart Into a Pint Pot

Getting enough casks into a cellar can often seem like getting a quart into a pint pot. Most cellars however could take a least 50% more casks.
The Chadburn Cask Racking and Lifting System enables casks to be stacked two tiers high, at the touch of a button. The powerful lifting system will position 9, 18 or 36 gallon casks and it doesn't use valuable floor space.
Even manual cask tilting becomes a thing of the past. Casks are automatically tilted as the beer is used, and the remaining waste is just ullage giving an increased beer output of around 2 pints per cask.
That's not all! Complying with Health & Safety at work 'lifting guidelines' - is at the touch of a button.

Telephone or fax Chadburns today for details of the Cask Stillage & Lifting System.
Chadburns Ltd. Park Lane Bootle Merseyside L30 4UP
Telephone 0151 525 4155 Fax: 0151 525 4150

CHADBURNS *LIMITED*

DUREX VENDING SERVICES - QUALITY WITHOUT COMPROMISE

YOUR CUSTOMER WANT QUALITY CONDOMS
- More than nine out of ten people still rate their pub as their usual place of purchase for condoms*
- Eight out of ten people want condom dispensers to stock Kitemarked condoms*
- All Durex condoms carry the BSI Kitemark, a symbol of quality, and the CE marking which means that Durex condoms conform to the requirements of the EC Medical Devices Directive.

CHOOSING DUREX VENDING SERVICES - A SIMPLE CHOICE FOR A QUALITY SERVICE
- Durex vending machines are installed, restocked and maintained free of charge
- Each packet of Durex condoms sold through your vending machine can earn you commission

TO FIND OUT MORE ABOUT DUREX VENDING SERVICES AND THE BENEFITS TO YOU AND YOUR CUSTOMERS PLEASE CONTACT: DAVID SEWELL - 01992 451111

* Figures taken from the SRA Health Monitor Survey

SWAFFHAM DISCOUNT CARPETS

Specialists in contract and domestic floor coverings.
Backed by 35 years experience.
All sizes of beds including waterproof contract type.

Members of Guild of Master Craftsmen

Tel & Fax: 01760 722775

The Publican's Handbook

FUJITSU GENERAL (UK) CO LTD

Comfort control in licensed premises is an important issue. Today's customers expects comfortable temperatures all the year round.

The need for heating has never been questioned; what could be more welcoming on a cold day than a sympathetically lit, warm, bar or restaurant to persuade customers to spend their money? Air conditioning, however, has often been considered an unnecessary expense. After all, how many really hot days do we get in the course of an average British summer and surely the most economical way to deal with them is simply to open a convenient door or window.

This may have been an effective when most of the population worked in non-air conditioned offices and factories. But just as commerce and industry have discovered that efficiency can be improved by providing staff with a cool and comfortable work place, so, many licensed premises have seen increased profitability by providing an equally comfortable environment for customers.

But we do provide optimum comfort to staff as well as a pleasant working environment for customers? Air conditioning is the answer but what type of system should be installed?

Constant volume, variable air volume, fan coil units, chilled ceiling beams, split systems.....the demand for air conditioning has brought a range of system types each offering various benefits.

The most popular local system is the 'split' system, so called because the condenser or chiller unit is positioned remotely from the room unit, usually in a convenient external location. The two pieces of equipment are linked by flexible hoses which carry the refrigerant.

Initially seen as a single unit capable of serving a single area, split systems have benefited from improved control, on-board intelligence as well as ducted versions which make split air conditioner a viable option for the open area.

These systems offer savings in capital and installation costs, and some units include a reverse heat pump which extracts heat from the outside atmosphere and uses it to warm a building. Under some circumstances this 'free' heat can replace other forms of heating and is particularly valuable in unseasonably cool weather by allowing the user to warm an area without resorting to a central heating system. With Fujitsu wall units, heating and cooling is precisely controlled, governed by the auto-changeover

40

program which ensures that temperatures are maintained at pre-set levels.

The equipment itself has been refined to the point where it is compact enough to be used for installations in places which would have been considered impractical, such as narrow space between the top of a door and the ceiling.

Like any nightclub the Talk of the Coast Night Spot, opposite the pier on Blackpool promenade, tends to get hot and stuffy when it is full. With 300 people regularly crowding in, measures had to be taken to keep the temperature down and the air fresh.

Fujitsu ceiling mounted cassette units provided ideally suited to the task. With limited wall space and no suspended ceiling system, the five units have been mounted centrally, directly onto the ceiling in purpose made enclosures to match the ceiling finish. The central location allows maximum use to be made of the 4-way air distribution vents, supplying cool filtered air to the nightclub.

Users can know take advantage of the compact size, near silent operation and most importantly low cost of split air conditioning systems to specify a system that will suit most applications. The Fujitsu range includes floor standing, wall and ceiling mounted, ceiling cassette and window mounted models.

Self-checking diagnostics, 'energy save' routine and zone control, which allows up to 16 units to be controlled from a single liquid crystal remote controller, are all standard design features.

The Fujitsu slim wall unit provides air conditioning without taking up valuable space.

bar clear all the time or nearly all the time for customers waiting to be served, don't provide stools at the bar.

But the same bar stools which are impractical during busy sessions provide a welcome facility for customers at other times. If this is the case, they can be stored out of the bar area during busy sessions.

Glassware

Glassware can be an important marketing device.

A drink presented in an inappropriate glass does nothing to encourage the customer to drink the product or return to your outlet. A drink in an attractive glass will create interest among other customers and help to sell your products. Customers will remember that their gin and tonic tasted much better in your nice tall thin glass with ice and lemon than in the half-pint sleeve they were served with at the pub down the road.

Branded glassware can further enhance the presentation of products and act as a marketing device. Badged glasses differentiate drinks that would otherwise look the same. Another benefit is that they are often provided free of charge by the brand owner, thus saving you money.

These benefits must be weighed against the disadvantage that your staff will spend time trying to find the appropriate glass and at busy times will inevitably use the wrong one.

Toughened glasses have the advantage of reducing the number of breakages, but you should consider whether this fully offsets the additional cost involved in buying them.

Whatever type of glassware you decide is right for your pub, it has to be truly clean. Glasses should sparkle, and not be watermarked, smeary or covered in lipstick. The best way to achieve this is with a mechanical glasswasher.

There are many types available, all of which vary slightly in the way they operate. However, they all wash your glasses and then coat them with a chemical called rinse aid which dries the glass by causing the water to sheet off it.

The best way to ensure clean glasses is to have a clean glasswasher. Clean the filter every day and make sure the water jets are not blocked, and clean the inside of the wash tank at least twice a week to stop the build up of dirt and bacteria.

You must also use good quality chemicals in the machine. The best cleaning fluids are non-caustic. Caustic cleaning fluids eat into the glass and cause etching after a couple of months which is detrimental to the appearance of your glasses (this is not so much of a problem in soft water areas).

A glasswasher should operate at a wash temperature of 45°C and a rinse temperature of 60-65°C. If your machine operates at lower or higher temperatures, it will not clean efficiently. If it has a mechanical dosing unit for the detergent, this should be set by the company that supplied it. If the chemical has to be put in by you add 2-3 squirts of detergent, using a pelican pump, every 4-5 cycles.

Air conditioning for all seasons.

Think air conditioning and you think summer. When the weather hots up, air conditioning brings cool relief from the blistering heat and stuffy conditions. **But Fujitsu air conditioning offers so much more.** Our climate control systems deliver year round comfort. So whether it's 30° or subzero outside – inside will be just perfect. Combined with ultra-easy installation and reliability that just won't quit, it's the perfect solution – all year round. **For more details and our free guide to air conditioning, call us on 01707 278100.**

Please send more information and my free guide.

Name
Company
Address
....Postcode
Telephone .... Fax

Return to: Fujitsu General (UK) Co. Ltd.
154 Great North Road, Hatfield, Herts AL9 5JN. Fax: 01707 273911

you'll be glad you fitted...

FUJITSU
air conditioning

Wall • Cassette • Ceiling • Floor • Duct • Window

Rinse aid is usually inserted by a mechanical pump built into the machine, often self-calibrated.

In hard water areas, a water softener will improve the effectiveness of your glasswasher. If you have a water softener fitted to your machine, you should ensure that you follow the instructions provided.

Lipstick appears to adhere to glass better than it does to lips, and even the best glass washing machines will not remove a thick layer. To get rid of it, wipe the rims of the glasses before you put them in the machine.

There is always a tendency to dry your glasses with a cloth when they come out of the machine. If your machine is working correctly and your glasses are stored on glass mats and not directly on a shelf, there should be no need to – they should dry on their own. A residue of the detergent in which the cloth has been washed will be left on the glass. This inhibits the rinse aid from working properly and your glasses will not dry efficiently.

Common problems of glasswashers, and their solutions are shown in the following table.

Fault	Check	Action
Machine will not fill or rinse	Water supply	Open stop tap fully
Machine not washing effectively	Filter, wash jets, detergent	Remove and clean blocked filters. Unblock wash jets. Use correct amount of detergent
Glasses not drying	Detergent, rinse aid	Ensure correct amount is being used
Condensation on glasses	Rinse aid, glass storage	Use correct amount of rinse aid, do not store glasses on a flat surface
'Blooming' on glasses	Detergent	Use non-caustic detergents
Excessive foaming in wash	Rinse aid, tank water	Reduce amount of rinse aid being injected; ensure machine has not been cleaned with high foam detergent, eg washing up liquid

Bar Design and Merchandising

Thanks to Honeywell, the atmosphere in this hotel couldn't be better.

"*The equipment has helped to clean the environment and adds to the image of the hotel.*"
Callum Scott, Assistant Manager, Channings Hotel, Edinburgh.

Today, more and more companies try to offer solutions to environmental smoke problems in public places. Just look at the ads in this magazine!

But, time and again, our customers tell us that only Honeywell offer the real solution. For the past 40 years Honeywell have been perfecting the art of clean air technology. Our air cleaners, located unobtrusively on the ceiling, remove smoke and other pollutants which can spoil customers' enjoyment and make staff's working conditions unpleasant.

We have a national network of approved distributors who take care of all cleaning and other servicing, leaving you with a hassle-free, perfect atmosphere for your customers and staff.

If you want to find out more, call this number today:

0800 909000

Helping You Control Your World **Honeywell**

Oak Flooring

Specialist suppliers and installers of naturally beautiful, easily maintained, heavy duty wood floors in oak, ash, maple, birch, afzelia, walnut, olive.

Plank, strip or parquet patterns. Design, manufacture, supply and installation by our own craftsmen.

Scandafloor Ltd
Lytham St Annes
Lancashire FY8 3HT
Tel: 01253-714907
Fax: 01253-729348

The Publican's Handbook

Poor air quality is the source of many complaints in public places, and it is well known that one of the most frequent causes of poor air quality is tobacco smoke. Using extractor fans or relying on air-conditioning are partial solutions which can increase energy costs enormously. Opening windows and doors can temporarily help, but it is not always practical and can cause even more problems because of draughts, especially in winter. A blanket smokeban is not always feasible: a number of restaurants which recently introduced total smoking bans saw their business reduce drastically, and had to quickly reverse the policy. A separate smoking room is a fair and viable alternative but without an air cleaner the problem of tobacco smoke will not go away. Smoke will spread from the smoking room into the other areas annoying customers and staff. The growing concern of indoor air quality today means that providing a healthy environment in public places has become a legal requirement. The only solution to this problem is the installation of an air cleaner. Today there are many products on the market but Honeywell offers the most cost effective products, as proved by recent independent tests. Thanks to our 40 years expertise and state-of-the-art technology, our units can quickly and efficiently remove smoke within the designated area, and are needed even when separate air-conditioning or ventilation systems are already installed. But our unit can tackle more than just tobacco smoke. They will remove other annoying pollutants such as dust and pollens, giving you and your customers an altogether cleaner atmosphere. There are over 4 million successful installations worldwide, in all types of buildings: from the factory floor to the open plan office, from the restaurant to the local public house. All our customers are delighted and in many cases restaurant and hotel managers have told us that the installation of our air cleaners has boosted their business: their own customers are happier and more at ease and therefore eager to go back, while staff provide a better service.

A Honeywell air cleaner can bring you other benefits, too! It can save you money on heating bills and protect investments made in decor and soft furnishing from the staining effect of tobacco smoke and the damage caused by dust and pollution. Fabrics and furniture will last longer, making the whole environment more pleasant, be it a pub, a restaurant, or smoking room.

Would you like the freedom to breath? Then Honeywell air cleaners are the answer!

How does a Honeywell air cleaner work? The answer is, very simply and very efficiently.

Dirty air is drawn into the ceiling mounted units where the particles are electrostatically charged and then attracted to a series of aluminium plates. Clean air is then expelled in all directions along the ceiling driving dirty air into the centre of the room where it is drawn up to be cleaned again. Some units are available with infrared remote control to allow you to switch the air cleaner on and off more easily. Honeywell offers a wide range of units with a choice of either white or wood effect finish to harmonize with any decor. The maintenance of a Honeywell air cleaner is completely hassle-free: periodic washing of the plates is the only routine service required. We have an excellent national network of approved distributors who will take care of all service and cleaning requirements to ensure maximum efficiency at all times.

So, providing a breath of fresh air to your customers and staff is no longer an impossible task if you install a Honeywell air cleaner. Remember, everybody stands to win: yourself and your business.

If you are interested and you want to know more, see our advertisement in this magazine and call 0800 909000.

Bar Design and Merchandising

In a pub like this, atmosphere is all important.

"The equipment helps us maintain exactly the right atmosphere for our customer."
Jim McDonald, Licensee, The Prince of Wales, North London.

There is more to creating the right atmosphere than meets the eye. In fact the naked eye can barely see the most unpleasant elements of the atmosphere, such as tobacco smoke, dust and pollen. These particles are too small to be filtered out by most other kinds of air filter.

For the past 40 years Honeywell have been perfecting the art of clean air technology. In our ceiling mounted air cleaners, electrostatically charged particles in the dirty air are deposited on to a series of aluminium plates. Clean air is then expelled in all directions along the ceiling driving dirty air downward and into the centre of the room where it is drawn up again to be cleaned.

In short, tobacco smoke, dust particles, pollen, even small micro-organisms, are removed.

We have a national network of approved distributors who take care of all cleaning and other servicing, leaving you with a hassle-free, perfect atmosphere for your customers and staff.

If you want to know more call this number today

0800 909000

Helping You Control Your World **Honeywell**

Health and Safety Notes

The Food Safety (**General Food Hygiene**) Regulations 1995 require a 'high degree of personal cleanliness' from persons who work in a food handling area, which includes bars, as the legal definition of 'food' includes drink. For this reason, staff should not smoke behind the bar because smoking involves hand to mouth contact. This does not prevent staff smoking elsewhere provided they wash their hands, before serving again. Bar staff, therefore, need access to a 'suitably located' hand basin with hot water, soap, and hand-drying facilities. Depending on where the nearest alternative is, a facility is commonly provided at the bar itself.

Where food is being served from the bar, there are particular food safety issues to consider in addition to the hand-washing facility. In particular, do you intend to have food on display and if so for how long?

The Food Safety (**Temperature Control**) Regulations 1995 apply to foods which may support food-poisoning organisms. The regulations allow for the one-off display of food outside the prescribed temperatures for specific periods (up to four hours for cold food and up to two hours for hot food). However, it is good practice generally (and a specific requirement where the exemptions do not apply) for hot food to be kept at or above 63°C and for cold food to be kept at or below 8°C.

You also need to consider how you intend to protect open food while on display. If you have domestic pets they are a potential source of contamination and their access to food-handling areas needs to be appropriately controlled.

Finally, care needs to be taken with regard to **ice production**. 'Potable' water should be used, and ice machines and freezers need to be kept clean. The use of trays to make ice may result in an undesirable level of handling, as does allowing customers to help themselves. Ice buckets should be kept clean and covered and regularly emptied. Scoop handles should not come into contact with the ice.

As part of the health and safety **risk assessment** required of everyone in business (see Chapter 4 Hiring and Firing), issues to consider with reference to the bar area and people working in it include:

◆ glass breakage;
◆ the condition of the floor (in terms of slipping and tripping);
◆ how to reduce the potential for violence to staff;
◆ measures to reduce the exposure to tobacco smoke and the potential effects of passive smoking;
◆ access to the cellar (where applicable). If a cellar hatch is located behind the bar it is vital

Bar Design and Merchandising

The first establishment to be bought by the new group was The Brothers, a large two bar pub in Glasgow's Saracen Street, which although maintaining a reasonable amount of regular custom, was clearly not realising its full potential.

Strathmore Taverns has now completed a major refurbishment of both the bar and lounge with quality of fitments, equipment and decoration being the key factor throughout.

As has been the case with Keane's previous pubs, once renovation and redecoration is completed an increased flow of trade is generated, so the variety of drinks available and the presentation of these becomes critically important.

One item of equipment that has caused publicans everywhere many sleepless nights is the ice maker, and as The Brothers had a long history of broken down, unreliable machines, Keane decided to opt for the best that was available. City Refrigeration in Glasgow provided him with a Hoshizaki 200kg per day machine that provides the pub with enough ice to last the hottest summer night with the bars at full capacity! Also its stylish good looks complement the new bar area.

Hoshizaki is the world's leading manufacturer of ice machines and is renowned for total reliability and quality and although every machine is supplied with an all encompassing two year parts and labour warranty, they are built to last for many years.

"The Brothers is attracting a lot of new customers," sums up Keane, "and I want to ensure that their first impression of the place is a good one - which includes drinks being perfectly presented - because we want them to return."

HOSHIZAKI CRACKS BARCODE

One of the most fashionable bars to have opened in London's Soho is Barcode. Owned and managed by Stephen Bond, Barcode is a monument to contemporary design. The interior is stark and modern with the strongest statement being made by the galvanised steel bar running the length of the room.

Drinks are served very cold, with ice being used copiously to pack glasses to the brim. As the ice machine was to be a dominant feature of the back bar area - facing customers - it was vital that it not only performed well, but looked good too.

Stephen selected the new Hoshizaki IM130 polished stainless steel ice maker which produces up to 130kgs of ice per 24 hours and has a massive built in 55 kg storage bin to ensure ice availability, even at the busiest times.

The removable, cleanable air filter helps to ensure maximum efficiency whilst dramatically reducing servicing and maintenance.

All Hoshizaki machines are built to last and come with a full 2 years parts and labour warranty.

HOSHIZAKI

55 CLIFTON ROAD, CAMBRIDGE, CAMBS CB1 4FR
TEL: 01223 412277 FAX: 01223 412377

Reliable Ice Machines are a Must for the Pub Trade

Eating and drinking out has become an integral part of everyday life and is no longer a treat reserved for high days and holidays.

One of the biggest areas of growth has been within the pub market. Most pubs now cater for today's sophisticated consumer with many providing comprehensive menus or even fully fledged restaurants, and all pubs have had to consider both the choice and presentation of the drinks they offer which includes serving them with a generous amount of ice.

The drink driving laws - and alcohol awareness generally - have also brought about changes in the types of drinks people consume as the increasing selection of low alcohol and soft drinks demonstrates, most of which are intended to be served with ice. Publicans are increasingly aware that an abundance of good ice improves the quality of a drink and are taking steps to ensure that they can provide it.

There is a maxim that bar personnel have often been heard to quote. "When you need ice you haven't got it and when you've got it you don't need it." Quite simply, the ice machines that the UK has been used to have traditionally chosen the summer months to break down or fail to keep up with demand, and, by the time they have been repaired or replaced, the busiest season is over! On top of this, the ice these machines produce often melts in minutes and merely flattens the fizz in the drinks they are intended to cool.

Hoshizaki, as the world's leading manufacturer of ice machines, supplies a wide range of very high specifications machines that will meet the needs of the busiest publicans in terms of both quality and reliability. Good quality equipment will last longer than cheaper alternatives and will remain reliable - an important factor that should be considered when setting a budget. Says general manager of Hoshizaki UK, Les Simmons, "We are totally confident in the quality of our machines and pass that confidence on to end users in the form of a full 2 years parts and labour warranty. There is no doubt that there is a very receptive market here for good quality, reliable machines that live up to their design specifications."

HOSHIZAKI

55 CLIFTON ROAD, CAMBRIDGE, CAMBS CB1 4FR
TEL: 01223 412277 FAX: 01223 412377

Bar Design and Merchandising

HOSHIZAKI IM RANGE IS STRONG ON HYGIENE YET LOW ON MAINTENANCE

Because the phrase 'cleaning and maintenance' translates to 'time and money' to licensees, bartenders and caterers the world over, these key areas are sometimes given a lower priority than is ideal - or are considered unnecessarily costly.

Therefore, when Hoshizaki - the world's leading manufacturer of ice makers - designed its IM range of machines, one of the key areas addressed was hygiene. By ensuring the IM range maintains the highest levels of hygiene possible, so cleaning and maintenance are reduced. This is achieved primarily by two special features. Firstly, a very hygienic closed water cell jet system is utilised and secondly, a fully automatic rinse and flush operates after every cycle. (Hoshizaki is the only European manufacturer to provide this). This combination ensures that - when used under similar conditions - Hoshizaki machines need substantially less servicing and maintenance than any other ice maker! Also, cleaning is minimised as bacteria are discouraged from establishing growth.

Coupled to this is the fully accessible and easily cleanable ice storage bin with its sealed door to prevent aerobacteria entering.

Water filters can also guard against some parasites. Hoshizaki offers 2 types of filtration, both of which are made exclusively for the Company to its own exacting specifications. There is a general purpose filter which will remove dirt, rust particles and other common debris, and a fine filter which will remove minute particles, cysts and water borne parasites. Both types remove 99.9% of chemical contaminants such as chlorine thereby generally improving the quality and taste of the ice.

HOSHIZAKI PROVIDES THE ICE FOR THE HEAVY DEMANDS OF THE BROTHERS

Having built a reputation for successfully renovating pubs with his Standard Taverns Group - now sold to Tenants - Dominic Keane has founded Strathmore Taverns

HOSHIZAKI

55 CLIFTON ROAD, CAMBRIDGE, CAMBS CB1 4FR
TEL: 01223 412277 FAX: 01223 412377

that a safe system of work incorporating appropriate protection to the opening is provided. The protection (eg chains or bars) needs to be far enough away from the opening to provide an effective barrier before anyone could lose their footing.

Health and safety in the **customer area** also needs to be considered including, for example, appropriate measures to avoid slips, trips and falls. If you have entertainments in the bar this may introduce temporary risks. The siting of performers and their equipment needs careful consideration to avoid exit routes being blocked and trailing wires. It is highly advisable to ensure that any power points used for sound equipment etc are protected by an appropriate residual current device (RCD). This safety back-up is generally a requirement for a public entertainment licence. Entertainments may attract more people than the pub is suitable for, and overcrowding can become a problem: where an entertainment licence exists, an occupancy limit is normally set.

Finally, consideration should be given to the use of glazed doors and other vulnerable glazed areas, and safety glazing needs to be used where necessary.

Legal Notes

The bar includes any place exclusively or mainly used for the sale and consumption of intoxicating liquor. So if a place in licensed premises is not so used, or the main use is not for the sale and consumption of intoxicating liquor (eg a room mainly used for dining), then the place will not be a bar.

Notices to be displayed in on-licence premises are:

1. The name of the licensee, usually displayed above the main entrance.
2. Details of any hours subject to a Restriction Order.
3. Details of a Supper Hour Certificate or Extended Hours Order.
4. Details of the effect of any Special Hours Certificate.
5. Details of the hours under a General Order of Exemption.
6. The measure used for the sale of whisky, gin, rum and vodka and the measures used for the sale of wine by the glass and carafes.
7. Price lists.
8. A tobacco sales notice under the provisions of the Children And Young Persons (Protection From Tobacco) Act 1991.
9. A conspicuous notice of the percentage alcohol by volume of a representative sample – commonly 30 – of drinks on sale (usually included in price list).

Bar Design and Merchandising

10. Notice, where applicable, of the effect of a Children's Certificate.

All packaged drinks with an ABV (alcohol by volume) of more than 1.2 per cent must be labelled showing their strength. It is important to be clear of the distinction between alcohol-free and low-alcohol drinks. To be alcohol-free, the drink must contain no more than 0.05 per cent ABV, and to be low-alcohol, no more than 1.2 per cent ABV. Such drinks must be labelled with their maximum per cent ABV.

Food hygiene is controlled by the Food Safety (General Food Hygiene) Regulations 1995, which set standards for the service of food and drinks. There is nothing in the regulations to prevent bar staff from serving a second or subsequent drink to a customer in the glass of their choice including the glass in which they had their first drinks, should they so wish. However, it is probably better practice to use a fresh glass, unless the customer insists on using the same one.

The Publican's Handbook

Planning the profit

SERVACLEAN's *sales director, Chris Royston, identifies the essential ingredients for financial success when considering a new or replacement bar serve*

It's an all too familiar story. A pub re-opens after a major refurbishment and hoards of customers, old and new, pour in to take a look. The owners - perhaps a major pub operator or maybe an ambitious free-trader - have just spent a fortune! Bright new exterior paintwork, an extended car park with neatly lined bays, new signage to announce a fashionable change of name or a new 'theme' - all very inviting. A re-designed interior, thick warm carpets, imaginative lighting, beautiful loo's (especially the "ladies"), re-fitted kitchen with menu to match, and the counter - a joinery masterpiece decked with shiny new dispensers offering a huge selection of beverages. But can you get a round of drinks before the friends you left sitting at the other side of the room think you've gone home?

Somewhere along the line many pub operators seem to have forgotten that most people visit a pub to get a drink. They seem to overlook the fact that a pub (and almost any other type of bar) is first and foremost a shop - it is there to sell a product and the more product it sells, the more successful it's likely to be. No one will deny that the vast majority of customers are attracted to a new or recently refurbished venue but nothing deters them more from coming back than having to queue at the bar for what can feel like an age and then being served by someone who is obviously working under pressure and isn't quite a courteous as perhaps they should be. Regulars - customers who come again and again - provide a sound base on which to build any successful business and satisfied customers usually tell their friends. Unfortunately, the converse also applies and one disgruntled customer can quickly spread the wrong kind of word to all and sundry.

One of the major brewery owned pub groups recently conducted a survey across a large number of its outlets to measure the efficiency of its bar service during busy trading periods. It found that the average customer consumed 2.68 drinks on each visit and that it took between 5 and 7 minutes to serve each drink - that's a total of 13 to 19 minutes "non-drinking time", spent queuing during each visit. Hardly "an age", you may say, but if most of this time could be eliminated many of their customers would buy another drink and that could represent **a 30% increase takings**... without any extra overhead costs! A substantial increase in business by anyone's standards and a massive extra contribution nett profit.

Why is it that so many customers are kept waiting for so long when all they really want to do is to hand over their money, re-join the conversation going on at the table and carry on drinking. Almost every time, it's the result of a total lack of planning behind-the-bar. Badly positioned drinks dispense, inadequate glass-storage areas, inefficient glasswashing facilities, not enough ice or fruit slices and many other small but important points, all slow down bar staff performance and hinder the profit-making process. doesn't have to be like that. A properly planned servery can run smoothly and produce an excellent return on the owners investment.

Our Company planned the replacement bar survey for holiday park entertainment bar two or three years ago. It's a good example because nothing else changed. Same room, same number of customers, same size of bar counter in the same position. Only the layout behind-the-

Bar Design and Merchandising

into your new bar

and the fitments were
…ged but the result was
…gering. Customers used to
…e "six deep" all night but
…n the new bar opened it
like clockwork and
…ne waited more than a
…ple of minutes to get
…ed. **Three less bar staff**
…**e needed** - more than
…,000 saving on the
…roll - and… wait for it…
takings increased by
… **four percent… yes**
…!

…, where do we start to
…eve the sort of bar
…ration that everyone
…ld like? Don't wait until
…joiner has almost
…pleted his work on the
…nter - start thinking about
…working area before the
…s leave the architects
…ving board. That way, if
…counter is found to be too
…ll (or too big) you can do
…ething about it before it's
…late.

…onsider the glasswashing
…lity first - can it be in a
…n next to the servery or
… it have to be accommo-
…d under the counter?
…ose a position in the
…nter away from the main
…omer approach and allow
…ugh space for a complete
…sswashing "system". A
… - preferably twin bowls -
…slops disposal, general
…ping down" and to pro-
…e a secondary manual
…h (with separate wash and
…e) in case of glasswashing

machine breakdown.
Somewhere to load the
glasswasher baskets - a mess-
free drainer shelf connected
to the plumbing waste either
above or to one side of the
machine. Take care in
selecting a suitable
glasswashing machine. It will
need to work hard - almost
non-stop at busy times - so it
may be worth paying a little
more for quality and
reliability. Most cabinet style
machines have a 2 minute
operating cycle but don't be
fooled into thinking that this
will provide 30 washes per
hour. Allowing for loading,
unloading and machine
"warm-up", the most
efficient operators will only
achieve twenty. If the
glasswasher basket carries 25
glasses and the machine can
operate 20 times per hour, the
throughput of 500 glasses
should be sufficient for 200
customers drinking two
drinks each per hour. Any
more than this and you really
need to be thinking of more
than one machine.

Most Environmental Health
Officers now insist on a
dedicated **hand washing**
facility within the bar
servery. A location close to
the gate & flap or between a
glasswashing position and the
serving area is sensible and
don't forget that hand washing calls for soap and a towel.

Now we come to what can
loosely be described as

"special equipment" and
planning requirements will
vary dependent upon the type
of outlet. If traditional ales
are to be served, you may be
tempted to go for full height
cabinet style beer engines but
they do use up a lot of space.
Counter-mounted hand-pulls
with convenient glass storage
space below, could be a
better option. "Compact
cabinet" hand-pulls provide
the best of both worlds by
achieving a traditional
appearance without
obstructing the valuable
lower storage area. A modern
"cafe-bar" theme may call for
a larger than average coffee
and snack servery. Limited
space in the backfitting for
refrigerated bottle display
cabinets - such as in an island
counter, may need to be
compensated by the use of
additional cabinets or
top-loading bottle coolers
under the counter. Glass-
frosters are currently very
fashionable and, an ice-maker
may need to be accommodated within the servery if there
isn't room elsewhere. All
these items of equipment take
up a lot of space, generate a
tremendous amount of heat
into the working area and
restrict the positioning of
draught beer and soft drinks
dispensers on the counter
above, so take care to plan
for no more 'equipment'
than you will need.

Choosing a suitable till
these days can be like

55

The Publican's Handbook

choosing a computer system and, just like computers, the technology is advancing apace. You will probably want to update to a new "model" in a couple of years and you can bet your bottom dollar that the replacement won't be the same size or shape, so plan for the future and consider as many possibilities as you can. Whether to position tills on the backfitting or within the counter is very much a personal choice but, if you choose the latter, remember that tills in the counter are at risk from spills, splashes and "grab & run" theft. A shelf with height adjustment, integral protective compartment for the drawer and, maybe, with a lockable cash-float drawer is worth thinking about. The space under the till is often a good position for a bottle skip.

Over the past few years, the American influence and holidays in the sun have increased customers' demands for heavily iced drinks. Who's complaining? **Ice is extremely profitable** and, if that's what the customers want, than give 'em plenty! Choose an ice-maker that will produce enough for all your needs and include ice storage facilities in the counter - an insulated ice-chest with connection to the plumbing waste and, preferably, with separate storage compartments for chilled wine bottles, fruit slices and other condiments as well as the ice. A rack for mixing liquors and cordials is a useful add-on. Space for a blender, with container rinsing facilities close by, will be needed if you intend to offer a cocktail menu.

The choice of **dispensers for beers, ciders and soft drinks** is possibly even wider than the choice of tills. Most of the individual, "brewery issue" badged dispense heads are fitted with the tap just above counter level and a "drop-down" drip tray which obstructs the storage area just below the counter top. Upright fonts or "T-bars" with higher taps and counter level drip-trays could be a better choice if space is tight and if you want to be able to reach most of the glasses without stooping. An 'Irish' themed bar may be more authentic if ales and stouts are dispensed from taps fitted to an 'Irish Beer Box' positioned over a draining platform with glasses stored below.

'Glasses'? We've got this far and we've hardly mentioned what is, arguably, the most important item of equipment in any bar. If you haven't got enough to start with, serving will probably grind to a halt just when you're beginning to make some money. And when you get started again you'll be serving cold drinks in hot, wet glasses straight out of the machine. Just the thing for good customer relations! Your glasses are one of the main links with your clientele - they need to be washed clean and stored hygienically. Make sure that you allow sufficient space for as many as you will need (**at least 2 $\frac{1}{2}$ glasses for each customer when the place is packed**) and that they're stored close to the position where you're going to fill them. Insist on storage shelves or racks that support the glasses "bottoms-up" with minimum rim contact, plenty of air space beneath the glass and a slide-out drip tray which will allow you to store glasses straight out of the washer and save you hours of laborious and expensive shelf-cleaning time.

Well, there you have it - or, at least most of it. Maybe you didn't think that there was quite so much to planning a profitable bar but, if you're able to integrate all the points we've made, you can almost guarantee a financially successful servery.

At every stage in your project, you are likely to be put under extreme pressure from well meaning architects, quantity surveyors, interior designers, builders and others, to compromise or reduce the specification of your carefully planned bar servery and transfer the cash they say will be saved, to some other section of the overall budget. **Give way to these pressures at your peril!** After all, this is the place in which you and your staff will spend most of your working life and, perhaps even more important, **the only point in the whole building at which you're going to take any money.**

56

Bar Design and Merchandising

the other side of bar design

Planned (free) by ServaClean to provide the best in hygiene & operating efficiency

Illustrated with easy to understand three dimensional C.A.D. drawings.

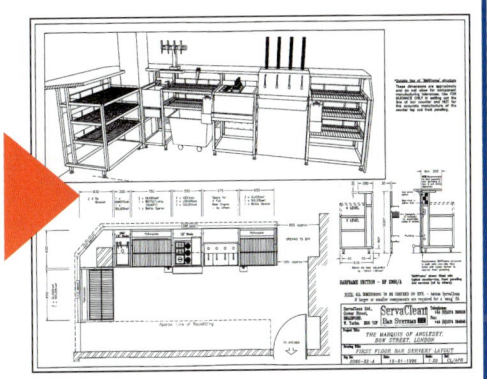

Manufactured in food quality stainless steel to last a lifetime.

Delivered ex-stock for quick and easy assembly… with just one screwdriver!

ServaClean®
Bar Systems

SservaClean Limited, Gower Street, BRADFORD, BD5 7JF

Tel: +44 (0)1274 390038   Fax: +44 (0)1274 394840

The Publican's Handbook

SATELLIET

Satelliet UK Limited
East Street, Farnham, Surrey GU9 7SY
Tel: 01252 724747 Fax: 01252 724454

SATELLIET

Fast growing Satteliet now one of the leading suppliers of furniture to clubs, bars and restaurants. This success is based on an impressive array of chair and table designs backed by quality, value and a clear understanding of customers needs.

The "European Collection", Satteliet's furniture offering, covers a wide range of styles and materials to suit any environment. Both traditional and contemporary designs are available, with chairs and tables in wood or metal to meet particular requirements. A new three storey showroom in Farnham, Surrey, is themed to stimulate the imagination of designers and clients by showing "real life" bars, clubs and restaurants. For too long customers have had to be content with catalogues, the odd chair and a myriad of phone calls and faxes. The Satteliet Showroom allows both designer and client to piece together the required fabric, wood or metal finish, chair and table sizes whilst working with the actual products.

The Satteliet Group of Companies has been established for over 25 years, allowing a high degree of quality and delivery control over source factories. Both in the UK and in close liaison with Mainland European sister companies Satteliet hold a vast collection of stock items, resulting in many products being available very quickly. The Group's involvement in manufacturing outlets also ensures immense influence with regards to design.

Bar Design and Merchandising

Hygiene 2000

Low Odour, environmentally friendly tough coatings for the Licensed, Restaurants and Hotel trades

TUF-COAT for walls   EPOXYCOAT for floors
PRIMING SYSTEMS even for cremic tiles

COATING
SOLUTIONS
LIMITED

UNIT 4 BROOK HOUSE YARD • SANDY LANE • OLD OXTED • SURREY • RH8 9LR
Tel: 01883 713599 Fax: 01883 717228

CURRENT HYGIENE REGULATIONS CAN NO LONGER BE SATISFIED WITH A "QUICK RUB DOWN AND A DECORATIVE COAT OF PAINT"

The use of more effective cleaning agents mean that specialised coatings are the order of the day. These resistant coatings must withstand repeated cleaning with a range of detergents, pressure washing and steam cleaning. They also need to be environmentally friendly, water based and have a low odour during application and drying. Importantly, they must be easy to apply.

HYGIENE 2000 is a range of coatings designed to meet this criteria. **HYGIENE TUF-COAT** is an epoxy/acrylic coating ideal for ceilings and walls. It can be overcoated in four hours and when cured will withstand repeated steam cleaning. **EPOXYCOAT WS** is a water based epoxy which can be used as a floor or wall coating. Whilst slower drying the cured film is extremely resistant. To compliment both finishes there are two priming systems. **SAF-T-SEAL** again a water based, encapsulating sealer for difficult or friable surfaces and **PRIMECOAT 33** is an adhesion promoter ideal where bonding is difficult especially ceramic tiles.

Westminster College's School of Hotel, Catering & Tourism Studies, established in 1910, was the forerunner of Hotel & Catering education as we know it today. Outstanding facilities with realistic work environments and a talented teaching staff together create a high quality learning experience which opens the way to exceptional opportunities in a dynamic industry.

The College is committed to advancing the professionalism of those working in the on-licensed trade by running courses of the British Institute of Innkeeping and the Wine & Spirit Education Trust. The three main qualifications we offer at present are the National Licensee's Certificate, covering the basic law and social responsibilities expected of licensees, the Qualifying Examination which contains management training, and the Wine & Spirit Education Trust Certificate, suitable for all people requiring additional knowledge of wine tasting and wine appreciation.

"Professionalism is the key to a successful licensed retail outlet"

The twelve NLC courses, three WSET courses and the Qualifying Examination that we have run during the past year have all had a excellent percentage of passes. All candidates have spoken highly of the courses and many have returned in order to add to their qualifications with another subject. By the time this handbook is published we shall also be offering the Advanced Retail Wine Certificate, which is designed to help retailers in the on-licensed trade maximise their profit potential and market their wine operations more effectively in this keen growth area. Other advanced certificate courses are being developed to deal with all aspects of the work of the Licensed Retail Manager. The School's facilities on both our Battersea and Vincent Square sites are being improved and extended to ensure that we have the ability to offer extensive practical training in this rapidly growing field. We also enjoy close links with local breweries and other organisations in the trade.

For more information about these or any other Westminster College courses please contact the Admissions Unit, Westminster College, Battersea Park Road, London SW11 4JR. Phone 0171-556 8001

CHAPTER THREE

TRAINING FOR LICENSEES

Andrew Palmer

Licensed retailing can give the right people, be they young, mature, male or female, a hugely varied and fulfilling career; and if you prove yourself, you can be offered challenging responsibilities at an early age.

But it's training that makes the difference between success and failure; and the industry has seen a sea-change in recent years in its attitude towards training and the delivering of business skills to licensees and staff. Training provides the tools for success in a happy, rewarding career in a challenging people-oriented industry.

The current upsurge in the availability of highly pertinent training, with qualifications recognised throughout the country, is revolutionising the industry and has been driven by the professional body for licensees, staff and industry suppliers, the British Institute of Innkeeping.

Traditionally, the public has never understood what is involved in running a pub and in-depth training has not been thought of as necessary. In fact just about everybody who hasn't tried it thinks they know instinctively how to run a great pub. It would be difficult to find a single regular of the 60,000 or so pubs up and down the country who does not sincerely believe that if only they were handed the keys to a pub - any pub - it would be a real money maker. And what a cosy life, too!

'All you've got to do is smile, keep the beer fresh, the loos clean, stick the wife in the kitchen, recruit an attractive bar maid,' goes the myth. 'Then you open the door and watch the trade roll in.'

Anyone who still believes that has an interesting three months or so to look forward to: bankruptcy, marriage break-up, poor health.... None of these consequences is unusual among those who, before taking a pub, didn't research the local market, sweat over a realistic one-, three-, and five-year business

Training for Licensees

plan, train the staff in customer care, or use all the training support available to learn motivational techniques and gain exemplary staff performance.

Time was when you retired to a pub. Many licensees would be ex-forces or policemen who had picked up their gratuity, done the minimum of training offered by brewers (a bit of cellarmanship and general book-keeping).

For most of the post-war period, apart from the hours, it wasn't difficult being a licensee. It was a trade that you picked up. Times have changed. The economic climate and growing competition from high-standard leisure alternatives mean that licensees now work in one of the harshest and least forgiving trading climates any sector of commerce has seen.

Rents are at a historical high, yet people are drinking less beer – consumption has declined almost annually since 1978 due to the decline of heavy industry, the trend toward home entertainment and concerns about health.

Business rates, excise duty, wages, the cost of compliance with health and safety and employment legislation all cheerfully rise each year. Pub professionals from junior staff to licensees must master every retailing discipline – purchasing, recruitment, financial control, marketing – to ensure they run a profitable unit.

THE RESPONSIBILITY

How many careers are there where almost immediately you may be put in charge of an established business with annual sales of £200,000+?

You have total responsibility for purchasing everything from beer to dry goods to garden furniture. You must recruit and motivate staff, you must know, or at least know where to find out about:

- the basics of food costing and control;
- food hygiene and processing procedures;
- drinks product knowledge;
- cellar skills;
- licensing law;
- gaming and betting legislation;
- rights of entry;
- refusing entry and service;
- weights and measures;
- other specialist topics.

You are the financial director, and must understand cash flow and working capital, cash control, VAT, budgets, stocktaking and information systems.

Employment issues are of prime importance to licensees, with their high proportion of casual staff and staff turnover.

- What are the rights of employees?
- How do you draw up their statement of terms and conditions?
- Are part-time staff entitled to the same conditions as full-time (yes, due to recent legislation)?
- What about disciplining staff and unfair dismissal with all the problems of possible claims against you?
- Do you understand the laws on racial, disability and sexual discrimination and how to stay within them?

- What about statutory maternity benefits and transfers of undertakings?

We haven't covered marketing, merchandising and best practice in selling, nor have we looked at the intricacies of health and safety procedures, Control of Substances Hazardous to Health Regulations 1988, the reporting and recording of accidents, risk assessment for employees and customers, the regulations concerning electricity, noise, fire and first aid.

In short, there's a great deal involved in running a pub which is profitable, where customers actually enjoy parting with their hard-earned cash, and where staff are happy and productive.

In licensed retailing you must prepare for success, and that means training. Training makes the difference between failure and an enjoyable and rewarding career. It is the key to success.

WHAT TRAINING IS AVAILABLE?

If you want to understand more about a successful career in licensed retailing there is a professional body that exists to guide people towards pertinent training and provide a network that may support you. That body is the British Institute of Innkeeping (BII).

The BII has varying levels of membership from graduate member upwards. It has worked with the industry, the Home Office and licensing justices' national bodies to develop a widely recognised and admired progressive series of qualifications that arm licensees with the knowledge and skills required for success. These include the Certificate of Induction Examination, the Qualifying Examination and advanced qualifications.

The BII Certificate of Induction Examination

This is a three-day training course that provides a knowledge of the basic technicalities and skills required in running a pub. It consists of two parts, and candidates must pass both to be certificated and allowed to apply for graduate membership of the Institute.

Part 1 tests the candidate's knowledge and understanding of:

- the health and safety legal framework, and the particular responsibilities placed upon licensees and staff by various acts and regulations;
- the practical and legal requirements of employing paid staff;
- the essentials of bar service;
- the essentials of cellar and stock management;
- the administration and operation of a catering service;
- basic principles of financial control and legal financial liabilities;
- maximisation of sales/profits through the appropriate marketing of the house and its products;
- the importance of customer service to the business.

Part 2 (the National Licensee's Certificate (NLC)) tests the candidate's knowledge and understanding of:

- justices' licences and other types of licence; permitted

Training for Licensees

Training For Success
By Guy Nottingham

Guy is the senior partner in Original Leisure a Company which specialises in the training and consultancy to the licensed retail, hotel and catering trades.

There are so many independent training courses on the market in the licensed trade these days, it can be extremely confusing for a new licensee to choose the most appropriate course to suit their needs.

Courses vary enormously in both content, duration, and the depth in which topics are covered. However, every individual, whether considering entering the trade for the first time, or an experienced operator, will have specific training needs.

As our business is so heavily people-orientated, and the skills, knowledge, and attitude of people running the business is by far and away the most significant contributor to the success (or failure!) of the business, investment in a good training programme is possibly the most important investment you will make.

In order to decide which is the most appropriate course for yourself, it is advisable to consider what you are trying to achieve, and what you hope to get out of your training.

WHAT DO I WANT TO ACHIEVE?

Training Courses can achieve a number of aims for the individual. These tend to fall into the following categories, which should be a useful guide in helping you to decide which training course is most appropriate for your requirements.

1) Qualifications.
Courses should enable you to pass any required examinations, in order to gain the qualifications you will require to enter the business. These include the british Institute of Innkeepers (BII) membership qualification, the National Licensees Certificate (NLC) and the Essential Food Hygiene Certificate.

2) Satisfying the Magistrates!
The training courses should be sufficient quality, duration, and carry the appropriate qualifications, to satisfy the licensing magistrates that you have the required skills and knowledge to run a pub within the legal requirements. Magistrates are becoming increasingly concerned about the frequency of the changes to licences in many pubs, and the requirements are becoming steadily more stringent. Many branches wish to see applicants with practical experience and full training - if you are relatively inexperienced, the course will need to be of a substantial length.

3) Satisfying the Backer or Brewery.
If you are seeking backing from a bank, brewery, or financial institution, one of the main criteria in the decision to back you will be your skill and experience. A business plan is meaningless, if you do not possess the required levels of skill and experience to deliver the results. Even for appointment to positions as Trainee within Managed House estates, many breweries now wish to minimise the risk they are taking, by appointing people who already have experience and qualifications.

4) Allowing you to plan your business.
A good training course should impart to you the skills and knowledge require to allow you to make informed decision about which type of business is appropriate for you, how to assess the viability of an outlet, and how to produce a business plan. If a training course helps you to avoid buying an outlet which is not viable, then this can save you a great deal of pain, loss and heartache later!

5) Helping you to be successful!
It is often lost, in the need to satisfy Magistrates and gain minimum qualifications, that the major purpose of training is to improve your skills. There is , quite frankly, little point to training, if it is not geared towards improving your knowledge, skills and abilities. A good training course should give you the tools with which to be successful.

WHICH COURSE IS APPROPRIATE FOR ME?

In deciding which course is most appropriate for you, it is important to consider the above factors, and highlight what you are hoping t gain from your training.

The level of training required will also depend on your previous experience and qualifications. Many existing and experienced licensees regularly go on training courses to "top up" their knowledge. This is a sign of strength, rather than weakness, as the market and the industry in which we operate is constantly changing, and it is the operators who recognise this and adapt to it who are most likely to enjoy ongoing long-term success.

A useful means of establishing the level of training which is required is to complete a review of your existing knowledge and skills. Original leisure regularly perform an Analysis of Training Needs, which enables a training course to be designed which is tailored to the specific needs of the individual. It is interesting that many experienced licensees will have little or no training needs in many areas, but real requirements in others - Marketing is one specific area in which many licensees need regular "top up" training, and Hygiene and Licensing Law constantly change, so re-training in these areas is common.

For those with little previous "hands on" experience, this option should form an important part of the training course. It is interesting to note that for many of the larger brewers, the Licensee Training Programme, which will often last up to 14 weeks, will include 8 weeks in-house training - learning all the "nuts and bolts" skills of running a pub. At the other extreme, a half-day course can only hope to scratch the surface of the knowledge required!

Original Leisure can be contacted by telephone (0113) 2773434 or by fax (0113) 2771889

The Publican's Handbook

Train to be a Success in Your Own Pub

Our Pub Management course offers two essential modules for everyone wishing to be a success in the licensed trade.

Off-job training in all aspects of successful pub management by an experienced independent company.

On-job training is by experienced training licensees in a successful pub.

Training for the National Licensee's Certificate and BII qualifications is included.

During the course delegates build up their own individual "Licensees Manual" to guide and help them throughout their career, which will be regularly updated to ensure their information is current.

SEND TODAY FOR OUR ILLUSTRATED BROCHURE AND DATES OF OUR NEXT COURSES

Original Leisure

YOUR SUCCESS IN OUR BUSINESS

Specialist Licensed Retail & Catering Consultancy, West Point Business Centre, Westland Square, Leeds, W. Yorkshire LS11 5SS
Telephone: 0113 277 3434. Fax: 0113 277 1889

Guy Simmonds

WOULD YOU LIKE TO RUN A PUBLIC HOUSE OR HOTEL??

We can help you make a success + lucrative living from your rewarding new career.

We run an *award-winning* highly acclaimed PUB TRAINING COURSE – leading to B.I.I. qualification – recognised throughout the licensed trade + brewing industry. Course designed for anyone thinking of buying/leasing a Public House/Hotel/Restaurant, for those entering the licensed trade on a management or tenancy basis. 3 day courses, held twice monthly in Working Freehouse. Recommended by Banks, Breweries, Solicitors, Accountants, Licensing Magistrates etc. *We also run a 1 day CELLAR COURSE, FOOD + HYGIENE COURSE. LICENSING LAW COURSE (N.L.C.).*

Brochure + Booking Forms
Tel: GUY SIMMONDS ON (01332) 865112
We train hundreds of people every year for a rewarding new career

WESTMINSTER COLLEGE

Please contact the Admissions Unit
Battersea Park Road
London SW11 4JR
0171 556 8001

This prestigious Hotel & Catering College offers licensed trade programmes in Central London.

• **Licensed Management Programme (British Institute of Innkeeping Qualifying Examination)**
Mondays 3-6pm for 18 weeks, starting 22nd September 1997 and 23rd February 1998.

• **BII National Licensee's Certificate**
All day Tuesday plus Friday morning, one course per month.

• **Wine & Spirit Education Trust Certificate**
Tuesdays 6-8pm for nine weeks, starting 30th September 1997, and 20th January and 27th April 1998.

Also tailor-made courses and consultancy services to companies.

hours; young persons; employment of young persons; gaming, betting and lotteries; exclusion orders; public entertainment; the Weights and Measures Act (Intoxicating Liquor) Order 1988 and other related laws; sale; of tobacco; credit; and notices;
◆ the social responsibilities of licences covering alcohol, drinking and driving, prevention of and dealing with violence, proof of age, drugs, door staff, pubwatch.

The National Licensee's Certificate is also available as a standalone qualification. Many licensing justices prefer new applicants for licences to hold this certificate as proof that they understand basic law and responsibilities.

The NLC as a stand-alone qualification is obtained by sitting a short multiple choice exam. Those without access to company training schemes can take a short course leading up to the exam, or simply buy the handbook from the BII.

The handbook for the National Licensee's Certificate, published by the National Licensee's Certificate Awarding Body (NLCAB) at the same address as the BII, can be used in conjunction with a training course or as a self-study aid for those who simply wish to sit the exam.

The Qualifying Examination

The Qualifying Examination (QE) of the BII is a more in-depth qualification with more emphasis on management skills and their application.

The QE consists of five parts and requires a minimum of five days' training followed by an exam. Candidates who fail one of the tests have to re-take that one only.

Part 1 tests the candidate's knowledge and understanding of Health & Safety at Work; drinks service; financial control; cash control and security; cellar management, storage and stock control; food service.
Part 2 is the National Licensee's Certificate (see above).
Part 3 tests the candidate's knowledge and understanding of selling skills; merchandising; customer care; management of internal and external areas; employment legislation; staffing; marketing: management skills.
Part 4 tests the candidate's knowledge and understanding of food safety and hygiene.
Part 5 is a practical exam and consists of tests in recruitment, training and cellar fault identification.

Advanced qualifications

The BII has developed a series of pioneering business building qualifications aimed at helping licensees and senior staff in pubs and pub/restaurants run a more profitable business.

These new qualifications will for the first time achieve a set national standard in their disciplines and will be recognised by employers throughout the hospitality industry.

1. Catering Management Certificate.
2. Financial Management Certificate.

3. Business Development Certificate.
4. Advanced Leadership and Motivation Certificate.
5. Customer Service Management Certificate.
6. Cellar Management Certificate.
7. Drinks Retail Certificate.
8. Wine Retail Certificate.

Although courses in these disciplines have long been widely available, the BII's new accredited courses address the need for a uniform standard set and approved by the industry.

In order to maintain high standards the BII is accrediting individual named trainers - not organisations - to run each of the courses. The trainers must be re-accredited each year.

Pitched at management level, the advanced qualifications have been developed by the BII in conjunction with licensees and management from leading brewers and pub groups. Each course has been developed by subject experts guided by an industry steering group.

Each course usually takes two or three days. The emphasis is on practical exercises and participation by delegates, and each course results in a certificate based on assessment and/or an exam.

Catering Management Certificate
This certificate is suitable for licensees new to catering operations or experienced practitioners wanting to improve the business. It is not about improving cookery skills, but managing all aspects of developing and running a profitable and effective pub catering operation.

The three-day course is specifically written for pubs and is based on an understanding of pub catering, not other catering establishments or hotels.

Licensees will learn how to improve the quality of food, speed of service and use of equipment. They will understand key marketing techniques and be stimulated into better menu planning and providing new ideas for food.

Split into four key areas, the course covers:

1. Introduction to the business.
2. Production management.
3. Sales, service and promotion.
4. Overall management.

Financial Management Certificate
Often the closest licensees get to financial management is when they compile figures or paperwork at the end of the quarter and pack them off to the accountant to produce something to satisfy the bank manager. This is not financial control.

This three-day course demystifies a complex subject and gives licensees confidence in using financial controls to run a better business. It will equip licensees with the basic financial skills needed to manage the entirety of a cash-based business and the emphasis is on efficient financial control and planning, and reducing financial service charges (banking, accountant's fees).

Components of the course include:

- calculating VAT and completing your own returns;
- recording weekly revenue and

Training for Licensees

How's your pulling power?

If you have a personality that will attract customers and the confidence to make the most of a successful independent business, now is the time to put your skills and experience to the test. Rapidly expanding and with ambitious plans for the future, Morland are now looking for a number of couples or individuals who will benefit from our professional support and advice and reap the rewards of their investment.

Our commitment to you is equal to our commitment to our beer – we won't pull a fast one. We believe in investing in your future and embarking on a long-term partnership for our mutual benefit. Like you, we want our money and reputation to be in safe hands. This is why we provide you with a wide range of consultancy services, an award-winning training programme and our highly respected business initiative – the 'Morland Business Builder'.

In return for your drive and enthusiasm, we can also offer:

- Security of tenure and the opportunity to benefit from long-term plans.
- A lease fully assignable after the initial two years, allowing your investment of money and effort to be realised at any time.
- Popular products, including the highly acclaimed premium ale 'Old Speckled Hen'.
- One of a large number of wide ranging refurbished public houses in prosperous areas throughout the country.
- No shortfall penalties.
- No privity of contract.
- No initial premiums.
- The profit from any investments you make.
- Generous discounts for all sales of beers and ciders above a fixed minimum level of barrelage.
- All machine income.
- A choice of famous guest beers, such as Draught Bass, Theakston's XB and Charles Wells Bombardier.
- The freedom to serve any wines, spirits, soft drinks and bottled low and no-alcohol products.
- All the advantages of having a regional brewer as landlord.
- A business loan scheme to assist you in any development plans.

If you think you have the pulling power to qualify for the acclaimed Morland 21 Year Lease, please contact John Erbes, Tenanted Recruitment Manager on 01235 540453, or write to him at: **Morland plc, The Brewery, Ock Street, Abingdon, Oxon, OX14 5BZ.**

Quote reference: **JE/PUB**

MORLAND
ESTD 1711
OF ABINGDON

Pubs with personality

67

Trade tips from Morland tenants

Morland is the second oldest independent brewer in the country and as such has a long history of helping licensees to serve their community and profit from their investment. The Tenanted Division is currently made up of 300 pubs with the majority trading under Morland's 21 Year Lease. An experienced team of Business Development Managers support the tenanted estate. Their personal commitment and attention to detail give Morland tenants the confidence to carry the business forward which is essential for success in today's competitive market. There are many recent examples of entrepreneurial licensees putting their confidence in Morland and it's lease with fantastic results. The partnership offered allows both experienced licensees and those new to the trade to maximise their potential as profitable operators. We've spoken to two Morland tenants about how they came to choose their current pubs and to get some first hand tips for those considering a career move into the licensed trade.

John Martin and his daughter Debra re-opened the Crown & Anchor, Maidens Green nr Windsor, in December 96 after a major refurbishment which required considerable investment from both the brewery and John himself.

John says, "I had been a Whitbread tenant for 24 years and when my wife was very ill with cancer I decided to come out of the trade to care for her. After her death I started to consider the possibility of running another pub with my daughter as joint licensee. Morland had a number of pubs for me to consider in this area and I chose the Crown & Anchor primarily because of the development. The potential is there to expand the facilities as the business grows.

I think it is vital that people have a clear picture in their head about what they want to achieve with a pub. Assessing the competition is also crucial, as is talking to people who are already in the trade. With my 20+ years of experience I know many licensees who are great friends of mine.

John Martin and Debra Keable, Licensees of the Crown & Anchor Maidens Green nr Windsor

Dave West, Licensee of the Vine at Long Wittenham nr Abingdon

Training for Licensees

The Maybush on the River Thames at Newbridge in Oxfordshire

The help and support I have received from them and the brewery has carried me through difficult times. There have been occasions when I have felt like throwing the towel in but today, with a thriving pub and restaurant business which is gaining a good reputation for itself in the area, I am very pleased and proud of the Crown & Anchor and being part of the Morland Team".

David and Denise West have just celebrated their first 6 months as tenants of the Vine in Long Wittenham, nr Abingdon. They got a taste for running a pub in the early 70's but had left to bring up their children. Both had careers, David as a computer consultant and Denise as a building society manager, but had promised themselves that one day they would fulfil their ambition of having their own pub. They considered several breweries and chose Morland after friends, who are themselves Morland tenants, recommended them.

David remembers, "We were very open minded about what type of pub we would look at but when I saw the Vine with its thatched roof and superb location I felt that the brewery couldn't have suggested a better place for us. Since moving in I have made some small changes and have plans to extend the restaurant area of the pub. I would say that it pays to take the time to get to know your customers. Sudden changes won't be welcomed, especially when the pub has an established reputation and people travel to visit you. Quirky ideas that suit your customers are a great way of introducing yourself as a new licensee. I have a board advertising Attitude Adjustment Hour, instead of happy hour, which has gone down very well here."

General advice from me would be to over-estimate your expenses for the first year. We have had several things go wrong unexpectedly and you really need some spare working capital to cope with the unforeseen. My final point would be to make sure you are wholeheartedly committed to the business before you sign your lease. I love being behind the bar but the hours are long and you have to be prepared to put a good deal of your life into the running of a pub. Once you are sure, go for it! There is plenty of freedom with these long leases, so you really can feel master of your own ship."

Morland are always keen to hear from prospective licensees. For an informal chat, please contact John Erbes, Tenanted Recruitment Manager, on 01235 540453.

The Red Lion at Northmoor, Witney, Oxfordshire

The Publican's Handbook

INN PRO
THE PROFESSIONALS INN TRAINING

The Heron Hospitality Centre
Hale Wharf
Ferry Lane
Tottenham Hale
LONDON
N17 9NF
Tel: 0181 880 9900
Fax: 0181 801 9740

TRAINERS AND CONSULTANTS TO THE LICENSED AND CATERING TRADES

ARE YOU CONSIDERING RUNNING A PUB?

If the answer is Yes then Inn Pro can help you with all the training and qualifications that you require to give you the best possible start in the business. Confirmation of a knowledge of Licensing Laws is fast becoming a mandatory requirement of a Licence issue by the Magistrates. Inn Pro are licensed to deliver courses carring a British Institute of Inn keeping (BII) qualification, whether it be the full BII Qualifying Exam or the Licensees Certificate.

If you or your staff are aged between 16 - 24 we are able to offer free training under the Government Modern Apprenticeship Scheme or if you are going to employ and unemployed person the Government Training For Work Programme both leading to an Industry recognised qualification.

WOULD YOU LIKE TO TRAIN AS A CHEF?

Inn Pro are now training Chef's in their own "live" restaurant. the training will qualify the students up to National Vocational Qualification Level 3, which is recognised as a fully qualified Chef at Management level.

WOULD YOU LIKE TO TRAIN AS A MAITRE D?

Inn Pro are now running waiter and waitress training up to level 2 for all your staff involved in table service, silver service and wine service.

WOULD YOU LIKE TO TRAIN AS A PUB MANAGER?

Inn Pro are still successfully running the Pub Management course up to Level 3, for all your bar staff and potential Manageers.

ARE YOU AN EXISTING LICENSEE OR CATERER?

If you are existing Licensee or Caterer and you need assistance to drive your business forward then Inn Pro are there to help. Inn Pro have a number of business consultants who are able to offer the best possible advice. All our consultants are highly trained and share a wealth of experience within the Catering & Hospitality Industry.

FOR ALL TRAINING OR BUSINESS NEEDS INN PRO ARE HERE TO HELP

Training for Licensees

expenses sheets and dealing with invoices, machine takings and till receipts;
- calculating gross profit, cost price and retail prices on products;
- putting together your own profit and loss account and setting budgets;
- stock control and how to identify stock loss and take preventative measures;
- setting sales targets and analysing the success of promotional events;
- understanding break even analysis and how to calculate revenue levels to cover your costs.

Business Development Certificate

This three-day course will give licensees the basic tools to help them assess the potential of their business and produce a strategy to achieve realistic objectives.

Starting with the widely used SWOT (strengths, weaknesses, opportunities, threats) analysis, delegates appraise the positioning of their pub and are made aware of demographic information available from key sources which gives a factual understanding of their local market and its potential needs.

Delegates write a concise business plan which includes realistic goals, strategy, timetables and resource planning. Intensely practical, the course aims to simplify business planning and strategy so that it can be used effectively in day-to-day management to achieve business goals.

Advanced Leadership and Motivation Certificate

The two-day intensive course aims to give practical skills in leading a workforce to achieve greater sales and profitability. Licensees focus on:
- the introduction of skills to encourage the formulation of precise business objectives and a system to measure success or shortfalls;
- how to encourage the team and individuals through positive leadership and motivational skills to take ownership of those objectives;
- managing performance in areas ranging from the good to the more difficult, eg attitude, and the specific, such as achievement of sales and profit targets.

Work on finalising the details of the Customer Services, Cellar Management and Drinks Retail Certificates is still in progress.

Wine Retail Certificate

This qualification focuses on providing the skills and information required by licensees who wish to promote wine sales in their pubs or bars. The two-day course includes:
- basic product knowledge and wine tasting;
- how to discern quality from the label;
- where to buy wines and how to store and serve them correctly;
- how to compile a wine list and match it to your menu;
- merchandising and selling technique;
- how to pick the most appropriate pricing strategy for your business and your market;
- eight steps to planning a staff training programme.

NVQs

One of the common qualifications taken by both experienced licensees and new staff are National Vocational Qualifications or, north of the border, Scottish Vocational Qualifications.

These are qualifications you can obtain simply by proving performance of everyday tasks to nationally recognised standards, whether you are an experienced licensee or new part-time bar staff.

NVQs in Catering and Hospitality operate on four levels of increasing responsibility, but you do not have to complete Level 1 to achieve Level 2 and so on; you do whichever Level you feel is suitable.

NVQ Level 1 Food and Drink (Bar)
NVQ Level 1 Food and Drink (Bar) is quite basic, but its benefit is that it standardises good procedures in serving. It is suitable for new and junior part-time staff. Most staff easily achieve Level 1, making them enthusiastic about progressing.

NVQ Level 2 Serving Food and Drink (Bar)
Level 2 Serving Food and Drink (Bar) covers the increased responsibility and technical skills needed by experienced bar staff who can work unsupervised. It is an excellent motivator for confident bar staff.

NVQ Level 3 On-Licensed Premises Supervision Management
Level 3 On-Licensed Premises Supervision Management is suitable for senior staff and is mostly used by assistant managers and licensees who are likely to be responsible for the day-to-day running and supervision of the pub. It covers staff training and supervision, contributions to policy, managing drink service and cellar operations, security, stock control, health and safety, and maintenance.

NVQ Level 4 On-Licensed Premises Management
Level 4 On-Licensed Premises Management is the highest level of NVQ currently available specifically for running pubs. It is suitable for those with total responsibility for maintaining and expanding the business and covers financial control, staff recruitment, training and retention, establishing and updating policy and procedures relating to customer service, health and safety and employment legislation, managing all aspects of drink service and cellar storage and evaluation, and maintenance of the pub and all equipment.

An NVQ Level 5 is in development and it is expected to cover responsibility for profitability of the business, and the planning and performance of own and others' work.

How to gain an NVQ
Traditional qualifications often involve attending a course and sitting a formal exam. You work for your NVQs literally as you do your everyday job, coached and assessed by your manager or training provider. NVQs confirm that you can do your job. They are ideal for people who hate exams, as the

Training for Licensees

Managing Money, Stock and Accounts
by Chris Beesley

Chris is senior consultant at Leisure Business Services the Leeds based specialist accounts and financial service to the licensed retail, hotel and catering trades.

MANAGING MONEY AND STOCK

The management of stock and finance may hardly be the most inspiring of subjects. In fact, to the majority of licensees it is considered to be the most tedious aspect of running a licensed business. However, it is essential to the success of any operation, and operators shun the control of stock and money at their peril.

The cases of licensees who are seemingly performing well, suddenly losing control of their business, are too numerous to mention. It is a common trap to fall into, to believe that because you have to improve the turnover of an outlet, that you are being successful. It is often the case that turnover improvements do not convert into improvements in profit. the most common causes for this failure are the failure to manage costs and control stock management.

MANAGING STOCK TO IMPROVE MARGIN.

The management of stock is really all about the control of gross profit margin. However, good stock management has implications for all aspects of the business - from the management staff, to the promotion and merchandising of products.

It is fairly common for a licensee who is worried about profits and cash to look at ways of cutting down on costs, and one of the first costs to go is often the monthly stocktake. However, this usually proves to backfire, as control over gross profit margin is lost. The cost of a good stocktake can be lost in a night of staff "fiddling" or in pricing a new product incorrectly.

A good stock taker will be able to give you much information which is valuable in the management of your business. The days when a stocktaker merely informed the licensee of the gross profit percentage are gone (in most cases!). Information on the profitability of individual products is essential for decisions regarding stocking of products, pricing, and which products to market and promote.

By analysing the sales mix in an outlet, stock management should enable the licensee to build sales and profits, whilst keeping stockholding down to manageable levels. The management of stock is effectively the management of money, as much of the working capital of a business is tied up in stock.

By comparing the sales information from your till system to your consumption of stock, a stocktaker should be able to tell you precisely which products are causing deficiencies in profit margin. It is in this way that wastage and theft can be minimised.

It is far more useful to know that it is bottles of Budweiser that are going missing, than it is to be told that you have a stock deficit of £80, but not know where the loss has arisen.

A good stocktaker is a key ally in the success of your business, and can offer extremely useful advice in controlling profits.

ACCOUNTS MANAGEMENT

Accountancy and book-keeping are the least favourite aspects of a business for the majority of licensees. very few licensed house operators have the skill, knowledge, or inclination to provide their own accounts, and so look towards an accountant to provide this service.

However, there are many services which are specific needs of the licensed house operator, which a non-pub specialist account may not be used to providing:

1) Budgets

The value of budgets is that you set yourself targets for turnover and expenditure, which give you a framework within which to operate. By budgeting, the publican is able to compare actual results to the targets which have been agreed, and to act on this information.

2) Managements Accounts.

Very few independent licensees are provided with regular monthly management accounts - but all the major managed pub companies use them as an essential tool. Regular information is essential to managing the business, by highlighting areas for concern, and putting you in control of finance.

3) Weekly prime controls

Weekly book-keeping should allow the operator to monitor turnover and cash expenses. The key cost area of wages can be managed on a weekly basis, which allows rotas tom be planned to ensure that cost targets are not exceeded.

4) Cash-Flow Management.

When cash-flow is tight, it is essential to monitor income and outgoings on a day to day basis.

In a 1996 survey of licensees by Leisure Business Services, 67% of licensees highlighted the need for accountants to specialise in the licensed trade, and understand the business. However, only 6% of those licensees surveyed believed that their accountants did this, and very few provided the full range of services highlighted above.

Unless you are a qualified accountant, with the time and inclination to provide all these services for yourself, a specialist licensed trade accountant should prove to be a major ally in the management of your business.

Leisure Business Services can be contacted by telephone on (0113) 2776169 or by fax (0113) 2771889.

CALLING ALL LICENSEES!
Improve your profits. Say goodbye to paperwork

- Full accountancy, bookkeeping and payroll service
- Practical advice on saving costs and making money from experienced Licensed Trade Professionals
- All you would expect from your accountant plus extra professional help to improve your business.
- Management reports and a Financial Health Check EVERY month
- Gross Profit/Stock Management Systems

Let us help you to run a happy, successful business.
Let us turn an hour of your time into the most profitable hour of your life.

OUR RATES ARE REASONABLE • OUR SERVICE EXCEPTIONAL

FOR A FREE NO OBLIGATION CONSULTATION

TEL: 0113 277 6169
FAX: 0113 277 1889

LEISURE BUSINESS SERVICES

West Point Business Centre, Westland Square, Leeds, W. Yorkshire LS11 5SS

---

qualification is confirmed by assessment.

They are also ideal for people who cannot take time out to attend formal courses and study for traditional exams. They fit in with the normal work routine and are particularly suitable for staff because they allow the licensee to train and assess practically and with immediate benefit to the business.

You may take them at any age, and as long as you need to complete. It may take a year to gain a whole NVQ, and involves completing a number of units which make up the total qualification for the particular level you want. Your work programme will include enough background study to ensure you have the 'underpinning knowledge' which is usually checked during the routine assessments.

Modern Apprenticeships
Modern Apprenticeships are a training route which takes young employees (aged 26 or younger) up to Level 3 NVQ. They are run jointly by a recognised training provider (brewer or college) and the licensee.

Funding and implementing NVQs
There are four ways to implement NVQs.

1. Licensees can form a small consortium to pool their resources and experience. BII members who are not part of large pub groups have co-operated on pilot schemes, notably in the South West, Hampshire, Kent and Herts and Beds sections. Licensees host feedback sessions where problems and best practices are shared. This method suits the

Training for Licensees

small pub best as training is usually only given when 10-12 people commit themselves to an NVQ programme.
2. Larger businesses undertake every aspect of the NVQ programme themselves in-house. Scottish & Newcastle Retail is an example.
3. It is possible to bring in external help for certain parts of the process such as pinpointing business requirements.
4. A Modern Apprentice who will be supported by an external trainer and assessor.

Funding is usually available to licensees for NVQ training through local Training and Enterprise Councils (TECs). All TECs have a list of training providers.

To find out more, contact your local Business Link which will advise on funding and support.

CHAPTER FOUR

HIRING AND FIRING

Christine Bradley

Every day, and without necessarily realising it, publicans are applying one or other of the current employment laws in their dealings with staff.

Employment law is complex these days and, while many publicans will have a reasonable working knowledge of it, this chapter will act as a reminder of the more important aspects which readers will encounter. Many problems can be avoided with a little forethought and pre-planning. What follows should not be taken as a comprehensive guide. There can be no substitute for recognising the potential exposure under unfair dismissal and other legislation and, if needs be, checking with a solicitor for confirmation that the steps about to be taken do not hold any hidden dangers.

THE CONTRACT OF EMPLOYMENT

There is a statutory obligation to provide a set of written minimum terms and conditions of employment to each member of staff, no matter how few hours he or she may work.

Properly drafted employment documentation can also be of great benefit to the employer. Once in place it will quickly become a valuable part of daily record-keeping, not just a burden of paperwork. Drafting even the most basic list of terms and conditions framed in general terms is good practice, even if it is only designed to comply with the minimum set out in the Employment Rights Act 1996, that is:

- ◆ date of commencement;
- ◆ dates of continuous employment;
- ◆ details of pay, hours of work, holidays, pensions and sick pay;
- ◆ notice provisions;
- ◆ any collective agreements;
- ◆ disciplinary rules and grievance procedures.

Doing more than the bare minimum is recommended, however. The more comprehensively the terms are set out the better, because reference back to the written contract will assist an employer in addressing staff problems as they crop up. In addition, detailed consideration of the clauses to be included at the outset of the relationship will enable you to be confident that you are operating sensible and proper systems so as to ensure full compliance with the law.

RECRUITMENT

When recruiting, remember that you need to ensure that you do not fall foul of anti-discrimination legislation, which now includes the Disability Discrimination Act 1995 which came into force in December 1996. The basic rule is to be careful not to treat any individual less favourably than others on grounds of sex, marital status, age, ethnic or national origin, or disability. All candidates must be assessed solely on their qualifications, relevant knowledge, experience and personal qualities. Equally, all candidates should be assessed on the basis of the same job-related criteria, regardless of marital status and/or assumed domestic responsibilities.

Job descriptions and recruitment literature should be drawn up to reflect accurately the requirements and duties of the job and should be referred to consistently throughout the recruitment process. Any explicit or implicit bias in the way a job is described and the duties are outlined must be avoided, so any job description or advertisement should be gender-free, ideally stating that you are an equal opportunities employer (and that you, therefore, have a written equal opportunities policy).

Interviewing – points to remember

In short-listing candidates, all applicants should be treated in the same manner, and the interview list should be drawn up with reference to a clear job description based on qualification requirements, skills, experience and so on. It is vital that special care is used to avoid setting conditions relating to physical strength or appearance unless such is essential to the nature of the job, eg where it could be argued that only one sex is physically capable of doing a particular job. Setting conditions is fraught with danger as these can give rise to an inference of indirect discrimination, as can selection based on qualifications or dexterity or a preferred age range.

When rejecting applications for interview, ideally a note of the reason for the rejection should be kept on file as evidence of the fairness of selection should your decision ever be challenged.

It is wise to arrange for applicants to be interviewed by more than one person so as to avoid any inference of personal preference or prejudice. Where this is not possible (and even if it is), careful notes of the interview should be kept. It is paramount that interviewers are careful to avoid asking questions from which discrimination could be inferred, particularly in relation to child care responsibilities; for example, it should not be assumed that a married female applicant will be unable to work during evening hours. For the same reason, questions should not be raised as regards an applicant's marital status and whether they have children, or in relation to an employee's religious beliefs. As these questions do not generally relate to the requirements of the job, interviewers are opening themselves up to unnecessary criticism by even raising them.

If it really is necessary to assess whether the performance of the job would be affected by the applicant's personal circumstances, this should be discussed without any detailed questions based on assumptions about marital status, children and domestic responsibilities. If it is necessary for the jobholder to be flexible, the requirements of the job should be explained in detail to all applicants and all applicants should be asked if they feel able to fulfil those requirements.

Once interviews have taken place, you should record your reasons why applicants were or were not appointed as objectively as possible. This may prove vital evidence should a claim of unlawful discrimination be brought. Disabled applicants have the right not to be discriminated against for a reason relating to their disability unless you can show that the discriminatory treatment in question was justified. Disability discrimination is in its infancy in the UK and the application of the Act to any particular situation is far too detailed to go into here. Suffice it to say that to justify discriminatory treatment on the grounds of disability, you have to show that your reasons were settled upon only after you had considered your duty to make adjustments to working practices and to the working environment to accommodate the requirements of individual disabled candidates (or for that matter existing employees).

EQUAL OPPORTUNITIES POLICY

To minimise your exposure to discrimination claims generally, you should have a written equal opportunities policy, particularly as these days industrial tribunals have the power to grant unlimited compensation.

An equal opportunities policy should provide a framework for ensuring that individuals are treated equally and fairly and that decisions on recruitment, selection, training, promotion and career management are based solely on objective job-related criteria. A written policy can also provide a defence if you are faced with complaints of discrimination, particularly sexual or racial harassment, suffered at the hands of other employees or even of a third party, for example if the stand-up comic booked to do a spot on your premises starts picking on members of staff on grounds of race or sex, or if a guest at a private party makes unwanted advances to your bar staff.

Given your liability for discrimination and harrassment by third parties, you should be able to show that you took reasonable measures to warn of the need to treat employees and colleagues equally and avoid discrimination and harassment. This will include setting up a procedure for dealing with complaints of harassment, implementing the policy through staff training

Hiring and Firing

and education, and even where necessary displaying notices warning third parties against behaving in a way which could be construed as discrimination or harrassment.

EMPLOYING ILLEGAL WORKERS – A CRIMINAL OFFENCE

Since January 1997 it has been a criminal offence to employ someone who does not have permission to live and work in this country. If convicted, you can be fined up to £5000 per offence.

It is up to you to check the status of new employees before they start work. To protect yourself, you should insist on having sight of the original of one of a number of documents which are listed in the regulations – a passport, a P45, a national insurance card and so on. Having seen the original document, take a copy of it for the personnel file, and you have a complete defence under the Act.

However, in complying with the Act, you need to be sure that you do not act in a way which could constitute, or be interpreted as, racial discrimination. The only way of avoiding this is to ensure that you ask *all* employees for this information, no matter how unlikely it may be that there are any problems about their right to work, since to act otherwise might be seen as treating a particular group less favourably on the grounds of their race which would be discrimination. Essentially, you should not make assumptions about an applicant's right to work or their immigration status based on their race or their national origin.

WAGES

Publicans need to know whether they can dock the wages of staff they suspect of pilfering or otherwise causing stock shortages. Provisions for making deductions to recover staff loans, cover damage to uniforms etc should be set out in the contract of employment; if they are not, written agreements should be made before staff loans are made or uniforms are handed over.

Other restrictions are set out in Part II of the Employment Rights Act 1996 which requires that in cases of cash deficiencies or stock shortages, no more than 10 per cent of the employee's gross salary for that payment period can be deducted in any one payment period. Deductions in respect of cash shortages or stock deficiencies which occurred more than a year before are also restricted. Breach of this statute can lead to a claim against you at an industrial tribunal and could result in you being ordered to repay the sums deducted.

It is only sensible, therefore, to ensure that there are internal procedures in place to enable the provisions of the Employment Rights Act, better known by its old name (the Wages Act) to be adhered to.

WORKING HOURS

In the licensed trade, more so than in many other business, it is prudent to build flexibility into working hours. The right to vary each employee's hours according to the needs of the business must be

79

specifically reserved in the contract of employment.

However, even though you should retain some power to vary your staff's working hours/days, you must not exercise it in an arbitrary, capricious or inequitable way, nor apply it excessively or oppressively, as to do so might breach your obligation of good faith which underlies any employment relationship. You should also be wary of insisting that an employee work longer hours than specified in the contract, and equally careful when seeking to reduce an employee's normal working hours, particularly if it means a reduction in the employee's normal earnings.

Considerations relating to the duty to provide a safe system of working and avoiding liability for stress-related illnesses should be borne in mind when drafting flexibility clauses. In addition, the impact of the Working Time Directive will have to be accommodated in the near future. It will probably provide for daily rest of at least 11, weekly rests of at least 24 hours, a minimum annual paid leave of four weeks, pro rata for part-timers, breaks for employees who work more than six hours a day, a maximum working week of 48 hours including overtime, and a restriction on night workers working more than eight hours at a stretch. It is likely that employees will be able to agree to work for more than 48 hours in a week, but it is clear that this will be subject to restrictions. When drafting contracts for new employees, it makes sense to ensure that your arrangements in relation to working hours take into account the likely provisions of the directive on the one hand, as well as reserve flexibility so as to assist you in dealing with the demands of your particular business.

TRANSFER OF UNDERTAKINGS (PROTECTION OF EMPLOYMENT) REGULATIONS

Care should be exercised when taking over a pub which is trading as a going concern. The Transfer of Undertakings (Protection of Employment) Regulations entitles employees transferring from one employer to another to carry on under the same terms and conditions as before, and if any dismissals are required, extra care should be taken to avoid exposure to claims of unfair dismissal.

The regulations apply to all employees, including part-timers, and dismissals of employees with more than two years' continuous service which can be shown to be connected with the transfer will be regarded as automatically unfair. The new owner will succeed in persuading an industrial tribunal that dismissals of this nature were not automatically unfair if he can show that they happened for an economic, technical or organisational reason entailing changes in the workforce. An economic reason could be where the profitability of a business cannot be sustained unless at current staffing levels. A technical reason could be where an employer wishes to introduce new technology and the existing employees do not have the necessary skills. An organisational reason

Hiring and Firing

INN ACCOUNTING SERVICES LTD

"Essential assistance to the license trade"

1. STOCKTAKING SERVICE

The Stock Report provides an evaluation of:

- Cost value of sales in any period
- Retail value of each stock line
- Gross profit achieved on each stock line
- Stock value held for each stock line
- Number of days stock held, based on the correct periods sales

SAME DAY RESULTS

2. FINANCIAL REPORT SERVICE

This service produces a Financial Report, similar in form to the Annual Accounts but with a greater emphasis on the analysis of the houses income and direct costs, with overheads being grouped into key controllable or fixed cost areas.

The Financial Reports are usually produced to the same accounting period to which the stock reports are produced. They provide a snap-shot indication of how the business is fairing. They provide essential information to enable the client to manage their business.

3. PAYROLL SERVICES

Whatever your payroll needs, we can help!

- fast and reliable processing
- strict confidentiality
- hourly or fixed rate payrolls
- weekly, monthly, periodically paid employees
- payments made direct to employee bank accounts via BACS
- summarised/detailed payroll reports and ledger journals prepared
- client specific pay slips designed, or detailed security ones

01332 348228

81

INN RELIEF SERVICES LTD

SELECTING AND PLACING TOP QUALITY MANAGERS FOR OVER 20 YEARS

- Founded in 1974, Inn Relief was originally formed to select and place relief managers into Licensed Trade Establishments.
- Based in Derby, we are recognised throughout the UK as one of the leading relief management and service agencies.
- With over 20 years experience of recruiting and successfully placing relief managers into public houses, clubs, leisure complexes and catering establishments, we have attained an unrivalled track record in supplying the best relief managers.

"OUR CHARTER TO YOU"

'We endeavour to provide relief or permanent management cover, in fitting with the establishments specific requirements, services and status, that will constantly meet or exceed your exacting standards and expectations.'

INN RELIEF SERVICES LTD

"1974 - 1997, 23 years service to the licensed and catering trades - providing temporary and holding relief managers"

INN RELIEF PERMANENT SERVICES

"Selecting and placing quality managers on a permanent basis"

INN ACCOUNTING SERVICES LTD

"Essential Assistance for the licensed trade - providing stocktaking financial reports and payroll"

109 London Road, DERBY DE1 1DG
01332 348 228

INN RELIEF
PERMANENT SERVICES

"Selecting and placing quality managers for over 20 years"

Inn Relief Services carry out an in-depth study of all establishments which register a recruitment need, to identify the specific skills and personal attributes, which the correct candidate will need to possess in order to successfully undertake the position.

ENSURING SUCCESS

One of the most valuable asset any establishment can acquire in order to ensure success, is the right team or person in management.

Inn Relief Services knows the importance of securing the right people. The services we offer are designed to ensure that the candidates selected, are specifically matched to your individual requirements, hence, reducing the risk of inappropriate management recruitments.

SERVICES AVAILABLE

- Immediate Relief Assistance
- Large Database Of Professional Managers
- Effective Advertising Of Vacancies In Appropriate Trade Press
- CV Scanning & Evaluation
- In-depth Interviewing
- Candidate Testing
- Final Interviews

"YOUR SPECIFIC NEED"

We will provide assistance in any individual or combination of areas within the recruitment process, right through to the total management of all your managerial recruitment needs.

01332 348228

INN RELIEF SERVICES LTD

"1974 - 1997, 23 years to the licensed and catering trades - providing temporary and holding relief managers"

THE COMPANY

- Established in 1974
- Specialising in providing relief management for public houses and licensed catering establishments
- **Professional and experienced staff**
- **Operating throughout Great Britain**
- Serving the major national and regional breweries and leisure companies

THE OBJECT

- Supply relief management of the highest calibre
- Allocating management contracts to match the experience, suitability and background of the relief management team to the particular assignment
- Short term holiday relief and longer term holding operations

THE RELIEF MANAGER

- Carefully selected following a lengthy assessment and reference cross-checking
- Required to have a minimum of three years experience in the managed house trade
- Required to maintain a security deposit of £1,000
- All relief managers are required to pay a daily premium to the company to indemnify clients against losses not arising from defalcation up to £1,000 over and above the security deposit

NEED A RELIEF?

Whatever the reason: holiday, sickness, dismissal, we can provide you with professional management.

01332 348228

Hiring and Firing

could be where the new employer wishes to operate at a different location and it is not practical to relocate the staff.

If one of these reasons exists, provided the dismissals are carried out fairly, they would most likely be found to be fair, thus avoiding liability for compensation. However, such dismissals may well fall within the definition of redundancy, so a redundancy payment would have to be made.

A prudent employer taking over a going concern will obtain the fullest information about its employees and seek the advice of an employment law specialist before embarking on any dismissals. As a minimum, information as to the employees' length of service, contracts of employment and the like are vital to avoid exposure in this area.

PART-TIME WORKERS

It is a common misapprehension that part-time employees can be treated in a different, even an inferior, way to full-time staff. In fact, part-time workers have the same rights as full-time workers in the same category and in particular, after they have accrued two years' continuous service, they acquire protection against unfair dismissal and entitlement to redundancy payments. In addition, to avoid discrimination claims, you need to ensure that part-timers have equal rights to any benefits, such as pensions and maternity leave, which are afforded to full-time employees.

Part-time employees, even temporary or casual workers, now have access to the same employment protection laws as their full-time counterparts and it is imperative that terms and conditions of employment are pro rata with the full-timers. Obviously, care must be taken to avoid discrimination, for example in relation to equal pay and the like.

DISMISSAL

To state the rule at its most simple, if after a period of two years' continuous service an employee is dismissed, he or she may have a claim of unfair dismissal. Protection against unfair dismissal is governed by statute, and you need to be able to demonstrate one of the following five potentially fair reasons for dismissal:

1. misconduct;
2. redundancy;
3. lack of capability;
4. work which would otherwise contravene a duty or restriction which has been imposed by statute;
5. some other substantial reason.

In addition, when dismissing it is important that the employer acts reasonably. You must follow a fair procedure when carrying out a dismissal, and this usually involves a process of warnings, investigations and consultation. Only in particular circumstances will an employer be able to dismiss an employee without warning (a summary dismissal). This normally arises in circumstances which involve a serious breach of contract such as gross misconduct (conduct involving breach of disciplinary rules and the like).

It is also important to bear in mind that for all employees - no matter how short their period of service or how few their number of hours worked - when dismissing (save for cases of summary dismissal) there are minimum statutory notice periods which must be complied with and these are as follows:

- ◆ service of less than a month - no minimum notice required;
- ◆ service of more than a month but less than two years - a week;
- ◆ service of over two years - one week for each completed year of service up to a maximum of 12 weeks after 12 years' completed service.

When dismissing, employers need to be sure that they have given the appropriate period of notice or they will be exposed to an action for breach of contract, in which case the remedy is damages for the period of notice which should have been given.

Where an employee is able to claim that he has been unfairly dismissed, the financial implications can be quite significant. Unfair dismissal compensation is commonly awarded under two heads:

- ◆ a basic award of up to £6300 (at May 1997), calculated on age, length of service and salary;
- ◆ a compensatory award up to a maximum of £11,300 (at May 1997) subject to the employee's obligation to mitigate his or her loss by getting another job.

Conduct dismissals are probably the most common types of dismissal and while small employers do not need to have disciplinary rules in place, the benefits of drawing these up will be well worth the trouble for even the smallest employer when the time comes for disciplinary measures. Bear in mind that a significant part of any employer's day-to-day relationship with employees (beyond the specific issue of dismissal) is governed by the disciplinary rules, so that spent in drawing them up will stand the prudent employer in good stead in the long run.

The following might be considered for inclusion by employers in the licensed trade:

- ◆ the right to search, rules on the consumption of alcohol at work;
- ◆ a no smoking policy;
- ◆ adherence to a dress code;
- ◆ rules as to compliance with security procedures;
- ◆ rules as to compliance with the laws relating to the operation of public houses.

Dismissals on grounds of ill-health is another area which can be fraught with difficulties. Employers need to recognise the competing pressures of, on the one hand, the need to have the work carried out, against, on the other hand, the employee's right to have sufficient time to recover their health and receive fair treatment. Obviously, employees who are frequently absent over a period due to unrelated minor ailments may find that their dismissal is by reason of their conduct rather than their capability,

Hiring and Firing

and to ensure that you properly ascertain the correct line to take in relation to ill-health dismissals, it will be important to ensure that dismissals are taken only after you are informed of the full facts and have followed the relevant procedural steps, dependent on the circumstances of any particular case. Once again, the prudent employer will have taken the trouble to set up a policy on sick pay at the outset.

Whatever the reason for the dismissal, as there is quite a high exposure to compensation claims and as pitfalls can so easily trap the unwary, the importance of seeking specialist employment law advice in the early stages, preferably before taking any action cannot be over-emphasised or seen as too cautious.

CONCLUSION

As will be appreciated, this is no more than an overview of the more relevant issues which may impact on an employer in the licensed trade. Employment law, more so than many other areas of law, is constantly changing such that no guidance notes will hold good indefinitely. Essentially, the advice is to recognise the complexities of this legislation as it impacts on any employment relationship by taking steps to prepare for problems that might arise and ensuring a solid footing based on laid down terms and conditions, policies and procedures. Above all, you need to recognise that you must proceed cautiously when dealing with problems that will inevitably crop up from time to time. As in many cases, licensees are responsible for the acts or omissions of their employees; it is essential to have in place a proper system of education and training so as to minimise your exposure. Careful record keeping, access to a basic source book on employment law and liaison, for more detailed advice with professionals experienced in the field should stand you in good stead to guide you through the minefield which is employment law.

⚠ Health and Safety Notes

If you have not previously been an employer and are not familiar with health and safety legislation it is advisable to seek advice from your local environmental health officer (EHO). He/she will be able to provide guidance and information on relevant requirements and explain how they apply in practice to your situation.

Even if you do not envisage employing anyone at the outset it is still advisable to do this as much of the legislation applies to self-employed people in respect of their own health and safety and, of course, there is a duty to safeguard the health and safety of non-employees such as customers and contractors.

(Note: unless otherwise stated leaflets referred to below are available from environmental health at your local council.)

As far as obligations towards employees are concerned, the **Health and Safety at Work Act 1974** requires employers to safeguard their health, safety and welfare. The Act also specifically requires that where there are five or more employees a written health and safety policy be provided. This comprises a general statement of responsibility and commitment, details of the organisation in place (key individuals etc) and the relevant arrangements (specific procedures, safe systems of work, training, etc). Guidance can be obtained from your local EHO, alternatively a booklet which you complete to create a policy can be purchased from HSE Books (01787 881165 – 'Our health and safety policy statement – Guide to preparing a safety policy statement for a small business').

The obligations placed on employers by the Health and Safety at Work Act are wide in their application and general in nature. More specific and detailed requirements are included in various sets of Regulations. To assist you in identifying and addressing the specific health and safety issues associated with your business, the **Management of Health and Safety at Work Regulations 1992** require that you undertake a 'risk assessment'.

This means simply identifying health and safety hazards associated with your business, assessing the risks posed and dealing with these risks as appropriate. A practical approach may be to consider aspects of the premises itself (eg awkward cellar access) and aspects of the activities that take place (such as different peoples' jobs, delivery procedures, entertainment events, etc).

In doing your risk assessment it is helpful to be clear about the difference between 'hazards' (the potential for harm) and 'risks' (the likelihood that harm will happen). It may be, for example, that while the risk is very low the hazard is so serious that preventive measures are appropriate. Also, it is useful to involve employees when making the assessment as they may have identified problems in practice that you have not appreciated. If you have five or more employees you must keep a written record of the main findings. The assessment needs to be reviewed periodically particularly where change introduces new hazards.

A guidance booklet, *Five Steps to Risk Assessment – A Step by Step Guide to a Safer and Healthier Workplace*, is available. This helps you to carry out the assessment and provides a means of keeping a record.

During any health and safety inspection you may be asked about risk assessment and (where applicable) be asked to produce the safety policy. Certain accidents are reportable to your local environmental health office in accordance with the **Reporting of Injuries, Diseases and Dangerous Occurrences Regulations 1995 (RIDDOR).** In any accident investigation the relevance

Hiring and Firing

of the risk assessment (and, where applicable, the safety policy) to the accident in question is likely to be considered. (A leaflet is available which explains which accidents are reportable accidents and includes a form to use). With regard to accidents there is also a requirement to keep a record of all staff accidents in an accident book.

Other legislation to be aware of includes:

- ◆ **The Manual Handling Operations Regulations 1992;** see the notes on these under Chapter 6.
- ◆ **The Electricity at Work Regulations 1989** which includes requirements relating to all aspects of electrical safety including the maintenance of the electrical installation so that no electrical danger arises (this includes electrical appliances as well as the fixed wiring). Periodic checks should be made to ensure that this is so. Various appliances are liable to greater wear and tear and therefore warrant more frequent examination. Also, anyone doing any electrical work must be competent for the job in question.
- ◆ **The Control of Substances Hazardous to Health Regulations 1994** (as amended by the COSHH (Amendment) Regulations 1996); see the reference to these with regard to hazardous substances in the cellar under Chapter 7.
- ◆ **The Personal Protective Equipment at Work Regulations 1992;** these require, for example, that appropriate personal protective equipment (including gloves, eye protection, etc) be provided where there are risks to health that cannot otherwise be controlled.
- ◆ **The First Aid at Work Regulations 1981;** these are concerned with the arrangements for and provision of first aid.
- ◆ **The Provision and Use of Work Equipment Regulations 1992;** which include requirements relating to the suitability and maintenance of work equipment, the guarding of dangerous parts of machinery, and training.
- ◆ **The Workplace Health Safety and Welfare Regulations 1992;** which are concerned with aspects of the workplace itself, eg the condition of the floors, the provision of handrails to staircases, the use of safety glazing where necessary, etc.
- ◆ **The Gas Safety (Installation and Use) Regulations 1994;** which are concerned with the safety of gas installations/gas appliances and work done on them.
- ◆ **The Employers Liability (Compulsory Insurance) Regulations 1969;** these require the provision of appropriate employers liability insurance.
- ◆ **The Health and Safety (Information for Employees) Regulations 1989;** these require specific information to be brought to the attention of employees. The poster (or leaflets) required is available from HSE Books on 01787 881165. There is also a requirement to consult with employees, either

directly or through a representative, under the **Health and Safety (Consultation with Employees) Regulations 1996**. A requirement also exists under the **Safety Representatives and Safety Committee Regulations 1977** to consult with trade union representatives where applicable.

◆ **The Health and Safety (Young Persons) Regulations 1997;** these relate to the Management of Health and Safety at Work Regulations and the risk assessment required under that legislation. The risks that might arise because of the lack of experience, lack of awareness and immaturity of persons under 18 need to be specifically considered and addressed. Information about risks and controls needs to be provided to parents of children under school leaving age. (You should note that there is already a requirement under the **Offices, Shops, and Railway Premises Act 1963** for young persons not to clean dangerous machinery if doing so exposes them to risk from moving parts.)

The above gives a brief summary of some of the health and safety issues to be aware of. The named leaflets and others which explain the various requirements in detail and help you apply them can be obtained through your local environmental health department or from HSE Books. A number of leaflets have recently been introduced to specifically assist small businesses. The requirements may seem numerous and complicated but, in general, compliance is straightforward; if in doubt as to what is expected of you seek advice. A thorough health and safety risk assessment will enable you to identify the risks that require attention and help you to prioritise them. Don't do this in isolation: involve staff, keep them informed and ensure that training needs are addressed.

Legal Notes

In many instances licensees are responsible for the acts or omissions of their employees. It is essential therefore that a proper system of educating and training staff is in place to ensure full compliance with the law relating to the sale of intoxicating drinks and the operation of public houses.

Ensure that you have a contract of employment. Simple forms of contract are available. Be aware of the necessity to have a disciplinary procedure and ensure it is implemented. Keep records carefully of any verbal warning, written warning, final warning or dismissal.

PAYE: Obtain the appropriate booklet on PAYE from your local tax office.

Employers' **National Insurance** contribution: Learn and understand the requirements.

CHAPTER FIVE

PUBLICISING YOUR PUB

Danny Blyth

THE GREAT OPPORTUNITY

Publicity is the key to successful marketing of your pub. It brings your business to the attention of a bigger audience, generating extra trade you otherwise might take years to build up. You needn't be a budding Max Clifford to make the media work for you. Nor do you need to spend much of your hard-earned turnover. What successful publicity calls for is some understanding of the media and its needs, a little imagination, plus the commitment to spend the time required.

Those publicans who have the healthiest of businesses are often the very same who enjoy regular good publicity. From an early stage in the trade they came to realise that time spent on being 'media friendly' was very well worth it. This chapter explains some of the basic techniques for your achieving the same.

GETTING YOUR TERMS RIGHT

The first step to understanding the media is getting your terms right.

PR is activity put into getting your pub editorial coverage. This ranges from calling the local paper to tell them about your big charity night to nominating your house for an award. It results in 'editorial' - an independent third party writing, then printing or broadcasting, a message about you over which you haven't the final say. Though PR involves time and expense it is not paid for.

Advertising is bought. You decide what is said about you and you pay the price. Mixing the terms confuses people, especially your younger bar staff. Quite confusingly, there is also 'advertorial', a paid-for advert reproduced to look similar to editorial and usually headed 'Advertisement feature' at the top of the page.

We shall concentrate on editorial - what you don't have to pay for but is most prized, as more people are likely to see it and take note.

NEWS VALUE

To be a successful publicist you

must understand what is 'newsworthy', or of interest to the media. Most newsworthy is the unusual: 'Dog bites man' isn't a great story, but 'Man bites dog' pricks anyone's ears. And so, while your putting on a new guest ale might be newsworthy among your regulars, it isn't front-page news outside.

In all your PR and publicity work, therefore, focus on your main events, like big-scale fundraisers, quirky anniversaries you celebrate at the pub or some praiseworthy community involvement. And keep things unusual.

PLANNING AND TARGETING

Planning and targeting is crucial to good publicity - which rarely falls into your lap. Start by looking at your local media and get to know it well. Read, watch and listen with the dual purpose of spotting opportunities for your pub and gaining a better understanding about what your local media considers newsworthy.

Try to develop a good relationship with the local paper and radio, letting them know that you are prepared to talk. Target individual journalists and ask them down to your pub - they don't receive many invites. Meeting journalists will help you understand what is 'newsworthy', those off-beat stories they most like to cover. They will also impress on you the importance of having a good photo opportunity at whatever event you are trying to publicise.

Maintain a file of all media relevant to you - papers, magazines, radio and TV. Your 'media list' should also include any existing (and new) contacts, alongside address and telephone details. And it should also act as a record for deadlines for receipt of information.

Use some spare time to call all media on your list and ask about how they'd like information sent to them and when. All media run to a deadline for publication or broadcast. Too often good stories aren't covered because the information arrives too late.

Whatever you do publicity-wise, make sure it is done for a purpose. Identify three or four key areas of your business you'd like to have some good publicity for, such as increasing restaurant trade of functions room hire and focus efforts toward them. The good publicist knows what he's about - and why.

Once you have your list of priorities and your media list, it is often a good idea to take time to map out a media plan of action for the year and detail any costs (such as the odd advert). A separate plan for each event is also time well spent. If say you have a beer festival each August, effective planning will allow you to get the story into the local CAMRA newsletter for the start of the month, the two local papers in the week before the event and radio the night before. Knowing and responding to the separate deadlines for each will maximise your chances.

CONTACTING THE MEDIA

There are two ways of letting journalists know what story you have to tell: telephone contact and news release.

Publicising your Pub

Telephone contact

Telephoning is best reserved for fast-breaking events of great importance, or if you have already cultured a good contact. If you really must call journalists:

- Call between 10.30am (after the morning editorial meeting), but before lunchtime (after which field trips are made);
- Always ask for the 'newsdesk' in the first instance;
- Prepare a concise outline of what you have to say;
- Be ready to note any request for further information they need (and get back quickly with the details if required).

News release

The more common way of supplying information is by the 'news release'. A news release is a brief outline of what is going to happen, the bare bones of a story for consideration by a news editor. PR pros have perfected this to an art, but you can often do just as well – if you follow the golden rules:

- Use plain white paper, headed in capitals, 'NEWS RELEASE';
- Type or laser print your details, using double spacing and wide margins;
- Keep it tight, use only one sheet of paper;
- Be accurate with all details like times and name spellings;
- End with a 'person to contact' for further information and include a telephone number;
- Address to 'The News Editor'

and mail in good time to meet the deadline.

As for the writing, the keyword is brevity. Add a headline and keep it short, like 'Soap stars wanted at local pub'. Get to the point and stick to it – don't ramble. The first sentence is crucial, and always make it alone your first paragraph, for example: 'The King's Head pub in Main Street is looking for lookalikes of TV soap stars as part of its fundraising drive for Main Street Primary School.'

The news editor looks to a press release to find out Who? Where? What? Why? and When? Address these needs in a separate paragraph. Our earlier intro grabs the interest and now needs to be followed up with the necessary detail. A paragraph on Why? will show that you are planning a fundraising night for the local school's computer fund. What? will show that you intend to have a soap opera quiz plus a soap lookalike competition with prizes. Carry on with the other questions, then revise by looking through your release again, asking all five key questions.

What improves your chances of coverage no end, is having a good photo opportunity: design opportunities into your plans. For instance, if you are organising a fundraising disco, why not make it a Spicy Spin Disco, inviting girls to come dressed as Spice Girls with the best-dressed gals winning prizes. A raunchy photo opportunity like this would be highly likely to get you onto the front page of most local papers.

A good licensee would be able to

93

ADVERTISING

As a licensee you'll be regularly plagued by requests for advertising. Here's a quick guide to surviving.

Advertising has two major forms: display and classified. Display is a full-page, half, quarter or whatever that appears interspersed throughout the news and features of a publication; classifieds are smaller ads as are found under the likes of 'For Sale' columns.

Never be rushed into anything – even that 'once-only bargain price'. Consider the publication the offer is coming in from and ask yourself if it is read by your target customers. Get the advertising agent to supply details of its readership and circulation. Also query what the offer is in terms of position. Does it mean your pub being listed among a host of others, perhaps giving you just pub name and address details set in a little pint pot illustration.

WHERE TO PLACE YOUR AD

The key to successful advertising is getting the right ad in the right media at the right time. And of course there is the issue of repeat messages – your budget might only allow for one-off adverts but these will never be as fruitful as a series. The best approach is choosing your time and not responding to one-off offers. This means planning things out again: who you want to reach and how and when.

If yours is an ale house you might choose to advertise in a CAMRA newsletter. If it's your food trade you want to boost you might like to go for a 'What's On' publication or the 'Eating Out' section of the local paper, whereas your accommodation trade might be better boosted by an ad in a tourist guide.

Whatever your choice of media, tailor the message to suit a particular target market. Keep the wording brief and to the point – the chances are that there isn't a brilliant copy writer inside you.

DESIGN

Then comes the design stage. An advert is either 'made up' for you by the publication, or you can have it originated by a pro like a graphic designer. No matter which route you take, insist they keep the design simple and in keeping with your pub's desired image.

Try to incorporate either an illustration or a photograph – these really do grab readers' attention. But ensure these are good quality – poor illustration might even lose you business so these are well worth paying for. Remember you can use devices like bold or italic print, or 'reverse print' (black on white). But do use these sparingly for

Publicising your Pub

greater effect. The same applies to colour, either full colour (which can be expensive) or 'spot colour' (a single colour in addition to black type).

The chances are that you won't be entirely satisfied by your first efforts. So to maximise your chances, always ask the publication or your own designer to first supply a 'rough' (an outline design) for your prior approval. Inspect this carefully, check whether they've followed your design specifications and look carefully for setting errors that might appear in the text – especially details on things like opening hours and telephone numbers. Mistakes here can be crucial. Apply the same checking procedure to the proof.

If, however, the publication messes things up for you by poor reproduction like fuzzy pictures and poor print quality, get right on the telephone to the advertising manager (not any executive you might have dealt with) and demand recompense.

COSTS

Finally a word on costs. Always look at the whole cost picture, both when you are called up by an ad agent and when you are proactively knocking on their door. Get them to quote for a range of sizes and for use of spot and full colour, and to detail any costs in making up your advert and supplying proofs.

If you are going ahead with an advert, always negotiate on price. Every publication, radio and TV station is open to negotiation on the full list price that appears on a paper's 'rate card'. And this is all apart from a 'series discount' (where there is a percentage discount for your taking space in a certain number of consecutive issues).

Be especially tough when trying a publication out for the first time. Dangle the carrot of further business for them if first, you get a good introductory price and second, if the response is to your liking. With ad people you are dealing with some of the thickest-skinned operators in the commercial world. Fight like with like.

fill the pub with his disco alone. The PR-minded licensee would get free local paper coverage before and after the event as well. The seasoned PR/licensee would get all this, and arrange some sponsorship from a supplier like Bacardi Spice, plus land himself some coverage on radio and in the trade press. You must think big and spend time on the telephone and writing press releases if the coverage is to start rolling in.

If sending releases, don't be put off by lack of success. Yours might have arrived the day a royal made a surprise visit to the area. By calling them up calmly to find out why, you may find there was a good reason for the story not being used, or they might offer to do something with your pub later. Never assume that you've a right to press coverage.

PRO-ACTIVE PUBLICITY

Once armed with all this know-how, you are finally ready to get pro-active and set things moving. There are three distinct stages to your development as your own press officer:

1 - The core business

First is to ensure that you are, and remain, primarily a publican and not a publicist. Good publicity might be successful in getting people to try out your pub for the first time, but to get them back on a repeat basis will need a tip top pub. Remember all this publicity lark is a bonus. Don't let the stardom get in the way of standards at the pub.

The best PR of all is always word of mouth.

The first pro-active move, therefore, has to be for you to go out of your way to develop standards and the unique features of your pub that might enable you to win awards. There are award schemes run by pub companies, trade suppliers, tourist authorities, CAMRA and a wealth of other organisations. They cover everything from floral displays to children's facilities. With most you can enter yourself by self-nomination, if not, you can arrange this through a third party.

Assess your strengths and enter. If you do win - or are even short-listed - let everyone know about it for a long time. Tell the press, then display any cuttings, use A-boards outside, tell everyone. Your publicity machine is up and running - and running on the basis of a solid pub business instead of hype.

Secondly, do the same for guide books. There are a plethora of guide books published today and being listed in any can only benefit trade. Spend an hour in WH Smiths perusing and targeting where you'd like to appear. Call the publishers for details on how listings are had (again you can sometimes arrange nomination) and get cracking.

2 - Free opportunities

Look at what opportunities are going begging. Often there is free publicity to be had out there which, on its own might only bring one or two extra people out per night, but as part of the overall package that is the image of your pub, can add up to something significant.

Publicising your Pub

At last! The pen for the job! *Registered Trademark*
PENS 4 CHALKBOARDS

BHMA Limited

46 Colours now available from 'flesh to metallics'
Waterproof or Wet Wipe, Large or Small.
You choose the colours
Order from ONE PEN upwards

We are never knowingly undersold, on single or bulk orders

To Order, Telephone 01353 776305

THE PEN FOR THE JOB

BHMA limited has been changing the face of pub retailing for the past six years. Based in Cambridgeshire, BHMA's director Patrick Huggins and his valued team have been driving the standards of in-pub merchandising and chalkboards with relentless aggression through training and product development.

Patrick spent the best part of 12 months before discovering a waterproof Japanese product that would write and stay on a chalkboard, and has developed it into a widely used medium. BHMA now has a brand of its own with all the qualities of the original pen, called quite sensibly: Pens4Chalkboards™.

The new BHMA Pens4chalkboards™ are available in 46 waterproof colours, and a range of wet wipes, no-one else offers this extensive range.

BHMA is also known for their much acclaimed merchandising and chalkboard courses, run all over the country for most of the licensed retailers and brewers. The constant rebooking reflects the courses' success.

The Directors of BHMA attribute their success to staying one step ahead, and explain that their name is the Greek word VEE-MAR meaning to step ahead.

BHMA also manufactures signs, banners, chalkboards and so on. They have a price promise, and are never knowingly undersold.

WESTMINSTER COLLEGE

Please contact the Admissions Unit
Battersea Park Road
London SW11 4JR
0171 556 8001

This prestigious Hotel & Catering College offers licensed trade programmes in Central London.

•**Licensed Management Programme (British Institute of Innkeeping Qualifying Examination)**
Mondays 3-6pm for 18 weeks, starting 22nd September 1997 and 23rd February 1998.

•**BII National Licensee's Certificate**
All day Tuesday plus Friday morning, one course per month.

•**Wine & Spirit Education Trust Certificate**
Tuesdays 6-8pm for nine weeks, starting 30th September 1997, and 20th January and 27th April 1998.

Also tailor-made courses and consultancy services to companies.

For instance, if you have regular music or entertainments nights, look to getting them included, free, in the 'Listings' sections of local papers and in 'What's On' magazines. Call up the person who puts that section together and ask how they like to receive details and when. Some licensees have devised their own form which they quickly fill in and fax to the appropriate editor every week.

Local radio stations often have a variety of guests from all walks of life in to review the papers on air. Why not call whoever is in charge of such a show and volunteer? You could take in a copy of a trade paper and chat about the top pub trade stories at the same time.

There are also opportunities to be the 'guest writer', from local papers through to publications like *What's Brewing*. Use them to get your pub's name spread wider. But do send a topical and lively contribution and not a whinge. Be positive about your business.

3 – Making your own news

After getting your pub in the frame for awards, and going on to exploiting what easy opportunities exist for you, you will begin to become 'media-wise'. You will now be ready and able to be more ambitious and get out to create the news, speaking to the media in advance of your big events, such as charity fundraisers or special celebrations for big dates like Halloween.

You might like to create a special newsworthy event for yourself by celebrating an unusual anniversary. The stranger it is, the more newsworthy; be sure to stress this while talking to the press (as well as telling them what a good picture your event will make). Choose a good, fun theme but choose so you can run the event well (events should always be for customers first and media second). Always try to get your suppliers to contribute to funding, pointing out you expect good PR. They're liable to be more helpful with the possibility of added publicity. As for inspiration, pick up on your pub's geographical or historical connections. Or you could have a core of regulars with an unusual hobby. Make things topical by relating your event to something in the public eye.

If, for instance, gardening is big in your area, why not hold – during the time of the Chelsea Flower Show – an 'Alternative Chelsea'. You could offer prizes for the weediest weed, most miserable houseplant and least appetising vegetables. Silly? yes, but also quirky and newsworthy – and worth a picture. But whatever you decide, proper planning and targeting involving pre-event liaison with the media will make or break the event.

What will also help greatly is involving your staff in your plans; properly briefing them about a publicity-driven event and taking on board their views and suggestions. The last thing you need is a microphone thrust in front of a member of staff uncomfortable in fancy dress, resentful of the occasion and not having a clue as to why your special event is being run.

Get out there and have some fun!

Publicising your Pub

Health and Safety Notes

In considering ways of promoting the pub regard should be had to its locality and the potential for **noise** issues.

People aggrieved by noise from your pub can complain to the local environmental health department. If an investigation into the complaint satisfies the local authority that a statutory nuisance exists or is likely to recur, a notice can be served requiring an abatement of the nuisance or preventing a recurrence. Failure to comply with an abatement notice may lead to prosecution in the magistrates' court. There is a right of appeal against a notice. The principle of 'best practicable means' applies (see notes on nuisance under 'Food').

While the majority of nuisances are dealt with by the local council, the Environmental Protection Act 1990 allows people to complain directly to the magistrates' court and magistrates can make an order in relation to the nuisance and impose a fine.

To avoid the above it may be useful to liaise with your neighbours, to check the noise level yourself by walking around outside the pub during events, and to stick to those sort of entertainments that create the minimum of disturbance.

If noise problems arise this could have implications for your entertainment licence (where applicable) and could potentially be brought to the attention of the liquor licensing justices.

Legal Notes

It is permissible to hold certain small lotteries, including raffles, in public houses. However, the promotion of lotteries is guarded by strict legal rules and licensees are strongly advised to obtain professional advice (from, for example, the local authority's licensing department) before allowing lotteries to be held on their premises.

There is a general prohibition on gaming in places to which (whether on payment or otherwise) the public has access. However, there are concessions for dominoes and cribbage which may be played for money (along with any other game which is authorised to be played on those premises). These games do not include games of skill such as darts, pool or billiards, where players wager with each other on their skill.

Other card games or gambling games must not be permitted without the court's authority.

The Publican's Handbook

However, even where gaming is authorised 'high stakes' are not permitted. Unfortunately there is no definition of what stakes may be considered as 'high'. Guidance can be sought from the Justices, the police, or the Gaming Board who issue guidelines from time to time.

If you are considering a Race Night or Bingo Evening, it may well attract the attention of the authorities and must not be 'the only or the only substantial inducement for persons to attend the event'. Even if considered lawful, the whole of the proceeds of the entertainment, after deducting expenses, must be devoted to purposes other than private gain.

In any event you must not permit any person under 18 years to take part in any permitted gaming. Bingo also constitutes gaming so you will need a Special Order from the Justices.

Be careful, as on summary conviction there is a fine up to £5000.

THE TRUE TASTE OF TRADITION

Kimberley Brewery, Nottingham NG16 2NS.

BEER AND CIDER

Ted Bruning

Catering may be the growth area of the pub trade, but that doesn't make wet sales any less important. Indeed, it could be argued that as dining becomes more and more central to the pub trade, attention to the drinks offering becomes not less important but more.

There are two reasons for this. First, diners are picky. They demand choice and quality, and they are well-educated about their drinks. They can tell a good wine from an indifferent one and a top-quality cask ale from a low-gravity club keg ... and they know how much it ought to cost.

Second, the profit margin on food is often poor. Catering is both capital and labour intensive, but there's a double squeeze on prices: consumers see the pub as a cheap alternative to the restaurant, even if the menus are similar; and big league competitors can afford loss-leading steak platters. It all drives prices remorselessly downwards, leaving the wet sales to make the business worthwhile.

The whole subject of wet sales has changed dramatically in the last 25 years as the widening of consumer choice has increased consumer sophistication. Both the Campaign for Real Ale and the micro-brewing boom which has seen the number of breweries rise from about 70 to nearly 400 started in 1972. More recently, the tied house system has been growing progressively weaker: the Monopolies Commission report, now a decade old, put guest ales on the bars of many pubs and also created the non-brewing pub chains which now own nearly one-third of Britain's pubs and can stock what they like.

In short, the days when a publican, whether tenant, manager, or loan-tied free trader, served only the company's wines, beers, spirits and minerals in the manner prescribed by the company, and neither needed nor wanted to know more, are long gone. Successful publicans today need to be as knowledgeable as their customers, and to appreciate and meet their expectations.

What is required, therefore, is a strategy.

101

In today's ultra-competitive pub trade, nothing can be taken for granted and everything must be thought out.

- ◆ Who am I setting out to attract?
- ◆ What do they drink?
- ◆ How do they like it served?
- ◆ What will they pay for it?

You may not succeed even if your offering is spot-on, but you'll sure as hell fail if it's not.

Whatever market you are addressing, there is one golden rule which applies to beers, wines, spirits, and just about everything else: find the right balance between quality and price. Even if your pub is bottom of the range in socio-economic terms, you have to offer your customers the best you think they can afford. Remember: people don't have to go to your pub, and if they feel, rightly or wrongly, that you're ripping them off, they won't come. If, on the other hand, they feel you're doing them proud, they'll be back.

Publicans seeking detailed information on the various kinds of drinks available, where they come from, how they are made, and so forth should at this point turn to writers such as Roger Protz and Michael Jackson (beer), and Hugh Johnson (wine), who have all produced encyclopedic and enjoyable works on their (and your) specialist subjects. This book assumes a certain base of knowledge among its readers; it can serve them best by helping them focus on a drinks regime which will most fully serve their purposes.

BEER

Beer sales may not be as high a proportion of turnover as they used to be, but beer is still Britain's most popular alcoholic drink and very much at the heart of the pub trade.

Few things say as much about your pub as the beer you stock. Are you carrying all the various ice lagers, prominently displayed? You're after the clubbers. Mild at 98p a pint? The old vote. Ten little-known real ales and two draught ciders? Students, CAMRA members, folkies. Two national brands of real ale and three Guinness taps? You're in Kilburn.

So what is beer? Put simply, it is the fermented result of adding yeast to a syrup derived from a cereal, usually malted barley, which has been dosed with hops. However, the number of variations in both ingredients and process makes for an almost limitless variety of beers.

Nobody should know more about beer than the people who deal in it, but sadly, this is often not the case. All publicans should make a point of visiting a brewery, and revisiting if needed, until they have a better than working knowledge of the business of brewing: the publicans who really know how to work their beers to best advantage are those with a deep understanding of what is, admittedly, a vast subject.

Cask and keg, bottle and can

Cask ales
'Real' ale is shorthand for cask-conditioned ale – ale which undergoes a secondary fermentation in

Beer and Cider

the cask so that when it arrives in the pub the yeast is still alive, generating an entirely natural head while creating a prickle of carbonation in the body.

Choosing a sensible range of cask ales is one of the seminal decisions facing a publican seeking an identity for his pub. Cask ale needs special handling in the cellar before it can be served: more of these two subjects later.

Keg ales

Lager and so-called 'keg' or brewery-conditioned ales are conditioned in a tank at the brewery and then filtered and pasteurised before being put into kegs. Keg beer lasts a good deal longer than cask ale, but has to be artificially carbonated in the pub.

Mixed gas or nitrokeg beer is treated in exactly the same way as keg, except that the gas added in the cellar is not straight CO_2 but a mixture of CO_2 and nitrogen. The technology was developed by Guinness in the 1980s and later adapted by ale brewers because the delivery was closer to that of cask ale.

The big advantage is that nitrogen is not as soluble as CO_2, so nitrokegs should be less fizzy than CO_2-only keg. Nitrogen also makes smaller bubbles, so the head will be deeper, denser, and longer lasting.

Two varieties of nitrokeg exist.

◆ The stand-alone brand, pioneered by Caffrey's (Bass) and Kilkenny (Guinness), tends to be a premium ale which straddles the line between ale and lager, offering the low temperature and low bitterness of the former along with the malty richness of the latter. One or other of these brands is currently a must-stock, although for how long is anyone's guess.

◆ Less high profile but likely to be more enduring is the mixed-gas variant of the cask brand: Thwaites Smooth, John Smith's Smoothpour and so on. Most breweries now offer mixed-gas instead of the old CO_2 keg, and most drinkers prefer the temperature and delivery to those of the old-style keg.

As far as stocking draught lagers is concerned, most publicans will find their options limited by the tie. It has become common to stock three: one session lager such as Carlsberg or Carling Black Label; one premium of European heritage such as Kronenbourg or Stella, and one premium non-European; eg Foster's, Budweiser, or Red Stripe.

There is now a fourth option: the 'authentic' European lager. Authentic draught imports – including Czech lagers such as Budwar, Pilsner Urquell, Zamek, and Staropramen, and Belgian speciality beers such as Hoegaarden – confer the stamp of quality on a pub.

Bottled beers

Bottled beers are catching on. Bottled premium lagers such as Holsten Pils and Grolsch have been with us for a long time, and ice beers have become must-stocks; you might also make capital, especially in September when holiday tans are fading, of stocking beers such as KEO or San Miguel, perhaps on special offer. This is the

The Publican's Handbook

A plug for a Beer that was born in a bathtub.

When Pete first mixed his inspired choice of various hops and malts in his old bathtub, Pete's Wicked was born. From this humble beginning, Pete's Brewing Company has grown into America's Premier Craft Brewery and has been voted World Champion Pilsner three years in a row. So if you want to plug a hole in your range call the stockists below.

Pete's Wicked

Bull & Taylor, Calderhead, Casa Julia, Coe Vintners, Euroimpex, James Clay, Nectar Imports, Peckhams, Philips Newman, The Good Wine Company, Waverley Vintners, Whitbread, World Beer Trading Company or call The Bright Partnership on 0171 721 7590.

The Modular Double Stacking System…
…Grows With You!

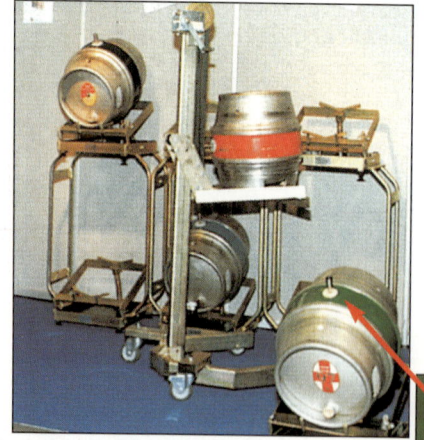

REDUCED ULLAGE INCREASED PROFIT!

Automatic beer valve. Simple to use.

Extends life of draught beers by days.

Eliminates excessive air.

Prevents contamination.

No need for Co^2 blanket.

All stainless steel construction.

Mermaid Industries Ltd., 30 Linton House, Catherine Street, Aston, Birmingham B6 5RS
Tel: 0121 328 5204 Fax: 0121 328 5351

Building success on flavour

H&B Henninger
SEIT 1869

Germany supports more breweries than any other country in the world, about 1,243 in all. Between them they produce some 5,000 beers in more than a dozen classic styles. As you would expect German consumers are very particular about their choice of beer, with only those who adhere to the highest standards achieving real success. Henninger rank along side the most successful of the premier brewers, and have (since 1869) built a world wide reputation based on quality, taste and a continuing commitment to excellence. We are sure it will become your premier choice Pilsner and as shown in other markets, the benchmark in quality and flavour.

Picture - The landmark Henninger Tower - over 300ft tall - Frankfurt /M.

SHACKLEFORD SALES Ltd
Russell House, 137-139 High Street, Guildford
Surrey, GU1 3AD. Tel: 01483 456644 Fax: 01483 456616

sort of flexibility that a creative approach to premium bottled products can offer.

Bottled ales, for too long meaning a choice between light, pale, sweet brown or sweet stout, are catching up. A good array of different labels in the chiller is a low-cost way of maintaining an exciting range of beers and gives the flexibility to suit customers individually: you can economically keep a stock of bottled Marston's Low C for a diabetic bitter-drinker, but you couldn't if Low C were draught.

Until recently almost all bottled ales were pasteurised and artificially carbonated, with the exception of a small number of specialities such as Worthington White Shield which were bottled with enough live yeast to generate natural CO_2 in exactly the same way as cask conditioning.

The number of these bottle-conditioned ales (BCAs) on the market has increased enormously in the last three or four years. BCAs have a number of advantages for the publican: they are premium products and command a premium price, and they offer an opportunity to stock a wide range of 'real' beers without the risk of stocking too many cask ales. At the time of writing, it seemed more than likely that the guest ale provision would be extended to embrace one BCA, which makes the whole genre doubly interesting.

One drawback is that being alive they do change, not necessarily for the better. Careful keeping in a cool, dark, and vibration-free cellar and sensible stock management should be enough to ensure they are served at their best, but an open attitude to customer complaints is essential.

One thing is certain: the bottled beer offering is no longer confined to the commodity range of light, brown, and stout; it is now an active part of the marketing mix.

Canned beers

These are all pasteurised and artificially gassed. Carbonated canned beers are now giving way to so-called draught in can versions which, like nitrokeg, contain both CO_2 and nitrogen. Draught in can beers contain nitrogen in solution, which on opening is released by a plastic device dubbed a widget, producing a sudden gaseous surge settling to a dense head. Publicans may be wary of stocking such beers unless strictly necessary, as they invite too close a comparison with take home prices.

Types of beer

Lager and ale are generally accepted as being subdivisions of beer, so the term 'beer and lager' is not strictly accurate. The main differences between the two are in the strains of malt, hop, and yeast used and in the conditioning or maturing process. Lagers should mature or condition for much longer than ales ('lager' means, very roughly, 'kept'), and at much lower temperatures – which also explains the difference in recommended serving temperature.

These differences, though, have always been very approximate, and the edges are blurring all the time:

◆ many ale brewers now use lager-type hops;

Beer and Cider

- some ales are brewed with lager-type yeasts;
- most ales and stouts are served at near-lager temperatures;
- many British lagers condition for half the time a premium bitter does.

The almost infinite number of variables in the brewing process means there are many styles of beer which publicans today need to be familiar with. The following is only a selection, but covers the main styles the publican is likely to encounter.

Mild
Once the favourite of workers in heavy industry, milds tend to be sweeter, weaker, and less hoppy than bitters, being a cheap, quenching beer which can be consumed in bulk. Milds can be dark or light and vary from 2.8-3.5 per cent alcohol by volume (abv).

Bitter
A rung up in hoppiness, strength, and price comes standard bitter, ranging from 3.5-4 per cent abv. Premium or best bitters range from 4-4.8 per cent abv, and there are even stronger ales these days which seem to fit the 'bitter' category better than any other, Morland Old Speckled Hen at 5.2 per cent abv being a prominent example. These merely serve to show how elastic the categories are. The rise of the guest ale market and the general trading-up process have given premium bitters such as Marston's Pedigree and Wadworth 6X dominance in the ale market.

Stout
Originally 'Stout Porter' – not a fat bag carrier, but a stronger version of porter (see below). Today, though, the term stout means either the dry or Irish style of around 4.5 per cent abv, typified by a strong flavour of roasted unmalted barley, or the much weaker sweet style of which Mackeson (3% abv) is the principal survivor.

British speciality beers
Various revived old-fashioned styles are becoming popular again, especially in bottle. They include old ales, exemplified by Theakston's Old Peculier at 5.7 per cent abv, and porter, the dominant beer style of the 18th-19th centuries, killed by malt rationing in World War I and revived in the 1980s. There is endless argument as to what porter was really like: since it was the first ale purpose-brewed for widespread distribution (the term has nothing to do with London market porters; it simply means 'portable', the best modern equivalent being 'export'), it would have been very hoppy (hops protect against infection), and highly alcoholic. It would have left the brewery in an incomplete state, the continuing fermentation and CO_2 production giving further protection during transit. Modern porters, however, tend to be only mid-strength. India Pale Ales were also developed for export, and exactly the same rules of strength and hoppiness apply as for porter, except that as IPAs were a later development they benefited from advances in the malting process and were therefore pale and clear. Today IPA, if it means anything,

107

GROWING RECOGNITION FOR ROBINSON'S ALES

Quality cask-conditioned ales from Stockport-based brewer Frederic Robinson Limited are becoming better known outside their heartland in the north-west. One of the brewery's ales, FREDERICS, has followed Robinson's Best BITTER by gaining recognition as an international medal winner. Other brands such as Hartleys XB, are also increasingly recognised through the guest beer market.

Last year, FREDERICS Premium Beer, the company's most recently introduced ale, won a bronze medal at the Brewing Industry International Awards. This followed the silver medal won by Robinson's Best BITTER brand 2-years previously. Available in 500ml and 275ml bottles as well as on draught, FREDERICS is brewed from an all British malt grist and the finest traditional aroma hop varieties. Beer experts from as far afield as North America and Japan attended the B.I.I.A. award ceremony in Harrogate, selecting the premium beer from a list of 59 entrants. Named after Frederic Robinson, founder of the company, the 5% abv brew has won an export order from the United States where British beers are growing in popularity.

Robinson's Best BITTER is the company's best selling brand, containing a full bitterness that is derived from choice aroma hops. With a 4.2% abv, the ale is much admired by real ale. drinkers for its rich head and pale, bright colour. Made from the highest quality ingredients, this brew is to be found increasingly in pubs across the country.

Hartleys XB is another popular real ale brewed at the Unicorn Brewery in Stockport. At 4% abv, this ale is cask-conditioned to be smooth and bitter, with a subtle tang of malt. Well known in the Lake District through the Robinson's owned Hartleys estate, it is famed for its rich body and is still faithfully brewed in the traditional way to an original recipe.

Other cask-conditioned ales in the Robinson's collection, produced at the Unicorn brewery include OLD TOM, HATTERS MILD and OLD STOCKPORT Bitter.

Strongest and oldest of the brewery's cask-conditioned beers, OLD TOM is available in 275ml bottles as well as on draught. The 8.5% abv strong ale, which was first brewed in 1899, is also known for the cat which features on bottles, pump clips and drip mats of the brand.

OLD STOCKPORT Bitter, named after the town where it is brewed, is a traditional ale with a 3.5% abv, that has a rich golden body and refreshingly hoppy taste.

A mellow, well balanced brew, HATTERS Mild has a 3.3% abv. It is synonymous with Stockport's famous hat making industry and is one of the few light coloured milds available.

All these ales are available across much of the country.

Traditional values and quality count for a lot at Robinson's which was founded in 1838 and is presently run by the fifth generation of the family. Products are still brewed to age-old recipes and a team of shire horses can still be seen working around the brewery as well as at shows across the country.

Only the finest tried and tested quality ingredients are used in the brewing process at Robinson's. Using their long standing relationship with British suppliers, they secure the highest standard malt and hops. The water used in the products is drawn from the company's on site bore holes and the yeast is taken from the same strain used for many years.

With a continued adherence to brewing tradition, it is no surprise that Robinson's ales are gaining growing recognition across much of the country.

Beer and Cider

As one of the oldest independent brewers in the country, Hardys & Hansons Kimberly Brewery is steeped in tradition. Brewing Three main ales, Kimberley best mild, kimberly best bitter and the stronger Classic, a selection of new ales as part of its cellarman's Cask range has also been launched recently.
With seasonal guest beers such as Rocking Rudolph, Frolicking Farmer, Crowing Cock and the award winning Guzzling Goose, the cellarman's cask range is achieving a terrific reputation throughout the country.
"Our Cellarmen's Cask range has proved a huge success in both our pubs, our traditional free trade and has opened many new doors to additional free houses in our area" said George Tunney, free trade and marketing manager. "In addition, we have received many orders from cask ale wholesalers and pub groups throughout the country, reinforcing kimberley Brewery's excellent and growing reputation as being one of the first cask ale brewers in the country".
Brewing technology has advanced greatly since the foundation of the original Kimberley Brewery, But not at the expense of taste. Traditional techniques and natural ingredients are used in conjunction with and the latest equipment to ensure quality standards remain continually high. Whilst measurement and control of ingredients are undertaken by computer control, once this has been completed the kimberley brewers "let nature take its course". Making the mash only takes one day, whereas fermentation takes the best part of a week, definitely a process which cannot be hurried. All Kimberley ales are brewed without the use of artificial additives.
Kimberley Brewery has been in operation since 1832, when a brewery was established less than 500 yards from the present site. In 1861 this original site was purchased by William and Thomas Hardy, with a new facility built known as the Hardy's kimberley Brewery Ltd , Stephen Hanson, meanwhile, had built Hansons limited Kimberley Brewery on the opposite side of the road in 1847. Having been attracted by the supply of excellent brewing water, both breweries thrived until in 1930, under increasing pressure from larger brewing companies and a lack of male successors to the Hardy's brewery, the two companies combined. Today, the family influence continues with Richard Hanson, being the great grandson of the original founder of the Hansons Brewery.
Last year, Hardys & Hansons p.l.c. reported a pre-tax profits in excess of £8m, whilst the company employs around 1,200 mainly local staff.
Hardys & Hansons own around 250 pubs, of which roughly 100 are Nottinghamshire, 100 in Derbyshire, the remainder being in South Yorkshire, Lincolnshire, Leicestershire, Staffordshire and Warwickshire.
Whether you are looking for a local with excellent comfort, good quality beers and sports and entertainment, an award winning rural house with superb home cooked food, or a major pub/restaurant catering for all the family, there is an
excellent choice of Hardy's & Hansons pubs to suit all tastes and needs. One of their best known pubs in nottingham is
Ye Olde trip to Jerusalem, generally regarded as the oldest pub in Britain. Established in the twelfth century, the inner walls of the trip (as it is known) carved out of the sandstone under the castle.
Recruitment for managed House is on an on going basis, with regular open days held for prospective tenants. Free trade loans are available, as well as competitive discounts supporting an extensive range of free trade beers. including Kimberley Cask Ales, Kimberley cool smooth bitter, Heineken, Carling Black label and Stella Artois.

Contact :Ken Anderson - Managed and Tenanted trade George Tunney - Free trade
Hardys & Hanson p.l.c Tel : 0115 938 3611 Fax: 0115 945 9055

means 'best bitter', although some breweries apply it to their standard bitters.

Barley wine
Traditionally the strongest of ales, barley wine is so called because by the time the yeast has struggled up to 9-10 per cent abv, it has also created a raisiny, vinous flavour. Only Whitbread Gold Label and Marston's Owd Roger matter today, but in times gone by brewers prided themselves on their barley wine.

Brown
Originally bottled mild, since the 1920s there have been two distinct styles - sweet or small browns, such as Mann's, and much stronger North Eastern browns, Newcastle, Maxim, and High Level.

Lager
Most of the beers we British call lagers are descendants of the beers first brewed in the early 19th century in Pilsen, in the Czech Republic. True Pilsners come in at around 4.5-5.5 per cent abv and are characterised by the softness and floral aromas derived from continental malt and hops. Long conditioning at low temperature should create a smooth, spritzy drink without the metallic tang evident in hastily made examples. A characteristic of matured lagers is that they are well-attenuated: that is, all or nearly all the sugar is digested by the yeast, leaving a strong dry beer suitable for diabetics. Holsten Pils is probably the best-known example. One of the best lagers, however, does not derive from Pilsen at all, but from Budwar. Czech-brewed Budweiser is not to be confused with its American namesake, and has opened the way for a flood of Czech beers such as Zamek, Radegast, Bohemia, Staropramen, and Urquell.

Continental speciality beers
The British market is becoming increasingly receptive to quirky Continental styles. First among these is wheat beer: that is, beer brewed from at least 50 per cent malted wheat. These beers are brewed chiefly in Belgium and Bavaria, with Hoegaarden the best-known example. They are soft and spritzy like lagers - although they count as ales, being top-fermented and warm-conditioned. The many odd flavours generated by malted wheat include cloves, banana, and even bubblegum. Belgian fruit beers, mainly cherry and raspberry (kriek and frambozen) are also building followings, as are Flemish strong ales such as Duvel and the Trappist ales brewed by monks, of which Chimay is perhaps best-known. Be warned: these beers can be immensely strong. The strongest Chimay is 9 per cent abv.

Beer in the cellar
In today's discerning market, beer quality is essential, and the publican's contribution to beer quality is top-notch cellar management. All breweries these days offer comprehensive courses in cellar skills, and no-one should go behind a bar without a solid grounding.

To a great extent keg and nitro-keg ales and lagers will look after themselves: they are designed to be stable on leaving the brewery, and the mechanical skills required on the publican's part to operate the dispense equipment satisfactorily can (and should) be learned and applied pretty much by rote.

Matters are very different when it comes to cask ale: to get the best out of the beer, the publican needs to be something of an engineer, something of an obsessive, and something of a connoisseur. This is not the place for an A-Z of cellar skills: all publicans are offered cellar training and should seize the opportunity; but there are areas which may have been insufficiently emphasized on some courses and cannot be repeated too often.

Never serve green beer. Many breweries these days send out ale which needs only to be vented and soft-spiled for a few hours before it is ready to be tapped, but this is not true of all beers. If you are serving unfamiliar brands, take the trouble to find out about their peculiar conditioning characteristics so that you can serve them at their best. Avoid floating filters and other devices which enable you to pull pints off the top of the barrel while the sediment is still sinking to the bottom: you may get some of the top breaks coming through, which will do nothing for your reputation, and the beer may be bright, but its flavour will still be immature.

Never return beer to the barrel. The financial savings are not worth the time and trouble involved – and they are certainly not worth the risk of infection and tainting which could end up with the waste of a whole barrel.

Choose the right cask size. Few real ales last more than three or four days after tapping, and few publicans these days would expect to empty even an 18-gallon barrel (kilderkin) of any but the best-selling brand in that time. Don't be afraid to order in nines (firkins) or elevens: the effort involved is well worth the return in terms of reputation, especially if you stock the range expected today.

Never flash chill real ale. It should be served a few degrees below ambient, and although the trend today is for ever-cooler beers, publicans should resist the temptation to serve real ale too cold. As well as killing many of the malt flavours, it prevents the release of CO_2, making the beer too gassy. It can also produce an unattractive chill haze. Temperature fluctuations, direct sources of heat, and draughts can have equally harsh effects, and too high a temperature is even worse. Maintain the cellar at a constant 50°F and the ale should be 52-55°F in the glass, which is about right.

Don't worry if beer from a sound barrel suddenly starts coming through cloudy. A proportion of the finings used to clarify the ale may settle in thin layers, producing a few inexplicably cloudy pints from a barrel which was clear minutes earlier. In these circumstances, pull off two or three more pints and you should soon work through the cloudy layer.

Think before using a cask breather. These devices, which fill the cask with CO_2 as the level of beer sinks, are useful in protecting slower selling lines from infection or oxidisation, and as the CO_2 is at atmospheric pressure it should not dissolve in the ale. Critics say they allow publicans to sell beers which are strictly past their best and cover up laziness in the cellar. On balance, it is surely better that the survival of slower selling lines, especially mild, in cask form should be secured by the use of a cask breather than that they be available in keg format only or, worse, withdrawn altogether.

Beer at the bar

Stocking policy
Most publicans want to offer as much choice as they can. But it's a temptation to be resisted. Attractive as a forest of hand pumps may be, if the throughput is slow, then quality will suffer. Few things dishearten the customer, especially a discerning one, more than discovering a pub serving a dozen of his favourite ales, none of them drinkable. For most pubs three or at a pinch four real ales are ample - a standard bitter, the brewery's own best bitter, a guest best bitter, and the brewery's current seasonal special. The public thirst for novelty is just as well served by constantly changing one or two of the brands as by trying to stock seven or eight at once.

This is as true of wholly tied regional brewery tenants as it is of publicans under a more liberal regime. For instance, a Greene King tenant has a choice of:

◆ a mild (XXD);
◆ two standard bitters (Rayment's Special and IPA);
◆ a world-class premium ale (Abbot);
◆ a stand-alone nitrokeg (Wexford);
◆ a complete range of seasonal specials;
◆ several lagers;
◆ two world-class strong bottled beers (St Edmund's and Strong Suffolk).

Greene King has been under consumer pressure to stock a 'foreign' premium bitter alongside Abbot, but tenants cannot really complain that their options are unduly restricted, even without foreigners.

Publicans who do decide to stock an unusually wide range of real ales should be confident of their cellar skills and should also give a lot of thought to the question of cask size: the firkin is ideal.

Guest ales
Cask ales are the only beers that qualify as guest ales under the Beer Orders of May 1990 (although at the time of writing the government was considering a European Commission suggestion that the scope should be widened to include bottle-conditioned ales), and even though it is several years old, the guest ale rule is still little known enough to be worth explaining.

It affects only two classes of publican: tenants and leaseholders of brewers owning more than 2000 pubs, and free traders tied to a big brewer by loan. These publicans may stock one cask ale of their own choice, from any supplier, above and beyond the beers supplied by their own brewery. Selecting from the brewery's own list of foreigners

BY APPOINTMENT TO THE ROYAL DANISH COURT
Carlsberg
Lager
CARLSBERG COPENHAGEN
Probably the best lager in the world.

The Publican's Handbook

CARLSBERG-TETLEY

As one of Britain's largest brewers and drinks wholesalers, Carlsberg-Tetley has both a reputation and a tradition to uphold.

With around 18,000 trade customers to look after and a portfolio of big name brands, Carlsberg-Tetley is recognised as one of the market leaders in the UK's highly competitive brewing and drinks wholesaling industry.

This position has not come about by chance. Carlsberg-Tetley has been serving the pub trade for almost two centuries, through its network of breweries which produces some of the most famous beer brands in the country.

Carlsberg-Tetley has three of the Top Ten selling beer brands in the UK, more than any of its rivals, while the company has a further seven in the Top 100 – according to the annual survey carried out by The Publican Newspaper, Britain's leading drinks trade title.

Brand names like Tetley's and Carlsberg are legends in their own right and have defined their respective bitter and lager categories in the UK drinks industry.

In its Yorkshire heartland, Tetley's is as much part of the scenery as Ilkley Moor. But Tetley's is a national brand too – one of huge significance, having given the traditional tight creamy head beloved of Yorkshiremen to a whole nation of appreciative bitter drinkers.

The traditions surrounding the brewing of Tetley's have been maintained but at the same time boosted by modern production techniques. Tetley's is still brewed in traditional 'Yorkshire squares' – the same style of two-tiered fermenting vessels that have been the hallmark of brewing in the county for the last 200 years. The beer is even brewed with the same strain of yeast as Joshua Tetley used in the last century and there are still Shire horses on the site – as there have always been.

Nowadays though delivery is a little more efficient than horse-drawn drays while brewing methods and production facilities have also been modernised to maintain the true taste of Tetley's despite the ever-increasing levels of beer production.

LAGER LEADER

In lager terms Carlsberg is one of the few truly global beer brands and is as well known in Britain as it is in Brazil, Bali or anywhere in between. Carlsberg has been brewed in Denmark since 1847, but it took until the Seventies for it to set up its Northampton Brewery. By that time lager had gone from being a rarity in UK pubs to an absolute must-stock for British publicans and now represents 52 per cent of the total UK beer market. Carlsberg can be said to have instituted that change in the nation's drinking habits.

The purpose-built Northampton Brewery produces up to two million barrels of Carlsberg Lager, Carlsberg Export, Carlsberg Special Brew and other associated brands every year.

But Carlsberg isn't the sum total of Carlsberg-Tetley's lager portfolio. Australian brand Castlemaine XXXX was also added to the rosta and quickly became a national name while Skol too remains a favourite with UK drinkers. Carlsberg Ice has quickly carved out a place in the exciting premium packaged lager market, backed by the pioneering expertise of Britain's first ever lager brewery at Wrexham.

With other brands like the esteemed Draught Burton Ale, which was chosen by CAMRA as the Champion Beer of Britain in 1991, Tetley's Mild and the Arrol's 'Shilling' beers brewed by the Alloa brewery in Scotland, Carlsberg-Tetley has a portfolio of beer brands second to none.

SPONSORSHIP BOOST

High profile advertising and sponsorships help keep Carlsberg-Tetley's brands in the limelight and marketing slogans like Carlsberg's 'Probably the best lager in the world' and 'Australians wouldn't give a XXXX for any other lager' are now ingrained in the national consciousness.

In pure football terms Carlsberg has become synonymous with the game. The brand will be sponsoring Liverpool Football Club until the turn of the century, while Carlsberg is also the official beer of the English Football Association which includes title sponsorship of the FA Carlsberg Vase as well as rights for the FA Cup and England matches played at Wembley.

Despite these links to the highest levels of English soccer, Carlsberg-Tetley has not forgotten the grass roots of the game and has created the Carlsberg Pub Cup – the annual FA-backed soccer competition for pub and club teams which sees the finalists playing out their wildest dreams at Wembley Stadium.

All these activities are underpinned in pubs and clubs across the country with innovative and business

Beer and Cider

CARLSBERG-TETLEY

building promotional activities for the company's loyal trade customers. Merchandising and promotions give those publicans the opportunity to get involved with the some of the most high profile advertising and sponsorships in the industry.

With this strength in brewing and brands, Carlsberg-Tetley is looking to the future with a host of new ideas. New product development is one of the key areas and it is the company's mission to be the most successful innovator in the drinks market. Last year Carlsberg-Tetley took the nitro-keg ales market by storm with the introduction of Calder's Cream Ale which was widely recognised as the most successful new beer launch in 1996.

LOYAL FOLLOWING

None of this would be possible without the company's loyal trade following. As Carlsberg-Tetley knows the UK has a drinking population of around 40 million and every one of them is a potential consumer of its range of beers. Trade customers are vital to that link between brands and consumers because they are the customers of Carlsberg-Tetley, first and foremost.

The On-Trade accounts for over three quarters of the company's business and within that the greatest number of on-trade customers are either individual pubs or clubs or small, regionally based chains of pubs – all serviced by a national network of local sales offices and distribution depots.

The On-Trade also includes four other main types of customer who all operate nationally. These are pub groups like Greenalls, Pubmaster and Allied Domecq Retailing – which is the company's largest single customer. National accounts represent more than 50 per cent of Carlsberg-Tetley's business and include hotel chains, restaurants and even ferry operators who sell beer as part of their wider operations.

As part of the total support service for all these trade customers, Carlsberg-Tetley also runs one of the largest and most comprehensive wholesaling operations in the UK under the banner of the Complete Drinks Service.

Wholesaling is something most consumers never see but for publicans and pub operators it is vital. Source of other products apart from beer like wines, spirits, ciders and soft drinks. Carlsberg-Tetley brings all these different product types together in a convenient and efficient package.

WHOLESALE REPUTATION

Within the wholesaling operation Carlsberg-Tetley has built itself an enviable reputation as one of the best wine suppliers to the On-Trade. Over the last ten years there has been an enormous change in British attitudes to wine and consumers' willingness to buy it. For publicans this represents another vital business-building opportunity – providing they can find the right wines at the right price.

Carlsberg-Tetley's Complete Drinks Service offers an impressive range of wines with nearly 500 on its current list, coming from 19 countries including China and Mexico. The list is revised each spring to reflect industry trends.

The range is broad enough to appeal to pub and club customers and stretches from house wines which retail at very reasonable prices to some of the most famous and expensive names in the history of wine production.

And because The Complete Drinks Service supplies Carlsberg-Tetley beers, plus wines, spirits, ciders and soft drinks, it can provide everything the busy publican needs with just one phone call, one delivery and one invoice.

The Complete Drinks Service is one of the ways in which Carlsberg-Tetley is evolving to meet the needs of trade customers. By providing the best possible package of quality brands coupled with efficient production and distribution, Carlsberg-Tetley is maintaining its reputation as one of the UK's major drinks suppliers and helping to boost trade for thousands of pubs and clubs across the country.

For more information on Carlsberg-Tetley's Complete Drinks Service call the Customer Service on 0345 820820.

does not disqualify a tenant from stocking one other cask ale not on the list. Any disadvantage arising from a decision to stock a guest ale, the threat of a rent rise, or withdrawal of discounts on brewery-supplied lines, is an offence and should be reported to the Office of Fair Trading.

Measures
Draught beers may only be served in multiples of a half-pint, with the exception of the 'nip' or third of a pint, which is making a modest comeback for strong ales or for sampling different beers where the choice is very wide. All mugs and glasses used for the sale of draught beers must be correctly stamped for size except where stamped metered pulls are used – this includes customers' own tankards.

At the time of writing the law regards the head on the pint as part of the measure, within limits: according to Brewers and Licensed Retailers Association guidelines the volume of liquid offered, including the collapsed head, should never be less than 19 fluid ounces or 95 per cent of a pint. Even then, the customer may ask for a top-up, which should always be given with good grace.

Refusing a top-up, or offering under 19fl oz, can lead to prosecution, although it is worth noting that the point at which the offence is committed is the point at which the glass is offered to the customer and the transaction is effectively completed. Prosecutions have failed because the court accepted that trading standards officers posing as customers had not given the bar staff a chance to finish pulling the pint.

The best way through the maze is to serve beer in 12- or 22-oz lined glasses, or even 24-oz glasses in areas where especially deep heads are the norm. If brim measures are replaced with oversized glasses as part of normal wastage replenishment there need be no extra cost. And the consequent reduction in loss through spillage, according to publicans who have made the change, more or less compensates for the advantage gained by not serving a full pint of liquid.

Beer dispense
Keg, nitrokeg and stout fonts and Keating pumps (keg taps dressed up to look like hand pumps) are delivered by the brewery; they should be operated in strict accordance with brewery instructions and their maintenance should be left to the brewery's technical staff. Controversy concerning dispense only arises, predictably enough, with real ale.

Northern bitters such as Boddington, Tetley and John Smith's in their cask version are correctly pulled through a quarter-pint piston, a swan neck, and a tight sparkler. This gives the ale the dense, creamy head prized by northerners but knocks much of the CO_2 out of the body of the pint and drives off some of the hop aroma.

Northern ales are brewed to withstand these effects; most southern beers are not. Sadly, since ales like those already named arrived in the South, many publicans and breweries have decided that one

DISCOVER CZECH BUDWEISER BUDVAR

OVER 700 YEARS OF BREWING TRADITION IN THE CZECH CITY OF BUDWEIS GUARANTEES THE QUALITY OF BUDWEISER BUDVAR LAGER
THE UK'S No.1 IMPORTED CZECH LAGER

PLEASE CONTACT: B.B. SUPPLY CENTRE LTD., SOLE IMPORTERS AND DISTRIBUTORS OF BUDWEISER BUDVAR
TEL: 0171-247 1252   FAX: 0171-377 6454

The Publican's Handbook

Supplier of fine Beers

Hard on the heels of the world discovering that Budweiser was Tony Blair's choice of drink at his now famous dinner with Bill Clinton at the Pont de la Tour restaurant recently, the Czech Republic's most successful export beer now takes fourth place in the on0trade PPl league. With the top five brands accounting for 65 per cent of the sales in this sector it is another tribute to the outstanding success of this honest South Bohemian beer. Without gimmick, gizmo or widget, year by year it has inexorably moved up the list of the UK's favourite drinks to become a have-to-stock item.

It's not just the Budvar in the 33 cl bottle that is making progress however. Clive Bygrave, on-trade national accounts manager of sole UK importers and distributors B. B. Supply Centre, reports that draught Budweiser Budvar is enjoying a growth rate well ahead of the 5.8 per cent enjoyed by the premium draught lager market overall. Currently plans are being developed by B. B. Supply Centre with one of their appointed draught wholesalers, Everards, for a major promotional push for Budweiser Budvar draught. This will include, amongst other things, new POS material emphasising the beer's real and unspoiled heritage which is becoming appreciated and understood by more and more drinkers.

"One of the key to the beer's success in the UK has been drinker to drinker recommendation," says Bygrave. "This means it has always achieved sound organic growth, not the ephemeral swelling of sales created by sticking a ton of marketing hype on top of the product." Very important is the universal appeal of the beer across a whole spectrum of drinkers. The target audience, it is true, are the 25-year-old to 30-something professionals but it embraces a much wider franchise taking in the well informed middle-aged drinker who wants a 'thinking man's' lager, or even the cask ale drinker who varies his diet from time to time. It also finds favour with women drinkers and strict vegetarians. The latter is because no animal or fish products whatsoever are used anywhere in the brewing or packaging processes.

It is in recognition of the broadness of its appeal that the Budweiser Budvar brewery has been spending a lot of time getting closer to its UK drinkers this year and this is one of the reasons why the brewery sponsored the trade day at the Great British Festival in August.

Despite all of the talk about Czech beers and the impact they are going to make on the UK scene Budweiser Budvar is still the only one that is here in the big time. "We don't even position ourselves as part of the Czech beer scene here," says Bygrave. "This is because Budweiser Budvar is an elite world lager located in the mainstream of upmarket beer drinking in this country."

Its success is due in no small part to the brewery's philosophy of putting quality before corner cutting and cost reduction and by its insistence that it can never be brewed under license but that every drop

Beer and Cider

has to be brewed on its own premises in Ceske Budejovice. This ensures that the characteristic Budweiser Budvar aroma, taste and finish stay the same way as the have always been. Only natural ingredients are used in its brewing including the unique water from the South Bohemian limestone table and it remains one of the few lagers in the world that are lagered for no less than 90 days.

At the time of writing still the property of the Czech state, the Czech government understands that the Budweiser Budvar brewery is not only a jewel in its own crown but a symbol of excellence throughout the world. It is this insight that has persuaded them to keep the excellence throughout the world. It is this insight that has persuaded them to keep the brewery Czech when it is privatised, this is most likely to be achieved by a management buy out. The sigh of relief on hearing this news, by drinkers and stockists alike throughout the world, was almost audible.

There are other great Czech beers waiting to be discovered a wider audience. One such is Gambrinus. Part of B. B. Supply Centre's portfolio Gambrinus is brewed by another all-Czech operation, the Pilsen Brewery Group. The largest brewers in the Cezch Republic, with a comfortable 24 per cent of the Czech market, its Gambrinus brew is by far the Czech drinkers' favourite beer and has the widest distribution of any in the Czech Republic.

Available in bottle or in draught form it is a honey coloured beer, slightly drier in taste than Budweiser Budvar and , although it lacks Budweiser Budvar's authority, its supporters in the UK are growing. Any beer that commands the respect of the Czech beer drinker (the whole nation consumes approx. 162 litres per head per year) has to be taken seriously.

Beers that have to be taken seriously are speciality of B.B. Supply Centre. Few can have more magisterial dignity than the Begian abbey beers. Their ecclesiastical patrimony is celebrated in the chalice-like Leffe branded goblet in which the beer should ideally be served, and there is nothing quite like a Leffe font for bringing ritual to the bar. Described by one publican as "a magnificent, technically advanced font that exudes quality and style" its very presence on the bar compels the drinkers attention. Spectacular front of house, behind bar it offers one of the most advanced dispense systems available, maintaining the beer in peak condition and as the same time giving the highest standards of hygiene. These fonts have been much in demand by outlets of all kinds over the country, according to B.B. Supply Centre who took over distribution on behalf of brand owners Interbrew some 12 months ago. Since the penetration, particularly of leading edge outlets, has enabled the brand to reach a wider audience than ever before and B. B. Supply Centre expects this trend will continue.

type of engine must serve all ales, and the old flat spout kit has been discarded. Some brewers, though, have resolutely clung to their traditional beer engines; CAMRA has pitched in and so controversy has arisen.

There is no need for argument so long as the publican respects the opinion of customers who express a preference. By all means install swan necks and tight sparklers, but simply instruct staff to loosen the sparkler on request. It takes very little trouble and, by raising the opinion of consumer as a connoisseur, pleases the customer enormously.

Hand pumps are not the only method of dispensing real ale. Until recently, metered electric pumps were common in the Midlands and North West. They have the advantage of delivering an exact pint, but many customers think they are keg taps. Metered or otherwise, electric pumps are necessary where there is an unusually long pipe run between cellar and bar. The quality of the beer should be unaffected.

Another form of cask ale dispense gaining favour is the simplest: gravity, with the ale being poured straight from casks on stillages behind the bar. Many connoisseurs say this produces the best results of all methods of dispense: it is visually highly appealing, and it eliminates the waste of line cleaning, pulling off, etc. However, it does lead to problems of temperature control, atmospheric taint (although there is little evidence that this really occurs), and stock management. It is not really advisable as the usual means of dispense, but it works well in such alehouse operations as Whitbread's Hogshead pubs.

CIDER

It is always puzzling that cider should be classed virtually as a style of beer, since by any practical definition it is a wine, being no more than the fermented juice of apples or, in the case of perry, pears.

Be that as it may, cider is usually served draught by the pint like beer or in 33cl bottles like lager; and it is as an alternative to beer that it has enjoyed the fantastic success of the last 30 years.

Until the 1950s, draught cider was rare outside the drink's western homeland, and even bottled cider was a minority drink. Many people didn't bracket it with liquor at all, despite its alcoholic volume of anything up to 8 per cent and until 1976, it wasn't even taxed as such.

In the 1950s, keg technology gave the biggest cidermakers the ability to despatch supplies of stable, consistent cider all over the country, and at the same time the decision was made to reduce the alcoholic strength of mainstream brands to that of premium beers. Given that cider was not taxed as highly as beer, it is no surprise that sales started growing, and barring one or two hiccups whenever duties were raised, they have been growing ever since.

Cider has succeeded largely through good marketing, tracking developments in the beer market and using the price advantage derived from its favourable tax status to gain an edge. Diamond White was developed by Taunton as the cider version of premium bottled lager, and what a success it proved to be. Only occasionally have the marketeers been caught on the hop, most notably in 1995-96, when they were ambushed by alcopops – and even then, they were able to turn things round by using highly processed and fairly neutral ciders as the base of alcopops of their own.

The commercially successful ciders are a long way removed from the farm produce from which they developed. But farm ciders have persisted, and in recent years have been enjoying something of a renaissance. Many real ale pubs like to have a polycask of farm cider in evidence on the bar in summer, when pints are passed across with many a bucolic wisecrack. These drinks have their place, and thanks to their favourable tax status can bring in a very good margin. But they have to be actively sold, and they are sensitive to the environment. Oddly enough, they are most appreciated well outside their traditional heartlands, where sales are if anything declining.

Health and Safety Notes

There are particular health and safety issues associated with **the cellar**. The first of these, the safety of the access has already been referred to with regard to trap doors behind the bar. Alternative access arrangements, such as steps, can also be hazardous. They should be properly maintained, adequately lit, kept clear and be provided with a handrail.

The cellar is the area where the majority of manual handling takes place, ie the lifting and moving of kegs, crates, etc. The conditions sometimes found in beer cellars – low ceilings and/or limited space – often make manual handling tasks more awkward. Specific legislation applies: the **Manual Handling Operations Regulations 1992**.

It is important that, where manual handling cannot be avoided, the risks of injury are assessed and appropriate measures taken to reduce them as far as is reasonably practicable. Appropriate measures include, for example, training in the correct way to lift and move loads and, possibly, rearranging the layout to reduce the amount of lifting and manoeuvring needed.

Some pub cellars are fitted with a lift or hoist to help reduce the level of manual handling. Particular requirements exist for lifts and hoists under the **Offices, Shops and Railway Premises (Lift and Hoists) Regulations 1968**. These include ensuring that the lift/hoist is checked every six months by a competent person covering specific aspects. (Where a lift is hand operated the check needs to be done every 12 months.)

BACK THE WINN[ER]

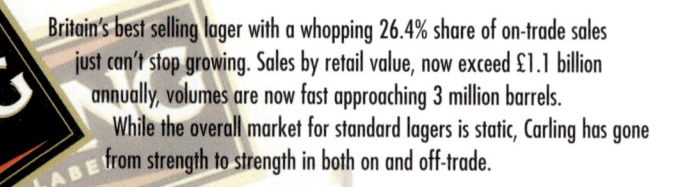

Britain's best selling lager with a whopping 26.4% share of on-trade sales just can't stop growing. Sales by retail value, now exceed £1.1 billion annually, volumes are now fast approaching 3 million barrels. While the overall market for standard lagers is static, Carling has gone from strength to strength in both on and off-trade.

NO ORDINARY LAGER .....
NO ORDINARY LEAGUE

90% OF MALES ARE HAPPILY MARRIED. TO ELEVEN MEN.

Carling is backed by the biggest sponsorship package in the UK – The FA Carling Premiership. An unrivalled marketing spend ensures that demand for Carling is driven through TV, Radio, Poster and press advertising, backed by extensive in-outlet tailored promotions.

Carling is always looking for new and innovative ways to promote itself and support the consumer and customers, whether it be through 'Shootout' (Carling's interactive football game for pubs) or the Carling website, now being accessed 4.3 million times a week.

CAN YOU AFFORD NOT TO HAVE CARLING ON YOUR TEAM?

- Britain's best loved and respected lager.
- A big revenue and profit earner commanding a price premium of up to 4p over rival standard lagers.
- Carling's fuller flavour and bite ensures it constantly beats competitors in blind taste tests – consumers prefer it to all others.
- Heavyweight marketing support, including the renewed sponsorship of the FA Carling Premiership for a further four years, driving consumers to seek out the brand in your outlet.
- Offers consumer variety – Carling is available in draught or 275ml bottles.

TO ORDER CARLING OR CAR[LING]

NG SIDE

The Carling line up brings an unrivalled combination of lager brands; Carling, with its classic sessionable taste, and Carling Premier with its unique smooth taste, that makes it effortlessly easy to drink.

CARLING PREMIER

Britain's fastest growing premium lager (increasing 30 times faster than the England and Wales premium lager market*). Drinkers clearly recognise that the brand brings something genuinely new to the premium lager sector.

With annual retail sales of over £100m (that's an annual sales volume of quarter of a million Brls), Carling Premier is a high margin, high throughput brand which is capturing the hearts and minds of lager drinkers throughout the UK.

IN A WORLD THAT'S LOSING ITS HEAD, A LAGER THAT DOESN'T

In addition to the quality of the product and unique font design, Carling Premier's success can be attributed to it's impressive marketing spend. Backed by highly popular advertising campaigns and close links with the nations music scene, the brands rapport with lager drinkers has produced results which have amazed even its most optimistic supporters. Carling Premier is also consistently supported through in-outlet tailored promotions and innovative merchandising.

HITTING THE RIGHT NOTE

- Britain's fastest growing premium lager.
- A high throughput, high margin brand (20p+ per pint v standard lagers).
- A brand which enjoys heavyweight marketing support to guarantee continue trial and increased loyalty.
- Singled out as the preferred premium draught lager in independent taste tests (source: MMR).
- Carling Premier is unrivalled on smoothness, coldness and sheer 'drinkability'.

*source: internal stats

PREMIER CALL: 0345 700 701

Make a clean save

For many years there has been a need for a system to reduce the significant costs and losses that arise from the weekly cleaning of beer and lager lines.

The Mirus Beer Saver has been introduced, following extensive trials and research and will achieve a guaranteed reduction in weekly cleaning costs by extending the cleaning cycle, assuming currently at one week to four weeks.

As its foundation the system incorporates technology that has been successfully used in a number of other industries particularly the water and oil industries where the need to maintain clean lines and pipes is as important as it is within the delivery system for BEER and LAGER.

The Mirus Group is appointing, throughout the UK, local Licensed contractors whose mandate is to establish a service to customers of all sizes a facility to supply the system as well as undertake line cleaning for those customers whose needs extend to this requirement. The contractors are fully trained in all related procedures and are in turn supported by a regionally based team of people.

After installation, which requires no special lines or power supplies, the user can expect a significant impact on their profitability, with the losses and costs being reduced by up to 50 per cent.

The system is available only on contract hire, with the contract term extending from a minimum of one month up to the current maximum of 36 months.

FOR FURTHER INFORMATION CONTACT:
Mirus Group Ltd
15 Wellington Road
Dewsbury, West Yorkshire
WF13 1HF
Tel: 0800 435792   Fax: 01924 456260

THE RETURN OF THE NON-RETURNABLES

The on trade is playing a key role in helping the UK achieve the ambitious recycling targets which the Government has set for the turn of the century. At the same time, 'green' publicans are saving themselves unnecessary costs and making a positive contribution to the environment.

If you currently dispose of your empties as part of your trade waste, then you should be talking to Berryman's, the largest independent glass recycler, processing around 400,000 tonnes a year (the equivalent of approximately $1^1/_2$ billion bottles). Glass which fails to find its way back into the 'recycling loop' is otherwise ending up as landfill, which makes neither financial nor environmental sense. Indeed, the cost of landfilling commercial glass runs into several million pounds a year.

The Government is committed to controlling the levels of trade waste by the gradual introduction of punitive taxes such as the recent landfill tax. Furthermore, legislative requirements regarding packaging waste will affect all areas of the leisure and catering industry.

Yet the solution couldn't be simpler. When properly handled, 'post-consumer' bottles (empties) can be re-processed to produce a precious raw material for re-manufacture by the glass container industry.

Berryman's operates a nation wide recycling scheme and is already calling on pubs, clubs and other licensed premises to which the company supplies wheeled or static bins in which to store empty glass bottles for collection.

We call on a weekly basis (more frequent if volumes dictate) using a custom-built fleet of modern recycling vehicles which collect the glass in three basic colours - flint (white), amber and green - for transfer to our state-of-the-art re-processing plant. Our drivers ensure a first class, hassle-free service, providing you with a cost effective way of disposing of your non-returnable bottles.

So, to save on trade waste costs, be seen to be 'green' by your customer and local community, and do your bit for the environment, contact Alex Brown on 01977 608020

The **Control of Substances Hazardous to Health Regulations** (COSHH) have particular significance to the cellar. These regulations require that no person at work be exposed to substances hazardous to health unless the health risks have been assessed and the necessary precautions have been identified and implemented. It is useful to clarify the difference between 'hazard' and 'risk'; a 'hazard' is the potential to do harm and the 'risk' is the likelihood that harm will arise. Where and how a substance is used may mean that the risk is low despite the hazard. You need to identify what activities involve exposure to hazardous substances and what risks to health may arise (short term and long term).

For a **cleaning chemical** such as beer-line cleaner the information on the label and that available from the supplier or manufacturer will enable risks to be identified. The appropriate measures include informing, instructing and training whoever does the job, and, in addition, the provision and use of suitable protective clothing (eg gloves, goggles and apron).

COSHH also applies to **carbon dioxide**, an asphyxiant gas in a pressurised container. It is important that relevant staff are aware of how to safely store and use carbon dioxide cylinders and for cylinder restraints etc to be provided. It is also vital that people understand and appreciate the dangers, know how to identify a leak and are aware of what to do. Anyone working in the cellar must always be able to make a quick exit. Further information and advice can be obtained from suppliers.

In some pubs **asbestos lagging** may still be apparent on pipework in the cellar. If such lagging is damaged or disturbed, there is a risk of asbestos fibres being released and, therefore, a risk of asbestos-related disease. If there is any cause for concern in this respect, professional advice must be sought: your local environmental health officer will be able to assist. You are obliged to protect your employees (and yourselves) from such exposure.

Finally, the procedure for **deliveries and collection** of empties may give rise to health and safety risks. The potential for injury to passers-by when the cellar flaps are open needs to be considered and appropriate measures implemented to ensure that the risk is addressed. (See also the health and safety issues raised under 'Hiring and Firing'.)

Beer and Cider

Air Products Heads to the TOP

TOPGAS™, Air Products' range of dispensing gases and gas mixtures for the drinks industry, is quickly becoming the choosen product for the licensed trade. The Topgas range of gases includes pure CO2 and Nitrogen as well as gas mixtures to meet every need in dispensing beers, stouts, lagers, ciders, soft drinks, mixers and wines.

TOP QUALITY FOR PERFECT PINTS

Topgas gives you the opportunity to improve the quality of all your dispensed products. By ensuring a consistency of presentation from the top of the glass to the bottom and from the first pint to the last, Topgas will increase customer satisfaction. And by giving you the flexibility to store beers, stouts, lagers and soft drinks in their optimum environment, Topgas ensures that even slow moving products remain in top condition.

With Topgas you can feel confident that your drinks will flow smoothly and that your customers will be served a perfect pint every time.

TOP NOTCH CUSTOMER SERVICE

As a Topgas customer you can also expect a quality of service that is second to none. The purity of our gases, the speed and reliability of our delivery service and the exceptional condition of our food grade cylinders makes Topgas the best choice for the licensed trade.

With a rapidly expanding network of over 150 outlets in the UK, Air Products' Topgas service offers all the advantages of a local supplier with all the support of a national team. Most of our outlets are able to offer a SAME DAY DELIVERY service and all provide a cylinder collection service.

MD30: SAVING YOU TIME AND MONEY

Air Products' Topgas cylinders come in a full range of sizes. Our most popular cylinder is the successful MD30 mid size cylinder. The MD30 not only offers three times more gas than the traditional 14LB brewery cylinder, but also reduces your cylinder changeover needs saving you time and money. With one cylinder instead of three you will save on rental charges and free up valuable storage space.

With TOPGAS™ from Air Products you can continue to serve the perfect pint AGAIN and AGAIN and AGAIN.

For perfect pints every time... get TOPGAS!

Now you can improve the presentation quality of all your kegged products by using TOPGAS – the specially developed range of Nitrogen and CO2 gas mixtures from Air Products.

TOPGAS enables you to:
- Produce a thirsty looking pint!
- Eliminate fobbing
- Reduce wastage
- Pull pints faster

FOR FURTHER DETAILS ABOUT TOPGAS™ AND YOUR NEAREST OUTLET CANTACT OUR CUSTOMER SERVICES DEPT. ON
0345 020202

AIR PRODUCTS

CHINEHAM, BASINGSTOKE RG24 5TE

The Publican's Handbook

Legal Notes

The sale of draught beer and cider must be made of either one-third pint or half-pint measures, or multiples of half-pint. There are exceptions for bottled or canned beer or cider.

Where **brim measure glasses** are used, a measure may consist of liquid and a reasonable head. The recommendation of the Brewers and Licensed Retailers Association is that the liquid content of beer and cider, once the head has collapsed, should not be less than 95 per cent of any of the permissible measures.

The law requires that **price lists** are clearly displayed in order that customers are able to know what the prices are for food and drink offered for sale. Where there are 30 items or less on a menu or list, the prices of all items must be shown. However, it is sufficient to display the prices of 30 selected items from a larger range.

There are separate rules in respect of categories or items listed together, and in respect of the listing of wines and mixed drinks: see Price Marketing (Food and Drink on Premises) Order 1979.

All prices must be VAT inclusive. Any service charges or other extra charges must be indicated.

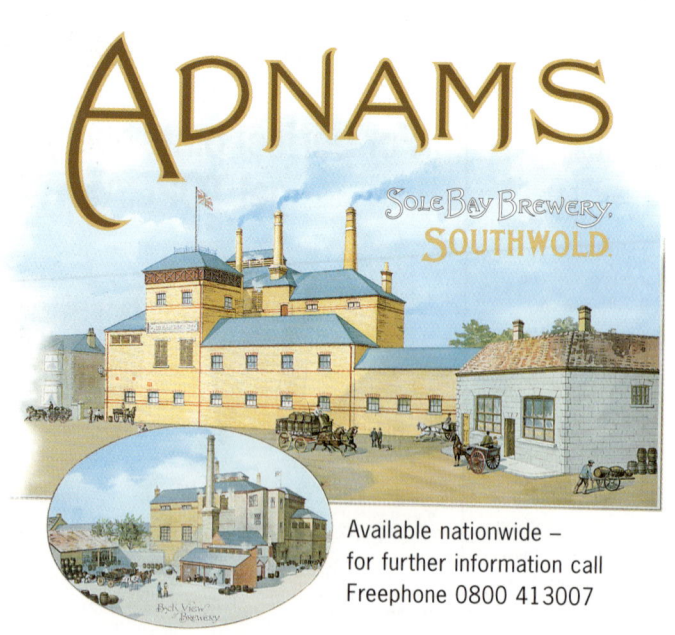

ADNAMS

Sole Bay Brewery, SOUTHWOLD

Available nationwide –
for further information call
Freephone 0800 413007

From Suffolk's Oldest Brewery, Britain's Finest Beer.

ADNAMS SOUTHWOLD

TAVERN

The Nations Leading Drinks Distributor

- ✓ CHOICE FROM ALL THE BRAND LEADERS ✓
- ✓ FREE DELIVERY ✓
- ✓ EXCEPTIONAL CUSTOMER CARE ✓
- ✓ REGULAR INCENTIVES AND PROMOTIONS ✓
- ✓ MOST COMPREHENSIVE RANGE ✓
- ✓ UNIQUE WINE PORTFOLIO ✓

For details of your local Tavern depot call
0345 002277
Head Office: Tavern Limited, Unit 12, Mercury Way, Barton Dock Road, Trafford Park, Manchester. M41 7LQ.   Fax: 0161 864 5050

The Nations Leading Drinks Distributor

Tavern Group Limited is the largest independent drinks distributor in the UK and supplies beers, wines, spirits and soft drinks to any outlet that has the freedom to determine its own source of supply.

Formed in April 1993, Tavern rapidly established a geographical network through acquisition and organic growth, in a process culminating in the acquisition of its major competitor Liquid Assets in late 1995.

The company offers an extensive and flexible product portfolio backed up by a comprehensive delivery, support and customer service package. It has a distribution network covering the length and breadth of the UK and is a genuine one-stop shop for drinks retailers of all sizes. In addition, all its employees combine both professional expertise and extensive knowledge of their industry.

> **It has a distribution network covering the length and breadth of the UK and is a genuine one-stop shop for drinks retailers of all sizes.**

With 23,000 customers and a turnover in excess of £200m per year, Tavern has achieved rapid progress. But there is still the opportunity for further growth and the company is dedicated to improving its service and enhancing its leadership position.

Tavern has been structured in order to make the perfect link between customers and suppliers - a link which provides the customer with the best service and the supplier with the most effective route to market. The Company has centralised many of its key functions, in support of its local operations. This allows us to pass on the benefit of our national status to our customers, while still retaining customer contact at local level.

Taverns pro-active approach to working with suppliers and its strong relationship with major brand names allows it quickly to identify brands with potential for success. But the company doesn't rely solely on big names and aims to seek out potentially successful products from a range of independent sources. This has led to Tavern developing a selection of exclusive products, which include Schlitz, a premium packaged American Lager, Orangina (on trade), Ruddles Smoothflow Bitter and Spoof, an exciting range of alcoholic carbonates.

These brands sit alongside an unmatched portfolio of draught beers, traditional ales, wines, spirits and minerals and our fully trained sales force of over 150 people is available to provide expert advice when required.

Tavern's aim is to source and sell those products which can enhance their customers profitability. Its experience and knowledge of the products which will succeed in a particular market and the way in which they should be promoted, are invaluable tools in helping both suppliers and customers to develop their business.

Tavern also manage and maintain a portfolio of quality products. It serves customers ranging from the largest multiple operators to the smallest clubs and recognises the differing needs of its diverse customer base.

Tavern have proved over the last four years that they provide a service level and portfolio of products unmatched in their market sector. With continual expansion and constant development for new areas of business, Tavern look set to continue their achievement into the next millennium and beyond.

> "experience and knowledge of the products which will succeed in a particular market and the way in which they should be promoted, are invaluable tools"

For details of your local Tavern depot call

0345 002277

Head Office: Tavern Limited, Unit 12, Mercury Way, Barton Dock Road, Trafford Park, Manchester. M41 7LQ.
Fax: 0161 864 5050

UNITED DISTILLERS

QUALITY AND PROFIT
WHICHEVER WAY YOU LOOK AT IT

United Distillers UK Plc, Registered Office: Cherrybank, Perth, Scotland PH2 0NG. Registered in Scotland. Number SC 135736
Tel: 01738 621111   Fax: 01738 638739
A United Distillers Company

CHAPTER SEVEN

WINES AND SPIRITS

Ted Bruning

WINES

Everyone drinks wine at home these days. Everyone is aware of the range available in supermarkets, and everyone has a shrewd idea of the correlation between quality and price. Publicans may not have to stock a range quite as wide as Tesco, but any pub that wants its catering to be taken seriously can no longer get away with a house red and two whites lurking inconspicuously on the bar-back.

Indeed, a growing number of publicans, especially in pubs with an accent on food service, are going to the opposite extremes and constructing restaurant-style wine-lists in a wholly commendable effort to make a positive marketing point out of their wine offering. While this is a great step forward, publicans must be careful to create a list that carries complementary brands, each offering a different style and price-point. It is no good having a red section which offers only cabernet sauvignons from around the world, for instance, and a white list composed entirely of various manifestations of chardonnay. A balance must be struck to offer wines of differing weights, characters, and prices, and if the publican is in any doubt at all he should seek advice from his supplier.

Quality is as important as choice, in both selection and service of wine. Drinkers today can spot a wine that has been incorrectly stored, either before or after serving, and will not accept it.

It is almost impossible for the publican, who has so many concerns, to master all the intricacies of wine service, which is a lifetime's pleasure and study. But it is vital for all publicans, especially those who aspire to any quality of food service, to be familiar with more than just the basics; and knowledge of wine starts with knowledge of France.

French wines are still the most highly regarded by the average drinker – far more so in the pub than in the take home trade, where New World and other non-French wines predominate. Perhaps this is because people like to spoil themselves when they go out, and French wines still have the cachet. Whatever the reason, publicans need to base their wine service strategy on the wines of France.

France

The best way to learn about French wines is to sell all you own, move to France, and do nothing but taste and spit for the rest of your life - impossible if you have a pub to run.

France has three wine making regions unequalled anywhere on earth: Champagne, Burgundy and Bordeaux. There are literally dozens of other appellations and regions but these are the wines your customers are likely to be most familiar with.

Champagne from the chalky north east of France is the world's greatest sparkling wine and will be dealt with under that heading.

Burgundy and Bordeaux at their best are probably the world's two greatest wine growing regions - although you pay a high premium for the name, and it takes great confidence to select a Burgundy or a Bordeaux suitable for the pub trade.

Burgundy

This is a picturesque strip extending from south east of Paris through Dijon down to Lyon. The main red grapes are Pinot Noir and Gamay, with Chardonnay and Aligote the principal white varieties.

The best-known appellations are probably Chablis (white) and Beaujolais (mainly red). But to confuse the non-expert, there are many other Burgundy appellations - Côte de Beaune, Côte de Nuits, Mâcon - and other famous names such as Nuits-St-Georges, Meursault, Pommard, and Pouilly-Fuissé (not to be confused with Pouilly-Fumé from the Loire) as well.

To make the labels even less intelligible, Burgundy wines are graded, in descending order, as Grand Cru, Premier Cru, Villages, and regional (ie, plain Burgundy, or Bourgogne).

Burgundy is sold in slope-shouldered bottles and should be served in an oversized goblet large enough to hold the vapours for nosing.

Bordeaux

Lying on the western seaboard, Bordeaux produces the red wines known to us as claret, as well as the finest sweet wine wines in the world.

Its principal red grape varieties are the tannic Cabernet Sauvignon, the Cabernet Franc, and the much softer Merlot. Its white varieties are Sauvignon Blanc and Sémillon.

Bordeaux appellations include Médoc, Graves, Sauternes, St Emilion, Pomerol, and Entre-Deux-Mers, and the names of the great chateaux will be familiar to most: Lafite, Mouton-Rothschild, Latour, Margaux, d'Yquem.

Bordeaux, both white and red, comes in a high-shouldered bottle and is best served in a rather deeper glass than the round Burgundy goblet.

But here's the heresy: publicans today must ask whether the wines of these regions are relevant to their trade. The wines command a premium which does not necessarily reflect their quality, and the labels

Wines and Spirits

are, frankly, no help to any but the initiated.

It all boils down to that balancing act between affordability and quality. Pubgoers in the main demand dependable and inexpensive. There are wine bars and dining pubs where there is a demand for great wines, but they are the exception. What most publicans and their customers want is a French wine which can retail at, say, £1.20 a glass or £7.20 a bottle, which will be dependably drinkable, and which for the publican will still yield a decent margin.

For most publicans the conclusion must be that Burgundy, and to a lesser extent Bordeaux, are a poor risk without the personal advice of a good and trusted wine merchant. Other regions of France produce wines of the right quality and price.

Other wine regions of France

To the east of the Bordeaux region lies Bergerac, whose sweet white Monbazillac wines once rivalled Sauternes. The region is now best known for its reliable and well-priced red wines, which come in a Bordeaux bottle and, for the purposes of most publicans, make a trustworthy alternative to claret.

South of Burgundy lies the Côte du Rhone. The Rhone Valley produces many fine and very expensive red wines including Châteauneuf du Pape, Croz-Hermitage, and the rare Côte Rotie, but the region's workaday wines are of excellent quality and sensible price.

The classic grape of the Rhone is the Syrah, also known as Shiraz, but here blending is the rule and a single wine can be produced from the juice of a dozen or more varieties. Rhone reds tend to be full bodied and robust and are deservedly gaining in popularity in the British market, although the whites are less well known.

Rhone wines come in a Burgundy-shaped bottle and should be served in a similar goblet; for most publicans, they will make an appropriate substitute.

The south of France produces enormous quantities of table wines with a huge array of labels from *appellation contrôlée* (AOC) to *vin délimité de qualité supérieure* (VDQS).

Traditionally the many regions of the south have produced cheap blended table wines for everyday drinking mainly in France. In the last 25 years, however, the industry has sought to move upmarket as consumption has contracted and expectations have risen. As a result there are now many wines from all over the south of France, from Gascony in the Pyrenees to the foothills of the Alps, which are performing well in the British market and which will be familiar to most pubgoers.

Publicans can generally trust such names as Côtes du Rousillon, Fitou, Minervois, Corbières, Vin de Pays de l'Hérault, Côtes du Ventoux, Côtes du Luberon, and Côtes de Provence to supply very drinkable wines at pub prices.

Of the many white wines of the Loire, Muscadet (sometimes 'sur lie', or bottled with its lees) is the most important, and the most relevant to the pub trade. When good, it is the perfect companion to white meat and seafood – dry, yet

SEE THE LIGHT!
DISCOVER RIESLING.

Germany has one of the most wonderful climates in the world. For growing grapes.

Indeed, the exact direction a vineyard faces, its protection from the wind, a nearby river with morning mists are all factors to be considered.

Therein lies the secret of the unique quality of German Riesling. Everything must be perfect to grow a perfect Riesling grape. Some countries are too parched. Some do not have enough sun. Others do not have the right rainfall.

Which is why, although other regions with different climate zones may plant the Riesling grape, they can never achieve the subtle nuances that make German wine so distinctive across the wide range of flavours.

So for a perfect partner for good food - re-discover German Riesling.

For further information please contact
German Wine Information Service,
Lane House,
24 Parsons Green Lane
SW6 4HZ
Tel. (0171) 331 8800

GERMAN WINES
LIGHT AND ELEGANT
naturally

Wines and Spirits

Discover German Wines

How much do you really know about German wines? We are all familiar with Liebfraumilch, Piesporter and Niersteiner but there is so much more to Germany.

So many different styles of wine are made in Germany's 13 wine growing regions. Did you know about Germany's red wines or about the new drier wines with their modern packaging and easy to understand labels. Maybe it's time you started thinking of Germany as a "new wine country" - there is so much to explore and discover.

Riesling is the grape variety for which Germany is famous and it is highly rated by the wine experts, many of whom predict that it will be the next trendy grape variety after Chardonnay. The dry fruity wines are "New World" in style and will appeal to all those people who think German wine isn't for them.

And by offering quality German wines you can get your customers to trade up, which means increased profits for you.

With a wide variety of German wines available from dry to dessert wines and different grape varieties, there is really no excuse for not listing a selection of German wines.

So here are a few tips about how to promote German wines to your customers:

Wine by the Glass

Offer a Kabinett wine, particularly one from the Mosel region by the glass, the refreshing balance of fruit and racy acidity, often combined with lower alcohol, means that it is ideal for drinking by itself or with food.

Wine of the Month

Hold a German Riesling "Wine of the Month" promotion - many wine drinkers are looking for something different to Chardonnay. Riesling is the grape variety for which Germany is famous and is the grape for the future as wine experts say it is every bit as classy as Chardonnay.

Food and Wine Matching

Match German wine with food - your customers will appreciate the extra effort you have made to suggest wines to go with dishes on your menu and with the wide variety of German wine styles available this won't be a problem. For example, Spätlese wines (literally late harvest wines), taste a little bit richer and are perfect partners with oriental cuisine. So next time you add a stir fry, sweet and sour or any similar dish to your menu, suggest a Spätlese wine from the Pfalz region as the ideal choice.

Seasonal Activities

Summer barbecues provide the perfect opportunity to offer one of the new, dry style wines from Germany. These wines are dry, but fruity and they are great with chicken, fish, pork or by themselves.

Christmas is another ideal time to promote German wines. Try offering your customers a dry Riesling with their smoked salmon starter and perhaps a Riesling Kabinett to partner the turkey. Whilst Riesling Spätlese from the Pfalz has the richness and flavour to stand up to strong cheese.

For further information and suppliers of German Wines, Please contact:
GERMAN WINE
INFORMATION SERVICE
LANE HOUSE,
24 PARSONS GREEN LANE
LONDON SW6 4HS
Tel: 0171 331 8800
Fax: 0171 331 1970

buttery. Its recent popularity has led to overproduction, and much of the cheapest Muscadet is either dull and flabby or acidic. However, it should be possible for the publican to make a good margin on Muscadet without buying the very cheapest.

Alsace differs from other parts of France in that its wines are generally identified by the grape varieties from which they are made. Usually these are German - Riesling, Gewürztraminer, and Sylvaner - although French varieties are also grown, mainly Pinot Gris. Alsace wines come in tall German-style bottles, so the publican should treat them with caution: they can be expensive, and are unfamiliar to many British pubgoers who may think all Rieslings are Liebfraumilch and wonder why they are being asked £10.95 a bottle.

Germany

To many people, German wine is Liebfraumilch, a weakish, blandish, blended white wine in a tall brown bottle - the pilsner of the wine world. A lot of German wine is Liebfraumilch, and demand will force pretty much every publican to stock one brand or another (and some brands are better than others). It's a shame that mass appreciation of German wines in this country stops there, but as far as the average publican is concerned, it does.

One exception is that the high-quality, low-gravity Kabinett and Spätlese grades with their spicey, aromatic flavours make a delicious alternative to the rather heavy, oily sweet white wines offered in most pubs. If you have regular customers who drink sweet wines, you might occasionally vary their diet and tickle their tastebuds by trying them on the odd German variety: even if they don't like it, they'll be flattered by the attention.

German wines should be served well-chilled in flutes.

Italy

Italian wines have traditionally had little exposure in the pub trade, being seen as restaurant wines to be drunk with food - and Italian restaurant wines, at that.

Many of the big, meaty reds made from old indigenous grape varieties such as Nebbiolo (used to make the highly alcoholic Barolo and Barbaresco) are indeed best with food. The same is true of the lighter Chianti, made in Tuscany from the Sangiovese grape, and Valpolicella from Verona in the north east, and of the classic Italian whites, Orvieto from Umbria, Soave from the north east, Frascati from the very suburbs of Rome, and Verdicchio from the east. The lover of Italian wines may regard this as a harsh judgement, but in blunt commercial terms it appears to be true.

Italian wines are beginning to find their way into the pub trade nowadays for three reasons:

- ◆ As food service becomes more important to pubs, better known Italian wines come into their own;
- ◆ Younger drinkers have discovered the sparkling, low-strength Lambrusco;

Wines and Spirits

◆ The Italians have started planting varieties such as Merlot which make for easy drinking without food and offer excellent value for money.

Spain

The mass-produced, blended, poor-quality Spanish wines of years ago were staple pub fodder, pushed by breweries in the days when the full wine and spirit tie was in force. Spanish wines as a result earned a terrible reputation which the country's winemakers have been trying to wipe out ever since.

Nearly all Spanish wines that reach the British market are red, the best of them being Rioja from the north of the country. Made from the Tempranillo grape and usually aged in oak, red Riojas are dark and rich when young, paler and rounder after anything up to 10 years in barrel. (White Rioja is little-known in Britain but is also oak-aged and can be rather over-mature.)

Other Spanish reds which have been widely advertised are the alcoholic but light-tasting Valdepeñas from La Mancha, Navarra, just across the River Ebro from Rioja and not dissimilar, and Penedes from the coastal region just south of Barcelona.

Central and Eastern Europe

The former Communist countries used to produce the kind of wines favoured in their largest export market – the USSR – from native grape varieties. These have usually been too sweet, tannic, and tarry (in the reds), and too sweet and oxidised (whites) for western tastes. Exceptions have been the Riesling-based wines of Slovenia and Croatia, notably Lutomer Riesling, and the big red Hungarian Bull's Blood made from the indigenous Bikaver grape.

Now, however, the foreign exchange hungry Eastern Europeans have turned their attention to the lucrative western markets, Bulgaria leading the way with excellent value for money red Merlots and Cabernet Sauvignons and white Chardonnays, often blended with indigenous grape varieties.

The same is happening in Romania, although it is to be hoped that the excellent Feteasca variety will not be lost altogether, while Hungarian dry Muscat and Ugni Blanc are extremely acceptable drinking wines at a very acceptable price.

These wines have proved most popular in the ever price-conscious supermarket trade and have not succeeded in penetrating the pub trade – perhaps because consumers know how much they cost to take home.

The Americas

Vines arrived in the Americas with the first Western settlers – indeed, there were already indigenous vines growing grapes capable of vinification. Catawba is one survivor.

The wines produced from these grapes are of no great distinction, but the vines themselves proved the salvation of the European wine industries in the late 19th century, when they were devastated by phylloxera. It was found that American vines were resistant to the pest, and most European grapes are now grown on American vinestock.

However, nearly all of the North American wine that comes to Britain is of a different origin. Winemaking arrived in Mexico and south western USA with the Spanish, but until 30 years ago made only poor-quality 'jug wines' for the domestic market.

In the 1960s, this all started to change as Californian wineries such as E&J Gallo, Masson and especially Robert Mondavi started growing European grape varieties and adopting modern wine making practices, winning great success in export markets worldwide.

American winemakers not only grow and use the world's great grape varieties – Chardonnay, Merlot, Chenin Blanc, Riesling, Barbera, Pinot Noir, Cabernet Sauvignon – they have also developed some of their own: Zinfandel, Carnelian, and Symphony, to name a few.

However, US wines have in recent years crossed price barriers into higher brackets, and many publicans may decide they are no longer competitive.

The latest sensation from the Americas is Chilean wine. With their Spanish ancestry, most South American countries have had domestic wine industries for centuries: recent economic developments have persuaded them to seek dollars abroad.

Argentina's is the largest wine industry in South America, but Chile has been grabbing the headlines in Europe. Cabernet Sauvignons are particularly sought after and will make any pub's wine list look both adventurous and good value.

Australia, New Zealand and South Africa

Like the USA and Canada, these countries have old-established wine industries which until recently produced only mediocre wines for their domestic markets – although South African 'sherries' were popular in Britain in pre-Common Market days.

First Australia in the late 1970s, then New Zealand in the mid-1980s, and now with the overthrow of apartheid, South Africa, have all transformed their industries, producing high-quality wines from European grape varieties, especially the classics.

They have also applied themselves to developing more scientific wine making practices, especially the Australians. A generation of Australian oenologists, dubbed the 'flying winemakers', has been responsible for modernising the wine industries of whole countries in Eastern Europe and South America.

Hunter Valley, Barossa, Rutherglen and Coonawarra are perhaps the best-known Australian wine producing regions, with Wolf Blass, Brown Brothers, Hardy's, Lindeman's, Orlando, Penfold and Yalumba among the most prominent producers.

Soil and climate in New Zealand favour white grapes, especially Sauvignon Blanc. Cloudy Bay, Cook's, Hawkes Bay and Marborough are among the most familiar labels in Britain.

READS
WORLD OF WINE

TEL: 01628 850053
FAX: 01628 528336

THE CASE FOR SMALL BOTTLES OF WINE

The person who first stumbled across the joys of the fermented grape died some 8,000 years ago. We hope whoever he or she was had a long and happy life, for their discovery has helped the human race in their search for happiness ever since.

Judging by the sales of wine today, the search goes on in earnest. Wine is currently enjoying an unprecedented boom in the UK. Since 1984 off-sales of wine have grown by a staggering 82% (over the same period beer and spirit sales have declined by 12%). Indeed there is such a choice here, with wines of every grape, from every wine producing country, that this country now boasts some of the most respected connoisseurs in the world. (It was a London man, now working in Los Angeles, who was given a budget of £250,000 to buy some of the finest vintages in a sale of Lord Lloyd-Weber's wines.)

There is no getting away from the fact that wine is popular. The £5 billion pounds people spent last year buying the drink just underlines the point. It is a particular favourite of women and it is the drink both men and women like to have when they are eating. But it's a rare pub that serves a decent selection of wines - even when they do serve food. Indeed pubs generally have missed out on the boom. Only 6% of wine volume goes through the on-trade while wine now accounts for over 21% of total alcohol consumption in the UK.

WINE WINE WHINE

Why is this? It is not like publicans to let an opportunity go begging. One explanation could be that publicans are simply overwhelmed by the choice available. On the whole they are very conservative in the wines they choose to stock. Half of the wines in pubs are from France whereas the wines people are buying for themselves mostly come from other countries, from California, Germany, Spain, Italy and Australia. More recently there has been a growing interest in wines from Chile, New Zealand and South Africa.

You can see the problem for the publican. By the time he or she has got to grips with what is good and what isn't they could have got a degree from the Open University in viniculture.

On top of that there is the problem of storage. Once opened, a bottle of wine rapidly deteriorates. So unless a publican knows that they have a reasonable demand for a particular wine, they can end up pouring a lot of sour wine down the drain. It is enough to turn you sour about the whole idea.

SMALL IS BEAUTIFUL

Meet Geoff Read, a man whose mission is to persuade you that there is money to be made out of the grape. His concept is very simple. Give your customers the wine they want in a bottle size they can happily drink. So The Minicellar Range from Reads World of Wine comes in quarter-size bottles, the perfect size for a single serving. The range itself is comprehensive, representing all the more popular wines which have been carefully selected to appeal to the widest possible market. There are wines from all over the world, from Portugal, California, South Africa, Spain, Italy and of course France. The names and types of wine are known and respected, Ernest and Julio Gallo, Mateus Rosé, Frascati, Rioja. There is even a fine dry champagne.

Like all good ideas, you wonder why it hasn't been done before. (Well in truth it has, but you would have to pay for a first class ticket on an airline for the privilege. Even then the choice wouldn't be as large.)

However it is not an untested idea. The Minicellar Range from Reads World of Wine was launched in the Republic of Ireland three years ago. In that short time it has helped boost sales of wine, and quarter bottles have captured half of the on-trade market. The concept has also been launched in the UK and wherever the range has been introduced it has produced a dramatic and positive effect on sales.

BUILDING SUCCESS UPON SUCCESS

With one twist of the cap it does away with the problems of storage. Every customer gets a fresh bottle of their favourite wine. It means that every publican can now stock a respectable range of wines without having to know a whole lot about wine. (Point-of-sale material includes wine tasting notes which describe the individual charms of each wine). It answers women's grudge that pubs don't sell drinks they like, which, you've guessed it, is wine. In fact it generally answers a lot of grudges. Research shows that over 70% of consumers would like to see a wider range of wines in pubs. And well over half believe that when wine is served it is in a poor condition.

The Minicellar Range from Reads World of Wine will also help publicans take advantage of the new trends in the market. The most obvious being that pubs need no longer miss out on the growing interest in wine. But there is another trend from which the clever publican can profit and that is the move to eating out. (Some estimates project that by the new millennium we will be eating 25% of our meals outside the home). The automatic choice of drink for most people when they eat is wine. So with Reads World of Wine, the trodden grape may yet help the poor downtrodden publican.

Prices of Australian and New Zealand wines have risen as drinkers came to appreciate the quality of the offerings. South African wines should still be more modestly priced.

South Africa produces big red wines and oak-aged whites of equal quality. Paarl, near Cape Town, is the country's wine growing capital and home of the KWV co-operative; Stellenbosch is another famous region nearby, with Nederburg and Spier among its better known producers.

Sparkling wines

Champagne is not made by artificially carbonating an ordinary still wine but rather by inducing a secondary fermentation in the bottle itself – a highly skilled, labour intensive, and time-consuming process which accounts for the apparently inflated price of real Champagne.

Other sparkling wines, and indeed, ciders, are made by the *méthode champenoise*, but only Champagne may describe itself as Champagne. (The only other time you will see the word used legally is on a Cognac label: Grande Champagne and Petit Champagne are two areas of the Cognac region.)

If Champagne it is to be kept for any length of time it should be stored like all wines, on its side in a cool, dark, dry cellar free from vibration. It should be served well chilled (an ice bucket is optional) in flutes, not saucers. The bottle should be opened by wrapping the neck in a clean cloth, untwisting the tag of the wire cage and removing it, grasping the cork firmly, and twisting it with one end of the cloth. If correctly done, the cork should come away with a quiet 'pop', not a bang, and there should only be a wisp of vapour, not a rush of foam. The cork should never be allowed to fly: it reaches considerable speed and can cause injury. For this reason it is advisable for a member of staff, rather than the kind of exuberant customer who usually orders Champagne, to open the bottle.

Pub customers with anything less to celebrate than hitting the jackpot in a rollover week might flinch a little at even the lowest possible on-trade price for genuine Champagne. But there are occasions when patrons will want to break out the bubbly, and the wise host would be well-advised to maintain a small stock of something affordable.

Crémant de Bourgogne, a French sparkling wine made of the same grapes and by the same method as Champagne, is a very acceptable substitute, as are Freixenet and Codorniu from Spain, and most brands of Sekt from Germany, especially those made of the Riesling grape.

India produces a *méthode champenoise* sparkling wine called Omar Khayyam made of Chardonnay grapes, and this has attracted critical plaudits.

FORTIFIED WINES

Sherry

Britain is still one of the world's biggest consumers of Sherry, although our appetite for it continues to wane. The problem has again been partly one of image: for years, Sherry has been perceived as a sweet'n'sticky for maiden aunts, a Christmas tipple for near-teetotallers (although it always strikes me as supremely ironic that infrequent drinkers should, when they do imbibe, go for something of 17 per cent abv).

The name Sherry has also been debased over the years by so-called 'Empire' sherries: sweet wines from Cyprus and South Africa favoured by pre-Common Market tax regimes; and even worse by the ghastly British sherry: imported grape concentrate, diluted, fermented, and sweetened in processing plants in Leeds and elsewhere.

In the past decade these problems have been addressed: the name Sherry is now permitted only on labels of genuine Sherries from the Jerez region of southern Spain, while British shippers, notably Harvey's, have been strenuously seeking to refashion Sherry's poor image and give it the status it deserves as one of the world's most complicated and fascinating wines.

The beauty of Sherry today is that sophisticates and novices drink from the same bottle: the publican, therefore, has little to lose and much to gain from stocking a superior range of Sherries which will attract the sophisticated without alienating the less refined.

Sherry is made mainly from Palomino and Pedro Ximenez grapes and fermented in contact with the air, so that a thick yeasty crust known as the flor develops, beneath which the intensely sweet juices can get on with the business of slow maturation. It is a fortified wine: spirit is added to halt the fermentation before the protective flor develops.

After the flor has developed the unique solera system of maturation comes into play. This is a process of adding young wines to half-emptied butts of older ones. The process is intended to speed maturation, and the young–old mixtures are transferred to tuns of ever-older wines so that the bottle of Bristol Cream you open today will contain a trace – an infinitesimal trace, but a trace nonetheless – of Sherry that was already old when Nelson was still young.

Sherries come in many styles from dry and intense to sweet and rich. Fino and Manzanilla are dry and elegant – a Fino such as Tio Pepe, served lightly chilled, is one of the finest aperitifs there is. Amontillado is older, nuttier, deeper, but still dry, while Oloroso is matured in the open air to bake and burn in the sun. A true Oloroso may be concentrated to more than 20 per cent abv – but it is still dry. The sweet sherries – cream, pale cream, and brown – are versions of Fino and Oloroso sweetened and coloured with unfermented grape must.

Sherry should be served lightly chilled and always in the tall, narrow copita rather than the schooner.

Worth noting alongside Sherry is Montilla, a similar wine from a neighbouring region.

Montilla is made from the same grapes as sherry, and may actually contain a higher proportion of the old-fashioned PX, and Montilla wines are used in some Sherry blends. The methods of production are similar, and the finished wines are of a similar strength and character. But thanks to a quirk of British law, Montilla wines have long been regarded as poor man's sherry - a fact that publicans can take advantage of.

The principal difference between true Sherry and Montilla is that Sherry only reaches its final strength by the addition of spirit, whereas Montilla, made mainly of the naturally sweet PX grape, achieves 16-17 per cent abv naturally. Sherry therefore falls into a higher duty bracket - and Montilla offers similar quality for far less money. To the publican who holds functions, especially wedding receptions and office Christmas parties, this is a godsend: you can offer the father of the bride or office party organiser a brilliant deal and still get a good mark-up.

Port

Like Sherry, port is a fortified wine whose image has suffered somewhat in recent years and which is now making a modest comeback, especially at the high-quality end of the market.

The wines come from the rugged Douro Valley in northern Portugal, the name being a contraction of Oporto, the city at the river's mouth from which the wines are shipped and where the great port houses are based. In their unfortified state, Douro wines are highly tannic - one of the qualities which contributes to port's longevity.

Port classifications are confusing - deliberately so, a cynic may say, since the distinctions between Vintage Port, Late-Bottled Vintage (LBV), and Vintage Character are hazy to the layman.

- Vintage is the bottling of a single exceptional year;
- Late-Bottled Vintage is also the crop of a single year but matured in the barrel rather than the bottle;
- Vintage Character is a classification which has no legal definition but which falls between workaday ruby and LBV.

A good vintage character port is an excellent standby for the publican who wants to be able to offer his customers the odd hint of luxury without breaking the bank.

Port styles include:

- white port, an aperitif popular in France;
- ruby, the basic red style aged for at least three years;
- tawny, which can be bottled at five years but which is sometimes as much as 40 years old;
- single quinta (or vineyard), which is becoming a vogue alternative to true Vintage Port;
- crusted ports of legend, which are merely unfiltered blends left to mature in bottle long enough to grow a protective crust.

Port should be served in a goblet large enough to allow the vapours to collect above the wine. A generous measure is a very tempting send-off indeed for business diners with a few minutes to spare before going back to the office. I have, more than once, been unable to refuse the publican who approaches

Wines and Spirits

my table after dinner with the welcome but costly words: 'Port all round, gentlemen?'

Other fortified wines

There are many other fortified wines, but these are of little interest to the pub trade. Madeira, from the eponymous Atlantic islands, is perhaps best known and is unique among wines in that it should be stored upright. The styles include sercial, the driest; bual, which is medium sweet; and malmsey, the sweetest. Malaga, a fortified wine from south eastern Spain, had its glory days over a century ago and is becoming extinct as its vineyards vanish beneath hotel developments. The sweetest Malaga, dulce, is said to be a good match for chocolate pudding. Marsala is Sicilian and was once very popular in Britain. Today it is used almost exclusively as an ingredient in zabaglione.

Winemakers in Australia and America have also started producing fortified wines of very high quality. Excellent though many of them are, however, the great British pub is probably not their best habitat.

Dessert wines

One category of fortified wines that will interest publicans with a good dining trade is what the French call *vin doux naturel*, although the sweetness of the various southern French Muscats – Muscat de Frontignan, Muscat de Beaumes de Venise, Rivesaltes and others – owes more to artifice than nature. They are in fact lightly fortified, not naturally sweet like the sweet whites of Bordeaux, but their price point and the possibility of selling them as an affordable after-dinner indulgence can make them attractive to some publicans. Serve them lightly chilled.

Tips on serving table wines

Although today's drinkers are a lot more casual about wine drinking than they used to be, they still demand certain standards.

White and rosé wines should be cold enough for condensation to appear on the glass; you may also serve light reds this cold nowadays.

Wine must be fresh: even with the various wine saving devices on sale nowadays, 24 hours is quite long enough. If you disagree, try drinking the last glass in a three-day-old bottle yourself.

By-the-bottle sales are on the increase, which gives great scope for marketing ploys: some dining pubs offer a free bottle of house wine for diners eating at otherwise quiet times; some pubs have gone in for carafes (normally filled from a wine box) which represent good value for money and have a fun, street café, still-on-holiday appeal.

Bag in box wines have, by and large, been slow to catch on – paradoxically, since they answer all the practical questions of cost, shelf-life and temperature eminently suitably. The problem is image: but the customer may be completely wrong and still absolutely right.

Measures

Appropiate glasses, never more than half-full, should always be used: the standard measure of table wines is six to the bottle, or 125ml. This is also a good measure for the much stronger after-dinner wines, producing a glow which may entice the diner to call for a second. As a session drink, though, port is usually served in the same measure as a double of spirits or 50ml – not really stingy for someone who's going to be drinking it all evening. It is best offered in a small Paris goblet, which gives it room to breathe without dwarfing the measure.

SPIRITS

There are many interesting parallels between the beer and spirits markets in Britain's pubs. Whisky, like ale, was the unchallenged king in the 1950s, when gin was drunk only by naval types, salesmen with social pretensions, and aged flappers; brandy was more common at table than in the bar; and vodka was known only to the more effete members of the Diplomatic Corps.

The day Sean Connery first asked for a vodka martini, shaken not stirred, was a fateful moment for the Scotch whisky industry. The Bond films gave the first inkling to most English people that there was an exciting, cosmopolitan life to be lived beyond suburbia; that their aspirations could extend beyond a week in Bognor and a new Ford Popular; and that their boss need not be their social model.

From that moment white spirits – vodka and white rum, not poor old gin – began to outperform whisky, even as lager was beginning to outperform ale. (Is casting dark rum in the role of mild ale stretching this analogy too far?)

Nevertheless, whisky is still the single most important category in the average pub's profile of spirits sales.

Whisk(e)y

Whisk(e)y is basically distilled beer without the hops. It was invented by Irish or Scottish monks in the 14th or 15th centuries, using technology learnt from the Arabs.

Whisky or whiskey? The spellings are etymologically interchangeable, but it has become conventional to describe Scotch and its Canadian and Japanese descendants without the 'e' and Irish and its American offspring with.

Scotland is divided into four malt distilling regions:

- ◆ Highland accounts for most production, best-known names being Glenfiddich, Glenlivet and Macallan;
- ◆ Island includes Islay, which produces characterful malts such as Laphroaig;
- ◆ Lowland malts are becoming rarer and tend to be less interesting as singles, more used for blending;
- ◆ Campbeltown is reduced to two distilleries, one of them the supreme Springbank.

Single malt

The product of one distillery, generally aged for at least eight years, although a five-year-old Balblair is not bad.

Wines and Spirits

Vatted malt
A blend of single malts, common in the last century, but virtually extinct until supermarket chains hit on the idea of reviving it for their own-label generic malts.

Grain whisky
Whisky made on a continuous still rather than the traditional pot still. Cheap, and until recently used only for blending. A couple of single grain whiskies have been launched in the 1990s to try and wrest market share from white spirits.

Blends
A compound of malt and grain whiskies, whose price and cost rises along with the proportion of malt. Standard blends contain a third or less malt whisky, although there are no legal definitions and some of them can taste pretty malty. De luxe blends such as Chivas Regal and Johnnie Walker Red Label still occupy a small place in the market, while export blends such as Johnnie Walker Black Label, Ballantine's, and Cutty Sark have increasing cachet in the home market.

Irish whiskeys
These are made by a slightly different process from Scotch and tend to be smoother and sweeter. All the common brands are blends, although single malts are beginning to creep on to the market.

American whiskies
In very broad terms, Canadian whisky derives from the Scottish tradition, and US whiskey from the Irish. However, there has been so much cross-fertilisation over the years, and innovations dictated by local conditions (especially in the use of rye) that the distinction is meaningless. Canadian distillers have stepped in to fill the gap in the take home market created by the banning of sub-norm (less than 40 per cent abv) Scotches, but Canadian Club is still an important pub brand. One or more US whiskeys - Jim Beam, Jack Daniels, Wild Turkey - are must-stocks, as is the derivative Southern Comfort. A connoisseurs' brand of US whiskey is Maker's Mark.

Retailing whisk(e)y
Twenty years ago, a single Scotch was 50 per cent more expensive than a pint of bitter. Now it falls somewhere between a half and a pint. The margin is still good, but more and more pubs are finding that they have to take their whisky range upmarket. This is all part of the game of balancing quality and affordability; but with Scotch it is possible for most publicans to stock one or two really expensive whiskies, since the entry price of even £2 a single is still not beyond the reach of many customers (especially as the evening wears on).

Pub whisky has always been more upmarket than take home whisky anyway - you never saw sub-norm Scotches in pubs even when they were legal, let alone supermarket own-labels. In fact, brand leadership could be established by pricing up - Bell's eclipsed Haig that way, and Famous Grouse very nearly eclipsed Bell's.

Today Bell's, Teacher's and Grouse are the lowest common

Gordon's promises a taste of perfection

HAVE you ever heard the saying: "The first taste is with the eyes"? Now picture a gin and tonic served in a wine glass with a limp piece of lemon and a half-melted lump of ice. Then think of a 'Perfectly Served' Gordon's and tonic - the classic, long, cool drink which promises instant refreshment and 'innervigoration'. Which one do you think looks more appealing?

Not only does a 'Perfectly Served' Gordon's and tonic look and taste better - it also sells better. Last year, trials of the 'Perfect Serve' campaign throughout London and the South East showed participating outlets sold 20% more Gordon's than before - which is great news for the bottom line.

But how easy is it to do the Perfect Serve? First, take a tall, chilled glass and fill two thirds with ice. Pour a generous measure of Gordon's and top up with premium bottled tonic water. Add a wedge of lime, stir and present - it's easy!

How not to present a Gin and Tonic

Premium bottled tonic is recommended for quality and effervescence

A good wedge of fruit must be added

United Distillers has now made it even easier to benefit from the 'Perfect Serve' with a dedicated team helping to roll out the programme around the country.

To enrol on the Gordon's Perfect Serve Programme and make the most of staff training and dedicated point of sale materials, call 0800 833 143 to receive your Gordon's brochure and find out more.

Gordon's & Tonic
PERFECTLY SERVED

The 'Perfectly Served' Gordon's & Tonic

denominators in pubs, and all pubs stock at least one single malt (invariably Glenfiddich). Any pub except the most basic will stock two or three malts, and it has also become common to stock two or even three Irish whiskeys.

The next steps in going up-market are to stock deluxe and export blends and merchant-bottled single malts. The former have been described and most brands are known at least by name to whisky drinkers, but cask strength, single cask and over-aged malts from the merchant bottlers – Gordon & MacPhail, Cadenhead's, and the Scotch Malt Whisky Society – are the new *dernier cri* in whisky snobbery: they are not really for the average publican, but you never know. The joy of whisk(e)y is that it's an area where the publican has the flexibility to stock a brand just for one good regular.

Other spirits

It may seem a little brusque, but with all other spirits the rule is precisely the same as it is for whisk(e)y: chase the premium. It's the same as with canned beers: people may have them at home, but they want something a bit posher when they go out.

For instance, French brandy in pubs has to be Cognac (with Armagnac as a speciality). Even the most basic boozer can't get away with French grape brandies such as Three Barrels: the handful of brandy drinking punters may quite happily drink own-label sub-norm caramelised grape spirit in the house; but when they go out, it has to be the real thing.

The same is true with gin: Gordon's may be the most expensive gin people take home, but it's the lowest common denominator in pub terms, and if you want to diversify it has to be upwards into Booth's, Bombay Sapphire, and other premium brands.

White rum has to be Bacardi (or at a pinch Dry Cane); you may also stock a specialist brand such as Wray & Nephew, but only the scruffiest shebeen would stock anything less.

Dark rums are an interesting area: Scottish pubs until a few years ago did a lively trade in value for money brands – but only a certain type of Scottish pub. Standard dark rums may not do much these days, but the number of pubs stocking an overproof, especially Woods 100 or Pusser's, is increasing: is there scope for a Trafalgar Day promotion here?

With vodka, again, the action is in the upper reaches: Smirnoff Blue Label and Black Label, Absolut from Scandinavia, Stolichnaya and Moskovskaya from Russia and other authentic Eastern European brands – many of them flavoured with anything from bison grass to ginger and cloves – compete for space in the premium sector, while even in the standard sector newcomers such as Black Death from Iceland and Virgin Vodka are creating interest. The diversity is such that all sorts of promotions suggest themselves: do you know when Lenin's birthday is?

Liqueurs and specialities

Very careful stock control is called for here. As far as traditional liqueurs

Wines and Spirits

are concerned, the range you really need to stock is dwindling: how many advocaats or Drambuies have you served in the last 12 months, for instance? And can you actually open your bottle of blue Curaçao, or is the lid stuck to the bottle?

There's little point wasting £6 or £8 on each bottle of something that is really only held in reserve as a contingency: on the two or three occasions a year you're forced to say 'sorry, we don't stock yellow Chartreuse', the customer will probably settle quite happily for something else anyway.

Many of the bottles you see on the too-high-to-reach shelves are only stocked because there's an ethos left over from the 1960s, a hangover that says bars are cocktail bars and cocktail bars must stock Maraschino: they aren't; they mustn't; and why waste money on stock you can't sell?

Modern speciality drinks are more problematical: when young people ask for a new drink such as Bézique or Archer's Peach County or Bailey's or Malibu, you have no way of knowing then that Bézique and Archer's are going to sink like stones while Bailey's and Malibu are going to become standards.

The golden rule is: never order more than one case, on sale or return if you can, and don't order a second until the eleventh bottle of the first is finished. However persuasive the rep, however appealing the promotion, remember this: there are bottles of Bézique gathering dust on top shelves across the land. In time they will become collectors' items, but until then they represent unrecovered outlay.

Presentation

Spirits and speciality drinks benefit from correct presentation and service. For instance, a scotch on the rocks has to be served in a clean tumbler with ice that doesn't float.

British barstaff have never understood ice the way the punters do: the customer sees in his mind's eye a sparkling broad-based tumbler with three or four big cubes of clean ice filling a quarter to one-third of it and the spirit poured over, resting in the bottom of the glass. Barstaff seem to see a Paris goblet a quarter full of liquid, with two round-edged sad little bits of ageing ice bumping about listlessly on top. Part of retailing is seeing through the punter's eyes, and spirits service is one area where the visual aspect is both obvious and essential. (And while you're there – how about a clean white coaster like you get in New York?)

APPEARANCES

You can't overemphasize appearances. Going out is expensive these days: customers are liable to ask whether they're really getting their money's worth. The secret of success, whatever style of operation you're running, is to satisfy your customers' expectations:

- ◆ flirty barstaff familiar to the point of rudeness, or barstaff stiff and formal to the point of being French?
- ◆ customers sinking lager in pints or sipping Chardonnay with their little fingers stuck out?

You have to ask yourself the same question: do they think they're

153

The Publican's Handbook

getting what they're paying for? Are they having a good enough time to justify the £X they're spending? Will they come back? Will they tell their friends?

In short ... are they happy?

Legal Notes

When sold by the glass, wine must be in quantities of 125ml or 175ml. Again, a statement must be displayed indicating the measurers in use. It is acceptable to use both measurers. When sold in carafes, wine must conform to either 50cl, 75cl or 1 litre. All measurers can be used in the same premises. Again a notice is required. Spirits must be sold in multiples of 25ml.

Berentzen
The Original Apfelkorn

For Further Information please contact:
Amberstone Trading Co Limited, Suite 13, Cortland, George Street, Hailsham, East Sussex, BN27 1QN.
Tel: 01323 842880/Fax: 01323 842830

Berentzen
The Original Apfelkorn

Light Fruit Schnapps is the fastest growing category among discerning consumers. Berentzen Distillers, Europe's market leaders in this field offer a range of premium packaged Schnapps in 10 smooth and easy to drink flavours. Since it establishment in 1758, Berentzen has proceeded to capture the imagination of consumers world-wide and is now available in over 100 countries.

Reflecting its fun loving roots Berentzen has become synonymous with having fun and partying to the earlier hours of the morning. Popular with both men and women in the 18-24 year old market, they can be drunk neat or with a variety or mixers.

Berentzen Schnapps support includes branded chiller units offered on a self liquidating basis, event nights and impactful point of sale.

For further information please contact: Amberstone Trading Co Limited, Suite 13, Cortland, George Street, Hailsham, East Sussex BN27 1QN. Tel:01323 842880 Fax:01323 842830

CHAPTER EIGHT

CATERING

Tony O'Reilly

What makes a great pub? Traditional drinking houses all have ambience and atmosphere, a warm, friendly, relaxing environment, a scenic location, a cracking host, and good beer - all provided, of course, that there is sufficient custom to sustain profits.

These days, though, more and more drinking houses are not able to sustain profits solely on wet sales and are turning to food operations to boost income. Indeed, recent survey figures show that in many pubs the percentage of food to wet sales has reached 60:40, and a fair chunk of wet turnover is in fact wine purchased with food.

Some pubs are producing fine food to rival any two- or three-star restaurant. However, there are still those which have not yet mastered the art of satisfying the culinary expectations of their customers.

The following is advice for those considering introducing a food operation to their establishment. It might also be helpful to those who have not, as yet, achieved their culinary vision.

TRAINING

The first question to ask yourself is: can you cook?

You don't need to be a master chef to run a pub kitchen, but you do need a sound understanding of food hygiene, basic culinary skills, a little experience, a pinch of imagination, a flair for presentation and the ability to cope under immense stress, which is an occupational hazard.

Some may be able to get by without any training. But anyone keen to learn how to cook correctly should seriously consider going to college to get formal qualifications.

Colleges will not be able to teach you everything, but they will teach the fundamentals. If this seems the right choice, contact a local catering college for expert advice and guidance on a part-time National Vocational Qualification (NVQ) or a Scottish Vocational Qualification.

The college will probably expect you to be employed in the trade already, because NVQs and SVQs can only be taught and assessed in a realistic environment – ie, your workplace. Alternatively, the college may run a public restaurant which meets the criteria of realistic working environment.

Nowadays most breweries have in-house training programmes for employees and potential employees, and one or two of the major breweries offer basic City & Guilds Cookery Certificates aimed specifically at the pub trade, but these are not normally open to outsiders. A few run courses for would-be licensees, but cooking is usually only an element of the full programme.

But no matter what you learn in a training environment, it will never prepare you for 50 hungry diners – you have to experience that at first hand. Perhaps it's a good idea to try working as a trainee in a local restaurant. This won't make you rich, but it will help you gain the relevant experience and a good practical grounding.

Alternatively, you might employ the services of a consultant who will visit your establishment for a set period to construct a menu and gradually ease you and your staff into it leaving only when you feel confident and comfortable enough to work on your own.

PLANNING

Before determining an appropriate style and level of catering, find out what your market wants. Once this is established, you can begin planning the scale and pitch of your catering operation.

The best way to go about establishing your intended market is simply to visit successful pubs and restaurants in the surrounding area to give you a clear indication of the potential clientele.

If you prefer a more scientific approach, you can try the market research technique known as the mosaic formula, which profiles an area by type of resident and postcode to give an indication of disposable income within a given radius. It then finds out how far people are prepared to travel for a meal to come up with your potential customer base.

Even then, constructing and pricing a menu can be a little hit and miss. Most establishments aim for an average of 50-60 per cent gross profit. However, this might not be applicable to all dishes on the menu: for instance, there are seasonal fluctuations in the prices of fresh commodities.

Then again, many dishes cost only around a pound to produce and some, especially vegetarian, as little as 60p, but research has shown that as many customers are put of by suspiciously low prices as by prices that are too high. A charge upwards of £7 may be an average main course price, for no other reason than that is what people expect to pay.

I know of one particular company that takes the average local menu price as a basis then sticks 10 per cent on top, reasoning that as it is superior to other local establishments its customers will be happy to pay the extra – and it has to be said, it does work in this instance.

Catering

THE DINING AREA

Having established a style and level of operation, the next step is to create a matching ambience.

The first thing to remember is that there should be no conflict between drinkers and diners. Clearly designate an area for diners, and ensure that everyone is aware of it. Should the occasional drinker stray into the wrong area then don't be shy – all you have to do is tell them politely.

When it comes to a suitable decor for the dining area, there is no substitute for employing a professional interior designer – assuming you can afford one. If you can, make sure you brief them clearly on your ideas: after all, it's your pub and it should reflect the standards you wish to convey.

Don't let the designer bully you into something you don't want. Take the advice, but don't allow yourself to be swayed if you are not entirely happy with the suggestions.

If hiring a designer isn't an option and you have to do it yourself, avoid the false economy of buying cheap furnishings. They will fill the room, but how long will they last? Buy furnishings that are practical, of high quality, and above all hard wearing.

STAFF

If, for whatever reason, you will not be doing the cooking yourself, you will need both a good chef and a competent team.

How much you can pay will, of course, be entirely dependent on your projected overheads and turnover, and only you will be able to decide what you can afford. My research concludes that an average salary for a good pub chef is £200-250 a week with bonuses. It might be possible to employ a chef who will work for less, and good luck to you. But be warned that if you pay a low wage you can expect a high staff turnover, which does nothing to help establish your food business in its start-up phase and causes operational problems even at the best of times. Always be fair, and remember: if you pay peanuts you get monkeys.

If you employ an experienced chef you will need to set a menu that will be a challenge. If the chef is allowed to become complacent, there is the risk that boredom will set in, and this will eventually be reflected in the presentation of the food.

LUNCH AND DINNER

Food service is broken down into two sittings with very different patterns: lunch and dinner.

Lunchtime diners have little time and expect to be served quickly and efficiently, whereas evening diners are more leisurely.

As a rough estimate, a lunchtime diner will take 8-10 minutes to reach your establishment, where they will then have 40 minutes before they have to leave. You should therefore allow no more than seven minutes to serve their starter and 15 minutes for the main course.

There seems to be an internal clock ticking in waiting customers that rings after 15 minutes, where-

CINDERS BARBECUES
CATERING SYSTEMS

Barbecues designed for the Professionals

British made using high quality stainless steel and carrying a two year warranty, these units are the ultimate profit generating barbecues.

All units are quick and easy to use, clean, and transport – folding for storage and with a model to suit any occasion, place or time.

For further information please telephone: 015242 62900, fax: 015242 62955.

ALL MODELS ARE CE APPROVED

• THE • HOTELIER •
Total Grill Area – 1134 sq ins (7312 sq cms);
Total Heat Input – 54,000 Btu/Hr (16kW);
Weight – 137lbs (37 Kgs)

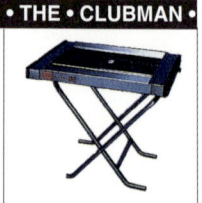

• THE • CLUBMAN •
Total Grill Area – 567 sq ins (3656 sq cms);
Total Heat Input – 27,250 Btu/Hr (8kW);
Weight – 83lbs (37 Kgs)

• THE • CAVALIER •
Total Grill Area – 567 sq ins (3656 sq cms);
Total Heat Input – 34,000 Btu/Hr (10kW);
Weight – 57lbs (26 Kgs)

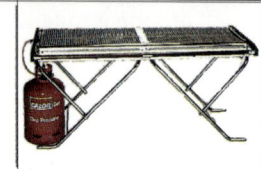

• THE • CATERER •
Total Grill Area – 1134 sq ins (7312 sq cms);
Total Heat Input – 68,000 Btu/Hr (20kW);
Weight – 103lbs (47 Kgs)

Viscount Catering Ltd

Manufacturers of Quality Catering & Refrigeration Equipment...

- Well known brand names in the catering equipment industry
- Wide range of products including light and medium duty gas and electric cooking equipment. Ranges, Convection Oven Ranges, Grills, Fryers, Steamers, Boiling Tables and Boilers.
- Combination ovens - gas and electric - 4, 6, 10, 24 and 40 grid.
- Refrigerated cabinets and counters.
- Back Bar equipment - boiling units, bain maries, fryers, griddles etc
- Taylor-made serveries and counters.
- Design and estimating facility available.
- Competitive prices.
- Showroom and demonstration kitchen
- 5 Minutes from M1 Junction 35 - visit our factory and see for yourself.

Moorwood Vulcan   LEE BISHOP   Sadia Refrigeration
Jackson   HENRY NUTTALL   Reg. No. Lloyds BE850283   ADVANCED COUNTERS & SERVERIES   Electroway
Registered in England & Wales No. 2656697

Viscount Catering Limited, Green Lane, Ecclesfield, Sheffield S35 9ZY
Tel: 0114 2570100 Fax: 0114 2570251

NATCO'S New Spicy Cashews

DRESSED TO IMPRESS

A NEW AND UNIQUE APPETISER FROM NATCO DESIGNED TO TURN HEADS

New Exciting Flavours ~ Uncompromising Quality

100% Large Jumbo Cashews ~ Dry Roasted

Specially Packed in Thick Foil ~ 12 Month Shelf Life

Naturally Flavoured ~ Without Added Oils or Preservatives

CONTACT KERRY 0181-903-8311

Really Delicious

upon the customer will start worrying about whether they will be served in time to eat and enjoy the food without having to wolf it down. You only get one chance with this type of customer and if you fail the first time they'll probably never dine with you again.

So you have got to get it right at the beginning, and if you do then they will most likely visit to dine in the evening as well.

Evening service is quite different from lunch. Diners have time to relax and socialise and usually expect to spend much longer dining. As a guideline allow 15 minutes for the starter and another 10 minutes after they have finished their starter before you serve the main course.

If you have a restaurant licence covering designated areas of the pub, there's no need to hustle diners out along with the drinkers at 11.20pm. If they're having a substantial meal, they can carry on buying drinks up to midnight Monday–Saturday and 11.30pm on Sunday, with the standard 20 minutes drinking-up time on top. From a staffing point of view, you will need one waiter or waitress for every 12 covers plus an additional person to take care of the bills.

KITCHEN CREATIVITY

It's great to have superb gastronomic ideas, but if they are not practical you are not doing yourself any favours or impressing your customers. Work through all new ideas carefully before actually offering them to the public. I have worked with many a publican who would change the menu because I was in their kitchen, and would add new dishes as they went along. On one occasion I found Hollandaise and Béarnaise sauce, both of which I enjoy making, added to the menu. It never entered the licensee's head to make sure he had enough eggs!

Whenever you introduce a new item, have a dry run at it – if only to time it and see how long it takes.

FRESH VERSUS CONVENIENCE

The balance to be struck between fresh foods and prepared dishes is a fine one which must take into account the standard and experience of your kitchen staff, what the clientele will expect, and whether you can charge enough to warrant buying fresh.

But how to define the term fresh? Meat is available pre-portioned and chilled in pouches; fish are sold gutted and skinned; potatoes can be bought ready peeled and cut for cooking. Are these fresh or not?

One important point is that the standard of pre-prepared dishes and ingredients has improved greatly in recent years. Gone are the days, I'm relieved to say, when the standard pub vegetables were frozen peas or tinned beans with chips, and when the best a vegetarian could expect was cauliflower cheese with chips and frozen peas.

In fact, there are few advantages in buying frozen foods other than they are convenient. I'm not knocking frozen foods, as there are many good-quality products available; but they can usually be distinguished from fresh and when people are

Catering

entertaining or being entertained they expect more.

My advice would be: whatever you buy, whenever possible buy fresh vegetables. There is no excuse not to as they are so easy to prepare and cook, and so cheap.

One of the drawbacks to using only fresh food is their short shelf-life, which means you spend half your time shopping. Fresh meat, for instance, should be purchased 2-3 times a week and vegetables and dairy products daily. Fish should be purchased fresh every day or as required. It makes no sense to buy fresh and then freeze it - you might as well have bought frozen in the first place.

There are some products, however, that have to be purchased frozen because there is insufficient trade to warrant buying fresh, eg exotic meats or tropical fish dishes. It is advisable in this case to get samples from various companies and compare prices to secure the best deal.

Frozen food needs to be correctly thawed before use, and a common problem is deciding how many portions to thaw. There are some that can be cooked from frozen, but unless you have enough - and adequately powerful - microwaves, you are limited in the number of frozen products you can cope with efficiently in a session. Frozen dishes are increasingly being superseded by chilled foods and, with major advances in chilling technology, you can purchase most products chilled with a fridge-life of up to 14 days. It usually needs only 8-12 minutes in a water bath to prepare chilled dishes before they are ready to serve.

What benefits does the microwave offer?

Standard microwaves are great for re-heating prepared dishes, but as far as cooking goes they have always been a non-starter with me.

I once worked in a West End restaurant that had 40 microwaves to cope with the volume of customers (about 1000 a night), and I'm sure the chefs used to glow in the dark as they went home. But all they were used for was to bring the food up to correct service temperature - economically, not very wise.

If you must cook with a microwave, your best bet is to buy a high-powered (not a domestic) combination microwave/conventional oven. These can bake potatoes in under 10 minutes, roast a rack of lamb in under six, grill a chicken breast in under four, and bake an individual pie lid in under three minutes.

PROMOTIONS

Themed evenings and events are a great marketing initiative, and provided you do your costings properly they can be a lucrative earner, with the bonus of drawing new custom as well as refreshing the jaded palates of your regulars.

Always research thoroughly to find out what excites your regular customers; but remember, their saying they would love to come is not the same as buying a ticket.

To attract a broad spectrum of customers always publicise forthcoming special events well in advance and as broadly as possible. To get free publicity in the local media, you might incorporate a charity fundraising element – that usually guarantees a few column inches.

The more outrageous and innovative your event is, the better. I heard of one publican who held a Caribbean evening and had two tons of sand delivered to the pub along with giant umbrellas, beach tables and beach towels ... in January.

Curry nights are another excellent promotional idea in the winter months, although curries are now widely referred to as baltis – the 'nouveau' term used to refresh Indian cuisine.

Thai cuisine is the new Chinese and another good idea for a theme evening. If you are not proficient in ethnic cuisine there are many companies producing good quality sauces that only have to be added to the meat to create the perfect authentic dish.

You might even consider trying a British regional promotion – you can always find genuine recipes if you look hard enough. But whatever you decide to put on, make sure you don't overstretch yourself.

CATERING FOR VEGETARIANS AND VEGANS

Catering for vegetarians is a must these days, and can be financially rewarding as the number of vegetarians is increasing steadily. Even so, it may not always be practical to cook fresh dishes daily for vegetarians. You might have to 'batch cook', cool, and freeze; or alternatively, you might want to try convenience vegetarian foods of which there are many now available.

One problem commonly encountered by vegetarians when eating out is lack of choice. They want variety just as much as anyone does, and what they tend to get is pasta smothered in a cheese or tomato-based sauce. This definitely doesn't go down too well with most vegetarians. I constantly hear them complain that if they're only going to be offered pasta, why do they bother to go out for a meal in the first place?

They expect more – quite rightly so, when they're paying for a meal out – and they demand an imaginative dish that will set their tastebuds tingling. If you're short of inspiration, there are many good vegetarian recipe books on the market. My wife and daughters are vegetarians and I have, over the years, built up a vast repertoire of imaginative and colourful meatless dishes.

Many people do not understand the difference between vegetarians and vegans. While vegetarians will eat eggs and milk-derived products, and some will even eat fish, vegans will have nothing to do with any food product derived from animal exploitation: no dairy products, no eggs, and definitely no fish.

Fruit and vegetables, pulses and nuts, and cereals of one sort or another are all suitable for vegans to eat but it's worth including one or two vegan-friendly dishes on your menu as more strict vegetarians can order them as well.

Some other tips useful in catering for vegetarians and vegans are:

Catering

A PINT OF MUSSELS, PLEASE!

Eating out is an important social occasion for many people. The good news for you, the publican, is that Pubs, Bars and Steakhouses are the leading sector in terms of the number of meals consumed out of home.

Putting FISH on the menu means greater opportunities for business development as fish has enjoyed a 12% growth in the last year.

QUALITY

Today's customers are very discerning and are demanding better quality foods. With this in mind the Sea Fish Industry Authority operates internationally recognised *Quality Award Schemes*.

The principal aim of the Quality Award Scheme is to provide buyers with the assurance that their suppliers have passed a very thorough, independent inspection.

CONVENIENCE

FISH is a food that is simple, convenient and nutritious. It is delicious, widely available, very easy to prepare and the fastest of all foods to cook. Fish and shellfish offer you, the publican, an unrivalled choice of flavour, texture and appearance and with at least sixty species available in the UK, the possibilities for producing delicious meals are endless.

Look out for the less familiar species of fish which are often less expensive yet command the same price per menu item as the more familiar species.

COOKING

Cooking is easy, requiring only the utensils and equipment normally found in a traditional kitchen. With the latest combination ovens, fish dishes such as seafood pie or lasagne can be cooked very quickly preserving the "home made" image.

Few other foods offer such a range of products. For establishments where time is at a premium or where staff skills are limited then there is everything from the simplest fish finger, through to the many top class convenience lines to the most elaborate of gourmet presentations. The choice is yours to fit your business.

OPPORTUNITIES

Putting fish on the menu will increase the business opportunities open to you but *you* have to convince your customers that your menu is better than the menu being offered by the establishment next door! Don't let them "mussel" in on your act!

Be enthusiastic about your fish menu. The "Dish of the Day" should stand out on the menu. This is often seen by the customer as being "good value for money" and should be just that!

It is important to cultivate customers and do whatever is necessary to retain them and encourage them to spend more money and/or return more often.

Children are strong prompters to parents in terms of visiting an establishment and in the type of meal eaten. Make certain that the menu includes popular children's dishes. Remember too, that children are increasingly sophisticated in their choice of food.

PROFIT

Profits can be increased by directing your sales to more profitable items, eg mussels. These are a very inexpensive item but their *perceived* value is high and may be served at any time of the year. A simple Moules Mariniere served with granary bread makes a very satisfying yet inexpensive meal to produce or make mussels a feature of your menu by serving them in a pint mug – this will certainly generate interest!

Smoked Mackerel and Apple Salad makes a light and refreshing change from the traditional paté as a starter or quick snack.

Fisherman's Chowder using a combination of white and smoked fish makes a very warm, nourishing meal, perfect for those winter lunch times.

Paté, Fish and Salad have witnessed the highest growth rates in the last 12 months; it is in this area that profits can be made.

Fish starters are relatively popular in pubs and hotels and account for in excess of 20% of all starters. Starters offer an ideal opportunity for sampling different fish for customers who are prepared to experiment.

The majority of pubs today have a bar menu. The potential for providing unusual fillings is immense as is the potential for profit. There are a variety of seafood fillings on the market. Try to prepare sandwiches fresh for each customer as nothing is more off putting than a dry curled up sandwich sitting on the bar. Today's customers eat with their eyes as well as their mouths so presentation is very important.

PROMOTIONS

Organise Seafood Evenings but make sure you advertise them! Many suppliers will assist in offering discounted product or promotional material to help with a themed promotion.

Boost your liquid profits by suggesting suitable drinks to accompany particular dishes. If you provide the drinks while your customers are studying the menu they will almost certainly need to have a top up before the meal is served.

Cheers!

Fish and Bean Bake

Metric		Imperial
1.25kg	cod or haddock fillets, fresh or defrosted, skinned and cubed	2lb 12 oz
2 x 15ml spoon	sunflower oil	2 tablespoons
2	large onions, sliced	2
2 x 420g	can baked beans	
	salt and pepper	
4	large baking potatoes, sliced and partboiled	4
60g	butter, melted	2oz
2 x 15ml spoon	wholegrain mustard	2 tablespoons

Preheat the oven to 190°C/375°F, Gas Mark 5

1. Heat the oil in a pan, add the onion and cook for 2 - 3 minutes. Place in a large casserole dish.
2. Add the beans, fish and season. Arrange the potato slices on top, brush with the butter and mustard.
3. Bake for 25 - 30 minutes.

Serves 10

NUTRITIONAL VALUES PER PORTION (APPROX) 294 Kilocalories; 29g Protein; 10g Fat; 24g Carbohydrate; 4g Fibre

Savoury Prawn Croissant

Metric		Imperial
455g	cooked peeled prawns, fresh or defrosted	1lb
340g	cottage cheese	12oz
2	avocados	2
	salt and pepper	
10	croissants	10

1. Mix together the prawns, cheese, avocados and seasoning. Refrigerate.
2. Cut the croissants in half. Use 2 x 10ml spoon (2 dessertspoons) of the prawn mixture to fill the croissant when required.
3. Serve with a side salad or on its own as a snack.

Serves 10

NUTRITIONAL VALUES PER PORTION (APPROX) 349 Kilocalories; 21g Protein; 20g Fat; 24g Carbohydrate; 2g Fibre

Fish and Tomato Gratin

Metric		Imperial
900g	haddock or whiting fillets, fresh or defrosted, skinned and cubed	2lb
8	tomatoes, sliced	8
4	cloves garlic, crushed	4
2 x 15ml spoon	fresh chopped parsley	2 tablespoons
	salt and pepper	
115g	Cheddar cheese, grated	4oz

Preheat the oven to 190°C/375°F, Gas Mark 5

1. Lay the fish in a greased ovenproof dish. Add the tomatoes, garlic, parsley and seasoning.
2. Sprinkle over the cheese and bake for 15 - 20 minutes before serving with a mixed salad or jacket potatoes.

Serves 10

NUTRITIONAL VALUES PER PORTION (APPROX) 134 Kilocalories; 21g Protein; 5g Fat; 2g Carbohydrate; 1g Fibre

Catering

LEMONY FISH FILLETS

Metric		Imperial
10 x 150g	plaice or lemon sole fillets, fresh or defrosted, skinned	10 x 5 1/4 oz
2	green peppers, deseeded and thinly sliced	2
2 x 15ml spoon	dry white wine	2 table spoons
5	tomatoes, chopped	5
3	lemon, rind and juice	3
	salt and pepper	
2 x 15ml spoon	fresh chopped parsley	2 tablespoons

Microwave Power: 800 Watt

To cook one portion:

1. Place 25g (3/4oz) peppers plus 1 x 15ml spoon (1 tablespoon) wine in a suitable container, Cover and cook on HIGH for 45 seconds.
2. Add half a chopped tomato to the dish, fold over a fish fillet and place on top of pepper and tomato mixture. Sprinkle with 1 x 15ml (1 tablespoon) lemon juice.
3. Cover and cook on HIGH for 2 minutes. Allow to stand 1 minute, season.
4. Garnish with parsley and lemon rind and serve with pasta or potatoes.

Serves 10

NUTRITIONAL VALUES PER PORTION (APPROX) 134 Kilocalories; 26g Protein; 2g Fat; 2g Carbohydrate; 1g Fibre

---

Active Solution Limited

• *Consultancy* • *Catering Equipment* • *Refrigeration* • *Shopfitting* •
And much more . . .
THE BALL'S IN YOUR C●URT!

ACTIVE SOLUTION is a Welsh-based company, able to offer its clients a wide range of services. Based near to the M4 for ease of access to motorways and main thoroughfares of Britain.

Active Solution and its associate companies can offer a range of custom-made stainless steel tables, extraction canopies and bespoke items; furniture and fixed seating is also available. A full and varied product range of catering and ancillary equipment, together with refrigeration, decor, soft furnishings and a wide range of floor covering.

Active Solution Ltd will be pleased to assist you in any of the above fields.
Unit 5 Glan Llwyd, Tyn-Y-Bonau Industrial Estate, Pontardulais, West Glamorgan SA4 1SG
Tel: (01792) 884500; Fax: (01792) 884700

What's fresh, live and very low fat?
NATURAL YOGURT
from DAIRY FARM PRODUCTS

Thick & Creamy Recipe now available
Tel: 01203 667162
For your local stockist

Manufacturers and Distributors of Live Natural Set Yogurt
Dairy Farm Products
7 Hales Industrial Park, Coventry CV6 6AN
Tel: 01203 667162 Fax: 01203 666287
(Also available in 5kg and 10kg containers for caterers)

- Don't serve a vegetarian crumble or other main dish made from the same vegetables you're serving on the side.
- An excellent meat substitute is Quorn, derived from mushrooms. But beware: vegans won't eat it because it is bound with egg; and some vegetarians may take offence if offered meatless products that resemble steak, a chop or mince.
- Vegetarian portions should be larger than equivalent meat dishes in order to yield the same nutritional value.

SUNDAY

With the gradual relaxation of licensing law, Sunday lunches have become the ultimate earner - and they're easy to do. But there are a few things to remember.

Roast the meat off the day before. I know there's nothing better than freshly roasted meat, but to maximise portions the meat needs to be cold before you carve it. Of course, you could always set the alarm for 5am so you can roast the meat on the day and still leave time for it to cool down to carving temperature - but I think not.

With a little planning and organisation it is possible to be completely prepared for Sunday lunch - with the soup simmering on the stove alongside the gravy, the cold starter and cold sweet in the refrigerator, the meat cooked and carved ready for service, the roast potatoes in the oven next to the hot pudding, and all the vegetables cooked in readiness so they only need to be re-heated in the microwave - by the time you open the doors at noon.

If your kitchen is always rushed on Sundays, it can be a tough decision whether or not to break the mould and serve the usual weekday sandwiches as well as the roast. When in doubt, fall back on the philosophy that whatever the customer wants you should give them. With planning and organisation there should be no problem serving sandwiches on a Sunday - and there is as much money to be made from a selection of sandwiches as there is from more substantial meals. If you still feel you have to discourage people from ordering sandwiches during the busy Sunday lunchtime session, don't just take them off the menu, try increasing the price instead.

FREE NIBBLES

If you've decided to put free nibbles on the bar, there's one golden rule to follow: disregard the cost.

Treating your customers will soon backfire if you appear mean. But if it is done well the returns can be highly satisfactory. A happy customer is the best possible messenger for your pub, far better than any advert on the radio, in the newspaper, or even on TV.

BARBECUES

Pub barbecues are a growth area and are an excellent way to increase profits: as well as a full restaurant, you can have a whole garden packed with diners.

This is especially true if your pub has lovely gardens or a picturesque

AUTHENTIC INDIAN CUISINE · Ruby · RUBY KING

The same taste - in your place!

Erroll E. Thomas, Director

Millions of pub goers visit Indian restaurants every week to enjoy **Authentic Indian Food.**

They do this because even though they may try Indian cooking at home, whether from a recipe book or with a sauce from a jar **Authentic Indian Food** is difficult to replicate.

Ruby King's Production chef has 22 years experience preparing **Authentic Indian Cuisine** from traditional Indian recipes, handed down through generations.

Ruby King has teamed up with pub caterers to put genuine Indian food in mainstream pubs.

The **Ruby King** menu has been recognised by pub goers throughout the country and is becoming a huge success; here are two ways to gain a portion of this profitable market:

- Add to your main menu a dish or two from our product list of 22 authentic dishes
- Offer the recognised **Ruby King ten item menu**, which caters for vegetarians as well as those who eat meat.

The **Ruby King** product can drive your gross return percentages to over 70% of sales and could prove to be your most profitable menu item.

We supply all our customers with **FREE** colourful merchandising and point-of-sale material; to generate impulse sales and create awareness and appetite building so increasing retail spend averages.

Those of you who offer the **Ruby King** ten item menu benefit from a national campaign, promoting your pub and the **Ruby King** menu to millions of pub goers.

clockwise from bottom: multi-use point-of-sale, poster and menu

My promise to you - **Ruby King** will continue to build product awareness to pub goers nationally, creating a reputation for high quality and good value, wherever you see the name **Ruby King.**

For a **FREE SAMPLE** and more details call:
01737 218517

… Ruby King at the Harvest Home…

Eileen & Roger at the Harvest Home

The Harvest Home is a friendly and traditional *Inn Business* pub sited in Beddington Lane, Croydon, Surrey.

The Landlord and Landlady, Roger and Eileen, make sure that there is always a good range of cask conditioned ales available - these are constantly changed to provide an interesting variety, but regular beers such as Bass and Ruddles are always on offer.

When it comes to pub food at the Harvest Home, Eileen and Roger are insistent on the best produce and ingredients when preparing their menu of traditional home cooked meals. Eileen recognised the need to include some ethnic dishes into their range, and was soon preparing her own curries.

Though the results were excellent, the process in creating authentic Indian cuisine was time consuming - inconvenient for the Landlady of a popular and busy pub. Eileen knew that if she were to trust someone else to prepare good quality, genuine Indian dishes for her, then they would have to be using absolutely fresh ingredients and traditional methods. That's when the Harvest Home put **Ruby King** on the menu.

We asked Eileen and Roger to tell us how **Ruby King** has helped them, and what their customers think.

Roger explained that **Ruby King** curries keep people in his pub longer because they "don't need to wander up the road to the local take-away"- and of course you always need a beer to compliment a curry...

Eileen said "People love it", and Roger commented that even *he* loves **Ruby King** even though he describes himself as "a steak and chips man".

Roger and Eileen found the point-of-sale cards and posters very helpful in promoting the product within their pub. This material makes an attractive display and compliments the other menu boards which display the pub's full range of meals.

If you, like Eileen and Roger, would like to offer high quality, freshly prepared Indian Cuisine, try ***Ruby King Authentic Indian Cuisine***. Your customers will toast your decision - you will have saved them the walk to the local Indian restaurant!

For a free sample and more details call
01737 218517

What is the pub goers dream?

A traditional English pub serving a good range of Ales, Premium Lagers, great atmosphere and next door to a great Indian restaurant, linked by adjoining doors.

Erroll Thomas, Director of **Ruby King Authentic Indian Cuisine,** is the son of publican parents.

His father pulls the pints and his mother does the catering. Thomas's mother spent many years competing in her kitchen with the best Indian restaurants, but found that to produce a top quality Indian curry takes hours. First, off to the market to select the the finest vegetables, meat or poultry. Secondly, locating the spices needed to produce an authentic curry.

Thirdly, having found the spices, you need to roast them to release those delicious aromatic fragrances. Then you must grind your spices once cool. Next you need to produce your own ghee. Now you are ready to prepare your ingredients for an authentic Indian curry.

After Thomas spent years in the kitchen assisting his mother with selecting, roasting and grinding spices, they still got 'pipped to the post' by local Indian restaurants.

Erroll Thomas decided that enough was enough. He head-hunted an Asian chef who has now been producing authentic Indian food for 22 years, together they developed the **Ruby King** concept; 'Authentic Indian food in the pub'.

They produce authentic products such as Lamb Rogan Josh, Chicken Tikka Massala, Chicken Madras, Tandoori Chicken, Lentil (Dhal) Curry, individually portioned, made to order and delivered chilled to pubs all around the country.

Ruby King cuisine has been independently judged on many occasions and has proven to be every bit as good as the best Indian restaurants.

Ruby King have many publican customers who they cook for each week, providing their publicans with authentic Indian products. These pubs can now provide high quality ethnic food to their customers without the investment of extra time spent in the kitchen and the market. These publicans know exactly how much each meal cost, so they can mark up their menu with the desired gross profit.

One such customer is the Harvest Home in Beddington Lane, Croydon, they have been enjoying the advantages of **Ruby King Authentic Indian Cuisine.** Eileen used to spend hours producing her own curries, now she invests time in more leisurely pursuits and they also enjoy a high gross profit from their **Ruby King** products.

Why is the **Ruby King** concept such a success? Erroll Thomas is fastidious in everything he does and is an extreme perfectionist. Starting with the produce that **Ruby King** selects; it has to be of the highest quality. The **Ruby King** food production team use traditional methods to achieve that authentic taste, consistently every time.

Ruby King is aware that no product walks off the shelf, so its marketing team, headed by Carol Brown is investing huge sums of money into a national campaign, aimed at pub goers, to familiarise them with the **Ruby King** name, authentic taste and great value.

After working in the licence trade and being involved in the catering industry for 11 years, Thomas knew what he wanted from a product.

"I wanted to produce food that was every bit as good as the best restaurants and at the same time save the licenced caterer time in the kitchen. I also thought that the product should come with its own menus, merchandising and point of sale material, too much time can be spent changing and preparing menus. When running a pub, your hours are long enough."

AMOY

PUB GRUB GOES EAST

The pub-goers ever-increasing demand for a diverse range of authentic ethnic food means that publicans must constantly be on the look-out for innovative and original serving suggestions that also offer them good margins.

Satisfaction Guaranteed

To satisfy both demands, try out Amoy's Frozen Dim Sum, a selection of exquisite pastry parcels containing a variety of fillings that will delight customers with their true authentic taste, and publicans with their excellent margin for profit.

A Taste of China

Amoy's Frozen Dim Sum is made in Hong Kong and China where for centuries thay have played an important role in traditional Oriental cuisine. The delicate shapes and textures of Amoy Frozen Dim Sum make them the perfect starter, light bar meal or buffet treat. They taste delicious hot or cold, and provide a mouthwatering centrepiece whether on a bar or table.

The range includes: **Wontons-** crispy flower-shaped Chinese pastry filled with prawn and Chinese vegetables or **Sichuan Wontons-** hot and crispy flower-shaped Chinese parcels filled with delicious chicken and Oriental Vegetables; **Shaomai-** delicate pastry dumplings filled with prawn, squid and Chinese Vegetables or **Ginger Shaomai-** with chicken and vegetables; **Sweet & Sour Potstickers-** crisp pastry parcels filled with tender chicken and vegetables; **Cocktail Spring Rolls-** Chinese vegetables hand wrapped in delicate pastry and **Five Spice Cocktail Spring Rolls-** which combine succulent pieces of chicken and vegetables with traditional five spice seasoning; **Samosas-** crisp triangles of pastry filled with a spicy prawn and Chinese Vegetable mixture.

Profit from Originality

So this summer, go for something truly original, give your customers a treat and make a good profit too! At only 21pence per piece, a three-piece portion costs only 63 pence. This gives publicans an excellent margin when included on the menu at £2.99 or more. Amoy's Food Service marketing manager, Arvind Devalia comments, "The beauty of frozen dim sum lies in the fact that once heated they retain their crisp texture and delicious taste. That's because they are prepared fresh in the country of origin and immediately flash frozen to seal in all the exotic flavours."

"We're confident that publicans and catering managers will love a product that can be prepared so quickly yet tastes so authentic", he continues.

Dip into Dim Sum

And finally, where there is dim sum there must be dipping sauce. Amoy has created a special dipping sauce recipe to perfectly compliment your dim sum menu ideas this summer.
For about 12 servings or approxiamately 400ml take:

1 x 150ml bottle of Amoy Light or Dark Soy Sauce
(light soy makes a lighter recipe; dark makes a richer flavour)
3 tbs Amoy Chili Sauce   3 tbs Amoy Sesame Oil
3 tbs tomato ketchup   3 tbs dry sherry

Simply put all the ingredients into a jar with a lid and shake vigorously. Serve in little dishes or ramekins, garnished with a few shreds of spring onion, fresh root ginger or sesame oil.
The sauce will keep for about four weeks if kept regfrigerated.

HP FOODSERVICE

Available from HP FOODSERVICE
on 0990 326 663

A Taste of the Orient

With eating out on the increase, it is important for publicans to make the most of the expanding opportunities. Pubs have their own unique environment which means that it is possible to cater for a range of customers whether for a complete meal or just a snack. The key to success is to offer an interesting range of quality food and to make the most of key times throughout the year.

Amoy offers a range of frozen Dim Sum - in Vegetable; Vegetable and Prawn; and Chicken varieties - which are a versatile option for any occasion. The Dim Sum are made in Hong Kong and China where for centuries they have played an important part in traditional Oriental cuisine. Each selection contains a variety of pastry shapes which can be served hot - simply deep fry in three or four minutes - or cold for a traditional taste with a difference.

At only 21 pence per piece, a three piece portion costs only 63 pence which provides an excel-

Amoy's Frozen Dim Sum are the convenient way to provide authentic eastern flavour

lent margin when included on the menu at £2.99 or more. There are a range of occasions when Dim Sum will go down a treat.

SUMMER LOVING

Literally meaning 'delicacies to touch the heart' Dim Sum are the perfect addition to any summer buffet or barbecue. Serve them with a selection of Amoy's dipping sauces - available in 6 x 1950g packs, Oyster Sauce, Sweet & Sour Sauce 12 x 383g packs and Amoy's Dipping Sauce 12 x 150 ml packs, will enhance any Summer feast.

BRING ON THE BAR SNACKS

Amoy Dim Sum is the quick and convenient option for a tempting snack with a difference. With a vegetarian variety too, there is something for everyone and an excellent chance to capitalise on the growth of Oriental cuisine.

EASTERN ENTREE

Dim Sum are the perfect starter for any meal occasion. The range ensures that all tastes are catered for, so why not offer one of the three varieties which are guaranteed to liven up any meal. For a starter with a difference why not serve Amoy

Chicken Dim Sum as an unusual entree in a steaming pot of chicken broth.

DIM SUM DINNERS

Dim Sum make an excellent light meal. Try serving with a salad and dipping sauces to offer a light meal alternative.

ORIENTAL NIGHTS

Theme nights are a popular and fun way to draw in the crowds. Starting in February and traditionally lasting 15 days, Chinese New Year is the perfect opportunity to party in style.

With increased competition in the high street and customers becoming more choosy it is vital for publicans to offer something different and theming the pub for a night of food and entertainment is a great way to get the edge on the competition.

You don't have to wait for Chinese New Year as Chinese food is popular all year round, so why not have a Chinese Night with all the decorations and trimmings. In addition to Dim Sum, Amoy has a secret in store for anyone who opens one of its Fortune Cookies, now available to caterers in 2kg packs. Each Amoy Fortune Cookie hides a traditional Chinese prediction inside and can be served for fun at a Chinese theme party.

If you're keen to build up the food side of the business, the forecasts are good, as eating out is predicted to rise by around 40% in the next five years. Ethnic foods are increasingly popular, with Chinese being one of the most popular and easy to prepare, so it makes sense to include some eastern fare on your menu.

It pays to opt for a brand that you can trust, for authenticity and premium quality, to ensure that you are giving your customers the very best.

If you would like more information or advice contact HP Foodservice on 0990 326663.

location – for instance on a riverbank or lakeside, or beside a canal.

Generally, barbecues do not detract from the ordinary restaurant trade: indeed, they can be a great boost to overall customer numbers.

Barbecue customers seek the relaxed atmosphere of eating 'al fresco', rather than the more formal restaurant experience, and while they may not be prepared to stand the expense of treating the whole family to a restaurant meal, they could well be happy to part with less money and have a family barbecue.

But organising a barbecue involves more than just cooking out of doors. First, you should assess your garden thoroughly, asking yourself some hard questions:

- Is your garden attractive enough?
- Is your garden big enough?
- Where will the barbecue stand?
- Do you have enough tables and chairs?
- Where will you store the food for the barbecue?
- Do you have adequate chill/cool facilities?
- How will you arrange the servery?
- How will people actually pay for their food – cash at point of sale or pre-paid ticket?
- What fire precautions or first aid do you need?

Next, buy the right barbecue. If you're not building one yourself (and if you are, build it bigger than you think you need), don't go for the cheapest type on the market: they don't necessarily last very long and will need replacing regularly. Go for something robust which will see you through the barbecue season and beyond without falling apart. In fact buy two: one for cooking on, and the other for keeping the food warm once it is cooked. Gas-fired barbecues are ideal as they heat up far more quickly than all-charcoal models.

Finally, you might also teach yourself how to cook properly on a barbecue and maybe have a practice run before trying it out on the customers. A hungry and expectant crowd doesn't want to wait while the barbecue slowly heats up; nor do you want to find that the barbecue simply isn't big enough and a backlog of orders is building up.

And the last thing you want is to find yourself panicking and serving insufficiently cooked food – which at best will be brought back by your distinctly unimpressed customers and at worst will poison them. A good tip is to part-cook some of the food in the main kitchen and then transfer it to the barbecue for finishing off.

If you are holding a special barbecue event and anticipate more customers than your equipment can cope with you might consider hiring specialist equipment for the occasion. There are also quite a few companies offering the right equipment and advice for special occasions such as ox or pig roasts.

One final tip: always use disposable crockery and cutlery as the good stuff has a tendency to vanish outdoors.

Cooking for the public is unquestionably a different ball game from cooking for family or friends, but they share the same basic philosophy – whoever you cook for, you are undoubtedly out to impress.

My personal outlook is: You are what you put on a plate. If it looks good, then you look good. If it's rubbish ...!

Health and Safety Notes

Requirements relating to hygiene are contained mainly in the **Food Safety (General Food Hygiene) Regulations** 1995. These are concerned with the conditions of the premises, the practices employed, and the personnel involved. As far as practices are concerned, the general regulations are supplemented by the Food Safety (Temperature Control) Regulations 1995.

Guidance on all aspects of the regulations is available from environmental health at your local council. There is also a book, the *Industry Guide to Good Hygiene Practices: Catering Guide* published by HMSO (ISBN 0113218990) giving guidance on complying with all aspects of the regulations. In enforcing the legislation, environmental health officers (EHOs) will have regard to that guidance.

THE PREMISES

As far as the premises are concerned there are general requirements, which include:

- cleanliness and good repair;
- layout, design, construction and size;
- the provision of suitably located hand basins;
- adequate lighting and ventilation;
- appropriate drainage;
- the availability of toilets;
- the provision of changing facilities for staff where necessary.

The Local Government (**Miscellaneous Provisions**) Act 1976 gives local authorities powers in relation to the provision of public toilet facilities at places of refreshment.

There is no specific requirement for staff to have separate facilities but this is preferable, especially for food handlers. Food hygiene legislation requires that toilets must be connected to an effective drainage system, must not open directly into rooms where food is handled, and must be provided with materials for cleaning and drying hands.

British Standard 6465: Part 1: 1995 provides guidance on the appropriate level of toilet provision. If alterations are made which increase the customer capacity, or if complaints are made regarding the adequacy of the facilities provided, or if an entertainment licence is applied for, then regard may be had to this standard.

If alterations are being made it would be advisable to discuss disabled WC provision with the building control officer at your local council.

Catering

When planning any changes it is useful to consult your local environmental health officer to enable relevant food hygiene and health and safety issues to be discussed and accommodated.

In areas where **food preparation or cooking** takes place, there are additional, more specific requirements regarding the nature of surfaces to be used (to enable effective cleaning), the provision of appropriate facilities for washing equipment and food, and the provision of fly screening to openable windows where necessary.

Despite rumours about what is or is not permitted, the regulations do not specify particular products. There is not, for example, a requirement to use stainless steel: it just happens to be a suitable and durable product. There are, inevitably, different ways of complying with the legislation depending on the budget available and the hygiene standard appropriate for the use. If you have any doubts about whether your pub complies, especially if the kitchen has not previously been used for trade or if you intend to expand the food side, you can get advice from the EHO.

Obvious though it may seem, if you are making changes because you believe the law requires it of you, it's worth checking that this is so – many don't, and end up doing unnecessary work, or doing necessary work wrongly. Similarly, if you are making changes because you want to, it may be advisable to check beforehand that when you've finished, the alterations will comply. In either event, doing so may save time and money.

THE PRACTICES

As far as practices are concerned, the fundamental requirement in the legislation is the need for a formal assessment in which potential food safety hazards are identified and methods of controlling them are specified.

Hazards include contamination by micro-organisms (in particular food-poisoning bacteria) or chemical or physical contaminants. Chemical contamination (eg the contamination of beer with line cleaner) is readily avoidable by the appropriate use and storage of cleaning products. **Physical contamination** (ie contamination by flakes of paint, insects and insect remnants and all other 'foreign bodies') can be avoided by good housekeeping and protection of food.

The biggest issue is avoiding the opportunity for food-poisoning bacteria to be introduced into food, to survive in food, and/or to multiply in food. If you are new to the food business and are not familiar with the conditions that food-poisoning bacteria thrive on and the practices that control them, training courses in basic food hygiene are widely available.

To assess the food safety hazards you need to consider all stages, from the purchase of supplies to the serving of the food. At each stage there are things that can go wrong and ways of preventing them from doing so.

There are a number of points at which controls are essential to prevent food safety hazards arising: for example, thorough cooking, correct handling and storage after cooking, thorough re-heating, and the prevention of cross-contamination. It is these controls that you need to monitor by, for example, carrying out **temperature checks**.

If you have barbecues these need to be included in your consideration of food safety hazards with particular reference to the potential for under-cooking of meat and for cross-contamination. It may be advisable to cook the food in the kitchen first to ensure that it is cooked through thoroughly and then, without delay, finish the dishes on the barbecue to give them the desired flavour. However you tackle it, barbecuing is a form of cooking which requires particular care.

The requirement for a proper assessment did not exist in previous hygiene legislation. In addition to the advice in the *Industry Guide*, general guidance on how to make sure you have complied with this requirement is available from your local EHO, as is information on 'Assured Safe Catering', one way of approaching the task. Another approach is SAFE (the Systematic Assessment of Food Environment), available from the British Hospitality Association (0171 404 7744).

Temperature control legislation has already been referred to in relation to the bar and the display of food. The regulations generally require that food which might otherwise give rise to a health risk must be kept at appropriate temperatures. For the most part, this means refrigerated at 8°C or below or kept hot at 63°C or above. Certain exemptions for one-off display have been mentioned. In addition, food which is cooked and then chilled awaiting use must be cooled as quickly as possible following the final heat processing stage. Quick cooling (eg through spreading food out, dividing into portions etc) is good practice in any event, in order to avoid risks from those bacteria that can survive cooking and subsequently cause illness if food is left at room temperature for too long. As a guide, it is advisable to cool food within 90 minutes. There are also requirements relating to the condition of raw materials/ingredients accepted by the business, the protection of food from contamination, and arrangements for refuse.

PEOPLE

There is a requirement for all food handlers to maintain a high degree of personal cleanliness, and to wear appropriate, clean clothing.

In addition, no person who has a condition (or is a carrier of a disease) that could put food at risk may work in any food handling area in any way which might contaminate the food with harmful micro-organisms. Anyone who thinks, or knows that they have, this type of infection must report it to the proprietor. The EHO can advise on what action to take if this situation arises.

Catering

Finally, anyone working in the food business must be supervised and instructed and/or trained in food hygiene to a level appropriate to the work they do. The nature of the supervision, instruction or training is not specified, but those involved in catering activities need to have a level of awareness which matches the risk involved with the food they handle. Many local authorities and colleges run short courses which provide an understanding of food hygiene issues and good practice.

THE FOOD SAFETY ACT 1990

It is this Act that provides local authority EHOs with the powers that they need to take action when necessary. It is also this Act which specifies the standards that food for sale is expected to meet. It is also this Act which, for some offences, provides a defence in law (a recognised excuse) if it can be established by a food business that all reasonable steps have been taken to prevent the offence occurring, and due diligence has been shown.

It is seriously worth considering whether, if someone did fall ill after a meal at your pub, you could be really confident that thanks to the procedures you have in place you could rely on this defence. There are various practices which are not specifically required by law, but which do help to show that due diligence is being shown and that the food safety risks identified are being monitored, eg the daily recording of refrigerator temperatures and/or the date marking of food cooked on site to assist with stock control.

HEALTH AND SAFETY RISKS

Particular risks may be posed by items of catering equipment such as slicing machines. Here, the provision and use of appropriate guards and the training of those who use and clean machines is essential. A safe system of work for both using and cleaning machinery is also important.

If you have staff under the age of 18, they may not clean machinery where in doing so they are exposed to risk. Also, the positioning of dangerous equipment needs to be considered to ensure that users are not likely to be distracted or knocked by others working nearby.

Other safety issues include the safety of gas and electrical appliances and the type and condition of the floor to avoid slips and trips. If a dumb waiter is provided, the testing requirements referred to for cellar lifts/hoists apply.

Finally, COSHH discussed in relation to beer-line cleaner and carbon dioxide applies equally to hazardous substances cleaning chemicals such as oven-cleaner.

NUISANCE

Nuisance complaints relating to food businesses usually relate to noise, smells or refuse. **Noise** is usually associated with music and/or the noise of customers (eg using beer gardens), although occasionally

The Publican's Handbook

IMPROVING YOUR SNACK SALES

In 1996, the UK spent £2.1 billion on snacks, with £177 million retailing through pubs. Over two thirds of the UK population will eat crisps, snacks or nuts in any four week period. Snacks are big business, they add to customer enjoyment and offer a huge opportunity to generate additional profit from the bar. Based on average sales, a pub can expect between £4-6,000 of turnover a year to be attributed to snacks – and that's just the start. Much higher turnover can be achieved by selling snacks more positively and by focusing on merchandising.

Why people snack in pubs

Independent research shows that snacks are seen as a treat. In pubs, people will eat snacks for a multitude of reasons including indulgence, habit, hunger, as a complement to food, fun for kids, and to soak up alcohol. It is important to recognise that snacks do not take away from prepared food sales – in fact they are often purchased in addition, for example with sandwiches, salads, dips and as pre-meal nibbles.

Stock the right product

In considering what products to stock, KP McVitie's, the No. 1 snacks supplier to the managed pub trade, urges licensees to carefully analyse their customers and what will appeal to them. KP McVitie's has a wide portfolio of brands but recommends a focused approach as illustrated by the table below.

Have the right displays

Snacks are an impulse purchase. By stocking the right product in the right place, pubs can achieve greater sales. Test results show that snacks sales can be increased by up to 18% if merchandised properly. For example, in an average pub, a KP McVitie's counter unit can mean an increase of nearly £1,000 per year in extra sales!

By following these simple guidelines KP McVitie's will guarantee increased sales.

1. Site snacks in "hot spots" such as next to the till, and in places visible from all sides of the bar.
2. Maximise space available by having a few packs from the full range in sight of all customers. Keep extra product in cases underneath the bar to enable supplies to be quickly refilled.
3. Strategically place snacks in each bar. Use wicker baskets, clip strips, carded nuts and branded counter display units – they are easy to display and eye-catching to customers.
4. Make use of promotional point of sale material and menu/chalk boards to communicate what is on sale. Promotions can increase turnover by highlighting snacks on offer in a bar. Think about conducting special promotions such as:
- Big value kid's offer – free packet of Skips or Hula Hoops with a soft drink
- A Meal Deal – free bag of McCoy's with a sandwich
- Low cost give-aways as competition prizes

5. Train staff so they are familiar with the pub's snack range and suggest they offer a snack with a round of drinks. In this way, snacks can become an extra item sold to every drinks customer.

In summary, Snacks are complementary to the pub experience and add interest to a customer's visit. By offering high quality products, you can generate significant additional revenue by converting drinks only purchases to drinks and snack sales.

BRANDS BY PUB TYPE

PUB TYPE	Premium Crisps: McCoy's, Brannigans	KP Nuts	KP Speciality Nuts: Cashews & Pistachios	Mini Cheddars	Phileas Fogg	Hula Hoops & Skips
Destination	✓	✓		✓		
Community	✓	✓		✓		
Town & City	✓	✓	✓	✓	✓	
Young Persons	✓	✓	✓	✓	✓	
Family/Food	✓	✓	✓	✓	✓	✓

Catering

Look Familiar?

That's just what your customers think!

Customer support telephone: 0151-220 4661

KP McVITIE'S

the noise of an extractor system may become an issue. Complaints about **refuse** are usually easy to avoid by ensuring adequate bin provision and emptying arrangements. **Cooking odours** are occasionally the subject of complaint, the likelihood, of course, depends on the type of cooking undertaken and the position of the extractor in relation to other premises. When carrying out any alterations, such as the provision of a new extractor system (for which planning permission may be needed), it may be worth considering the potential for nuisance and, where it seems likely, pre-empting this in terms of the type of system installed.

If complaints are made and the local authority are satisfied that a statutory nuisance exists, a notice requiring the abatement of the nuisance within a specified time can be served. Non-compliance may lead to prosecution in the magistrates court. It is a defence to show that the 'best practicable means' are being employed to avoid or counteract the effects of a nuisance. In attempting to establish this, the technical and financial implications can, along with other factors, be taken into consideration. A right of appeal against a notice exists. (For more on nuisance see Chapter 5 Publicising your Pub.)

GENERAL

Finally, all food businesses are required to be registered with the local authority under the **Food Premises (Registrations) Regulations 1991**. If you are not certain if you are registered, the EHO will advise and provide you with a form if necessary. There is no fee involved.

Registration with the local authority of premises used for food business is required by law. The local authority should be informed if:

◆ a food business is run for five or more days in any five consecutive weeks;
◆ a new food business is to be started (then 28 days' notice must be given);
◆ vehicles are used in connection with the business;
◆ there is a change of proprietor or if the business changes.

It is important to ensure that best practice is exercised in relation to food handling; that you are aware of current legislative requirements for food safety, hygiene, composition and quality; and that you take adequate steps to inform and train staff and carry out regular refresher courses.

Catering

Legal Notes

SUPPER HOUR CERTIFICATES

The usual permitted hours for licensed premises cease at 11pm weekdays and 10.30pm on Sunday, Good Friday and Christmas Day, with a 20-minute drinking-up time. However, in a restaurant or an area of a public house set aside for dining, it is possible to extend the terminal hour by one additional hour, subject to the sale or supply of alcohol being ancillary to a meal.

A Supper Hour Certificate is obtained by application to the Licensing Justices at any Transfer Sessions upon no less than seven days' notice. The fee is £10. The court will usually require a plan of your premises and the detailing of the area to which the certificate is to apply. Once granted, there is a requirement that you display a notice in the part of the premises explaining the effect of the certificate.

Where a Supper Hour Certificate applies there is a 30-minute drinking-up period. No new drinks can be supplied during the drinking-up period.

Abbots Coffee Co.

Have some of the finest blends of ground coffees available.

For use with

Espresso - Filter Machines

Bulk Brewers and Cafetieres

£71 + VAT per month buys a

UNIC DIVA - Automatic 2 Group Cappuccino Machine

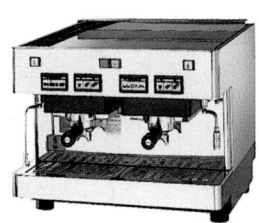

Call now on 01707 647390

Abbots Coffee Co., 2 Earls Lane, South Mimms, Herts EN6 3LT

The coffees we supply are prepared from the finest berries roasted-blended and packed to give a consistent quality and flavour.

We are independent suppliers of ground coffees for use with filter machines, Espresso/cappuccino machines, Bulk Brewers and Cafetieres plus a wide range of support beverage products i.e sugar portions, teas and drinking chocolate. Also an interesting selection of after dinner confectionery. We can also supply "own label" after dinner mints. Filter machines can be supplied on "Free-Loan" with no long term contracts and are maintained free of charge.

If you are looking for beverage equipment to purchase or lease we act as agents for "UNIC" Espresso/Cappuccino Machines and can also supply water boilers/Cafetieres, coffee perculators from the best manufacturers on the market.

If you are interested in our service and require further information please call the above number to arrange an appointment to discuss your requirements.

CHAPTER NINE

STOCK AND FINANCIAL CONTROL

Paul Adams

INTRODUCTION

You may think you have all the skills required for running a pub – welcoming customers, making sure they have a good time and even being able to throw out the inevitable drunk. But there is one other skill that is just as vital – you also need to be able to control your business financially.

It is often not appreciated that you, the publican, are controlling a business with a turnover of between £150,000 and £500,000 or more. Many businesses of this size will employ a book-keeper or accountant, but the publican normally does the vast majority of the work himself.

Unless you have experience of preparing accounts, you will need the services of an accountant to produce your accounts each year and agree your tax liability with the Inland Revenue. Their charges will be based on the amount of work they have to do and whether you trade as a limited company. The general rule is the more work you do, the less the accountant does and therefore the lower the charges.

The first decision you have to make is whether you should trade as a sole trader (or partnership) or a limited company. The major difference is that a limited company means your liabilities are limited to what you put into the company if it should fail. However, even if you are a limited company you may find you have to give personal guarantees for loans or to the landlord if you have leasehold premises. If you are unsure of the best route to take, it is worth paying an hour's fee to discuss your circumstances with an accountant or solicitor. Whatever decision you take at this stage can have major effects in the future if all does not go well. Another word of advice if you are going into partnership: do have a partnership agreement drawn up by a solicitor before you start so that all parties are clear on what share of

Stock and Financial Control

profits (and work) are due and what happens if one party dies or decides to leave. Many accountants and solicitors have a field day sorting out partnership troubles which could have been avoided in the first place.

Before you start or take over your pub, you must apply to Customs & Excise for a new VAT number or, in the circumstances, take over the existing one. In addition, notify your local Inland Revenue office to make arrangements to pay PAYE and National Insurance. You must also decide which bank to use for your business account. Generally, pubs generate the majority of their turnover in cash, so pay particular attention to the charges for paying in cash. If you already have a relationship with a bank the old adage of 'better the devil you know' probably holds true. You may wish to consider Girobank: their charges for handling cash are normally lower as they constantly need cash to pay pensions etc. In addition, post office hours are longer than those of high street banks, and there is nearly always a post office near your pub.

If there is significant food business, you will probably have to accept credit cards such as Visa and Access. Consider this well before the intended take-over date as it takes at least three weeks to process the application. Remember that the service charges made by the credit card companies vary from around 2.75-4 per cent, so it's worth shopping around and considering whether to use an electronic terminal. Although you have to rent these, from about £10 per month, and they need to be connected to a telephone line, the service charges are cheaper than paper transactions and they automatically check that the card is valid.

Quite often the question arises whether accepting a credit card over the bar for a series of drinks can be construed as supplying alcohol on credit (or slate). Strictly speaking, if no substantial meal is provided, this is illegal, although there is some doubt and I have never heard of a prosecution in this regard.

Another important thing to arrange is insurance for the pub. Apart from buildings and contents insurance to cover the normal risks of fire and burglary, it is essential that you have employer's and public liability cover. Simple accidents either to staff or customers, even though you would think it was their fault, can result in hefty claims for injuries. Do shop around for pub insurance – there are many specific packages that give good cover and they are all vying for your business.

If you are considering taking a leasehold premises, you need to be aware of what responsibilities and restrictions are being placed on you. The list of things you covenant to do and not do can be extremely onerous, and the landlord always has the whip hand if you end up in a disagreement. Make sure that your solicitor explains to you fully in simple terms what you are taking on.

RAISING FINANCE

Most people have to borrow money to help finance the purchase of a pub business, be it freehold or leasehold. A bank, finance company or building society will want to see projections of what profit you expect to make and also a cashflow statement. It is important that you understand the difference between the two - the profit and loss account records the income and expenditure of the business such as sales and overheads but excludes capital items such as equipment and furniture, and only takes income and expenditure into account in the period to which it relates. Cashflow on the other hand reflects every movement of cash whether it affects the profit and loss account or not. For example, suppose on the day before you take over your pub, you pay one quarter's rent of £5000 and £10,000 for the fixtures and fittings. Your profit and loss account at that stage will be zero as the rent was in advance and fixtures and fittings is a capital item. However, the cashflow will already show minus £15,000 as the cash has actually left your account.

Apart from the normal high street banks, you may wish to try other sources of loans. Some building societies now offer business loans, and there are lots of other financial institutions which also make loans. A good way of finding such funds is via the agent you are buying the pub through. The agent will also help with submitting an application and generally provide advice to smooth the raising of funds.

The bank manager will be particularly interested in the cashflow statement, as, although you may be able to trade profitably, you still need working capital to finance the purchase of stock, rent etc. You may even find that utility companies want a deposit if you cannot provide a history of paying for gas, electricity etc at a previous address.

Quite often you will hear the request for a business plan. This basically means you need to put in writing how you intend to trade the pub, what improvements and changes you intend to make, how much that is all going to cost, plus a projected profit and loss account and cashflow statement. You should also include descriptions of your own experience, whether in the trade or not, and provide assurances of your suitability to run a pub if this is your first venture.

STOCK AND CASH CONTROL

One of the major concerns of the pub business is to ensure all the cash gets into the till and that stock only leaves the premises by being purchased. Unfortunately, the business is notorious for employees stealing cash or stock, so you must be in a position to monitor the situation.

If you run the pub without employing staff you can be sure that no theft of stock or cash is taking place. However, you still need to be vigilant - it is not unknown for a drayman to short deliver an item if he thinks he can get away with it. I remember one pub that always seemed to have a stock shortage - it took some time to discover that beer stock kept in a locked yard was being stolen overnight at the rate of a keg a week.

For the larger operation with various staff involved, it is essential that a proper stock control system is in place. You must decide whether you feel capable of doing this yourself or employing an outside stocktaker. Another decision is what type of till you use – either a straight till or EPOS. This latter system records every sale by product and size and the till looks up the price at which it is sold. For this system to operate effectively all deliveries must be entered on the machine, plus any items given away, and an allowance made for any below normal sale prices, eg happy hour. Although this may seem time-consuming, it does allow any shortages to be pinpointed exactly. The alternative is to leave stocktaking entirely to an outside firm. Although I recommend stocktaking on a monthly basis, a lot of people feel quarterly is sufficient. The problem is that if the stock control is going awry, you need to know as soon as possible. An outside stocktaker will count all the stock on hand and then record all sales and deliveries of goods. This enables them to calculate the amount of stock used during the period. As the selling price is known for each item, and allowing for wastage, promotions and any other adjustments, it is easy to calculate the amount of cash that should have been received by the tills.

Charges for a stocktake vary depending on the size and complexity of the job, but expect to pay upwards of £60. If you feel confident enough and have the use of a computer, you could purchase a stocktaking package which will enable you to do the same job. However, great accuracy in checking all the stock on hand and entering deliveries is required, otherwise you will end up with a meaningless result. Personally, I think stocktaking is best left to the professionals so that you know you are getting an accurate result. The other benefit is that most stocktakers have a wealth of experience and can point you in the right direction for curing any problems.

Apart from losing stock due to pilferage, the other problem is to ensure you don't overstock your pub. Overall, you should aim to carry no more than two weeks' stock. This will vary according to your type of operation as, say an extensive wine list, will obviously take your stockholding higher. As a general rule, to work out your weekly order you should use the formula of twice your weekly sale less the amount of stock on hand. For example, if you start the week with five cases of tonic water and finish with two cases, you have sold three cases. Twice the weekly sale is six cases, less the stock of two gives an order of four cases.

If you do overorder on some items which carry a best-before date you can still sell them, probably at a reduced rate, as long as you make this clear at the time of sale. I would advise that you try to sell excess stock by reducing the price before the date in question is reached, rather than ending up with stock which has passed its expiry months before. Rotation of stock is important so that you don't end up with old stock buried under a pile of younger items.

SUPPLIERS

If you are a free house, you can obviously source all your products from any brewer or wholesaler. The market is highly competitive and you should shop around to get the best deal. Discounts for a one-off account of say 300 barrels can get up to £50 per barrel, which is about 20 per cent off the list price, so you can see there are good deals to be had. However, price is not everything: you must consider whether the brands a supplier is offering are right for your customers, because if you can't sell it, then no amount of discount helps you.

Items such as wines, spirits and food you can probably get at lower prices from a cash and carry rather than a company which delivers to your door. You must consider whether your time and transport costs are worth more than the amount saved. That said, I know a lot of publicans actually enjoy visiting the cash and carry – it gets them away from the pub and they can see what new products/offers are on the market.

RECORDS AND BOOK-KEEPING

Whatever level of financial knowledge you have, there is a minimum level of records you must keep. There are three government agencies that you need to be aware of.

1. **Customs & Excise** are responsible for collecting VAT, and these days they are judged by how much extra they can find to collect when they visit you. They have extraordinary powers to enter your premises and confiscate records if they think fit, so they are people to be taken seriously. Hopefully, you will not see that side of them as they will be happy with the records you keep. You can expect a visit from a VAT Inspector within the first year of trading as you will be paying a fair amount of VAT over each quarter.

   Although VAT on the face of it is simple in that you charge VAT on sales and before you pay this over you can deduct any VAT you have paid on supplies, it does get slightly more complicated. For instance, if you have a function room and let it for a meeting and don't provide any other services, you needn't charge VAT. However, if you provide refreshments in the price, then you do have to charge VAT. Also when deducting VAT paid on purchases you must be careful to get a proper VAT receipt from the supplier showing not only his VAT number but also the VAT amount and VAT rate (unless it is a small amount). Remember, if you don't have the right documentation, the Inspectors will disallow such claims and then you have to pay up, plus interest.

   The other important point with paying over your VAT is to adhere to the due dates. If you are even a few days late, they will issue a surcharge notice which lasts for a year. If your return is late during that coming year, you are automatically surcharged a percentage of the VAT due, plus a penalty.

2. **The Inland Revenue** gets involved on two counts: the collection of PAYE and NI on a monthly basis, and your tax liabilities on any profit you make.

   You can expect a visit from the Inland Revenue to check your PAYE and employee records, but

Stock and Financial Control

they vary tremendously, so you could wait years. Be careful though, as they can go back six years and charge you for any mistakes made during that period. The records you must keep for PAYE and NI are detailed in the Employers' Pack which you will receive when you register with them.

With regard to the Inland Revenue and your tax liability: this is normally done through correspondence with you or your accountant. However, if they are not happy with the figures or answers to queries, they have the power to go through everything with a fine-tooth comb. Bear in mind that they can issue an assessment for tax and it is down to you to prove that this is wrong.

3. **The Contributions Agency** is the department which checks to make sure National Insurance is being paid on employees' earnings and any benefits you provide. They take great delight in identifying any benefits given to staff which should have NI charged on them. For instance, if you pay for a taxi to take staff home at night, this is a 'benefit' and should have NI paid on it.

If they visit you, they usually check the PAYE records as well, just to help out the Inland Revenue. Why the PAYE and NI departments aren't combined into one is anyone's guess.

Computers

Computers soon become irreplaceable for your record-keeping and financial control once you have tried them. As mentioned earlier, you can get stocktaking packages off the shelf and you can choose from a number of accounting packages for small businesses such as Sage or Pegasus. They all come with good instruction manuals and as long as you follow them carefully you can use the information either to produce accounts yourself or to pass over to your accountant to finish off. If you do the latter, check with the accountant if they have a preference of package.

You can also use the computer to calculate wages payments. Keeping manual records is allowable and pretty straightforward (guidance manuals are produced by the Inland Revenue), but it does take time manually to calculate the PAYE and NI due on each person's wage, where the computer does it in seconds. The machine will also produce the year end returns up to 5 April each year for submission to the Inland Revenue.

An added bonus is that the computer is able to produce menus and posters whenever you like and to an extremely high standard. There are many such 'desktop publishing' programs around and most new computers come with a suitable package.

MAXIMISING PROFITS

The major effect on profit is obviously the amount of sales and the gross profit you can make out of those sales. It is difficult to give you any meaningful guidelines on what gross profit you should make as it varies so much between different parts of the country on selling price and what discounts you can negotiate on purchases. On wet take these can vary from 40 per cent to over 60 per cent and on food anything from 30 per cent to over 70 per cent.

Another large slice of expenditure for a reasonably sized pub is wages for kitchen and bar staff. Most managed houses work on a budget of 10 per cent for staff (excluding managers) where there is little food involved, but this can increase dramatically where the food take is high. Remember that although food gross profits can be very high, the wages costs for preparation, cooking and serving can mount alarmingly if you don't have tight control.

Many of your overhead costs such as rent are fixed, but there is scope to reduce other costs. Most fair-sized pubs can now shop around for gas supplies and make savings of at least 33 per cent over standard British Gas tariffs. The opportunity to do the same with electricity is on the horizon.

Another major cost can be rates. As far as pubs are concerned, the Inland Revenue Valuation Office fixes the rateable value based on the amount of business the pub is doing. This is reviewed every five years and can result in a change in the rateable value. If you think the rateable value is too high, you can appeal and have it re-assessed. This is a specialist field and I would advise you to use one of the many experts available. However, be careful who you choose as there are many firms who charge fees upfront yet never obtain any reduction. My advice is to stick to the rating departments of licensed valuers - they are all members of professional societies that ensure proper care is taken.

Finally, if things do go wrong and the business ends up in difficulties, take advice from your accountant or solicitor. A professional can advise on action for further financing or in the worst case how to minimise the financial burdens. If things go badly wrong and you have borrowed money from a bank or other institution, you will need all the help you can get as they always have the power to take any action to protect their own interests.

On a brighter note, the vast majority of pubs are successful businesses and provide a good living for the publican. It is a great business to be in and provides a varied and enjoyable way to earn a living.

Legal Notes

It is forbidden to sell or supply intoxicating liquor for consumption on any licensed premises unless paid for when sold or supplied, unless the liquor is sold with a meal and paid for together with the meal, or it is sold or supplied to a person residing in the licensed premises and is paid for together with the accommodation. This also applies to liquor sold to guests of residents.

Credit or debit cards may be used.

CHAPTER TEN

MAXIMISING MACHINE INCOME

Ian Chuter

Amusement machines are an essential part of the pub business. Like them or loathe them, they make a highly significant contribution to the profitability of most licensed businesses, and good management can boost machine income by up to 30 per cent. The secret to quite how much you profit from amusement machines lies in the relationship you have with your chosen operator.

ALL OPERATORS ARE THE SAME – AREN'T THEY?

Yes, in the same way that all cars are the same, all restaurants are the same, and Accrington Stanley's latest signing is as potent as Alan Shearer. Certainly at the most basic level they fulfil the same function, but in reality some provide an awful lot more, consisting of a wide range of business services.

I'M NOT INTERESTED IN FANCY SERVICES, ALL I WANT TO DO IS MAXIMISE MY MACHINE INCOME

That's exactly what operators are there to do. All of their services are geared to increasing your profit levels from machines. Operating amusement machines is a highly skilled business. Products popular in city-centre locations might not have the same appeal in community pubs. Not only should your operator be able to select the right machines for your business, they can also tell you what price of play to operate at, and with AWPs what percentage payout setting will get you the best return. An agreement between the industry and the Gaming Board of Great Britain states that the percentage payout on fruit machines will not fall below 70 per cent. Clearly this does not mean that for every £1 staked the player receives a minimum of 70p back. The percentage payout level is an

189

aggregate figure established over 10,000 plays. Percentage payout represents a variable whereby the licensee – in partnership and consultation with his/her chosen operator – can influence the level of machine income. And it doesn't follow that the lower the percentage the higher the income generated. For example, in community pubs where there is a strong regular clientele, a machine will perform best on a higher percentage setting, typically up to 84 per cent. In premises with a more transient trade the optimum percentage may be 78–80 per cent. And in extreme cases, such as on AWPs sited on or near railway stations where the customer is killing time, a lower percentage of approximately 74 per cent can be successfully operated. Although the price of play is limited to a 25p stake, this is a ceiling figure. It is possible to set machines on a 5p stake (20p plays for £1), 10p stake (10 plays for £1), 20p (five plays for £1) or 25p (four plays for £1).

SURELY CHOOSING AN OPERATOR LOCAL TO ME MAKES SENSE?

The national operating companies provide exactly that – a nationwide cover – so in practice they can offer a localised service but with the added attraction of knowing the national picture. Many customers have found that they are better off using an operator which has the experience gained from working on a national stage and across all sectors of the machine industry.

BUT SHOULDN'T I GO FOR THE BEST RENTAL PRICE?

The best price certainly doesn't mean the cheapest. Opt for the cheapest, and you could end up with an outdated machine which breaks down regularly, which isn't repaired on time and which doesn't take any money. If you take this route while the competition opts for the latest launch, which is regularly and promptly serviced, frequently collected, with the latest income protection measures against fraud, the likelihood is that you'll not only lose machine income, you could also lose some of your net sales trade as well. Although it's a cliché, there is a difference between price and value for money, and it is a difference that should be addressed.

WHAT'S THE BENEFIT OF CHANGING MACHINES REGULARLY – ISN'T IT JUST UNNECESSARY HASSLE?

Machines are changed only for business reasons: that is, to maximise your income. AWPs follow fashions, and having an older machine when your competitors - either pubs or betting shops – have the latest models will result in a drop in income. (Incidentally, it's important to recognise the competition posed by betting shops. Under the terms of the 1996 deregulation, they were allowed for the first time to site a maximum of two AWPs. There is a strong cross-over of betting shop and pub customers, and the siting of machines represents an extra tier of competition to the on-trade). The art to changing

Maximising Machine Income

machines is in the timing – that is, identifying when a certain product has peaked and bringing in a newer model before the income begins to drop. There is no set formula for this. Although typical machines will sustain income for up to 12 or 14 weeks, it may be that after the initial player learning curve income will begin to drop after six weeks. Conversely, a machine that your customers have learned to play and enjoy can last up to 20 weeks. It's certainly not welcome news for our colleagues in the manufacturing side of the industry, but we have sites where the same machine has generated excellent revenue for 18 months. However, I must stress that this is the exception. The decision on changing machines is a mixture of science and experience. As a national operator working across a spectrum of leisure sectors we have a wealth of data relating to the performance and product life cycles of machines. Combine this with an intimate knowledge of the amusement sector and a close relationship with all of the manufacturers, and you have the best possible credentials to make what is a crucial decision.

HOW BIG AN ISSUE IS SECURITY?

Machines, because they carry cash – particularly club jackpot machines which may have a float of £300 – are susceptible to crime. If a machine is physically broken into the loss is not just restricted to the cash box, but also relates to damage to the equipment and the resultant period of downtime. Fraud, or clever machine crime, is a separate issue which is sometimes harder to prevent. While it's impossible to claim that any machine is crime-proof, we can make life an awful lot harder for the criminally inclined.

To start with, machines should not be sited near exit/entrance doors. There have been examples of gangs simply lifting the machine and making off in a van. Machines can be supplied with alarm systems with tilt switches which will activate the alarm if the machine is tilted by more than a 45° angle. Security bars can be fitted in extreme cases.

Electronic Data Capture (EDC), which provides a wealth of information to assist in the identification of fraud, should be fitted. In straightforward terms, EDC is the machine equivalent of an aeronautical black box in that it provides us with detailed and valuable information. It can tell us what amount of money should be in the machine, when the machine was switched on and off, and how many times it has been played every hour of the day and night. By using EDC it is possible to identify the time of a fraud, allowing us to narrow down the list of potential suspects.

Front-line staff, including collectors, should be trained to identify signs of machine tampering which would remain unnoticed by laymen. Tell-tale signs include groups crowding around the machine, the winning of multiple jackpots, and multiple credits appearing on the machine. A significant proportion of machine crime is committed by organised gangs who move around the country. This being the case, it is vital that the authorities gather as

The Publican's Handbook

BAR TOP VENDING IS BIG BUSINESS

More and more pubs are realising there is money to be made from selling confectionery. While chocolate and beer may not be the ideal partnership, there is a definite on-trade consumer demand for the largest single impulse purchase in the UK. In fact 30% of all independent pubs now stock some confectionery*.

Pistachio nuts, M&M's, Skittles and Jelly Beans certainly get the taste buds going and can get your money working too. Proof is in our eating habits - we all love to nibble and no time better than when we're having a leisurely drink, whether that's in the pub, wine bar, night club, leisure centre or snooker hall- basically anywhere where there's a congregation of people.

IPH can supply machines and stock from their large warehouse in Surrey and deliver to anywhere in the UK, selling either direct to the site, or via their large operator network on a free loan basis.

IPH use only the classic Beaver range of machines. No other machine comes close on either durability, quality of finish or appearance, and with a wide range of body colours and finishes the combinations are endless, guaranteeing a machine to suit any location.

Although many pubs start with vending Jelly Beans and Pistachios, the product range is endless, from M&M's and Skittles to savoury and cashew nuts, from mints and Minstrels to chocolate peanuts and raisins. By updating and changing the stock this ensures that the customer never gets bored and the cash returns remain constant week in week out.

By choosing the option to buy, the machines are soon paid for - normally within 3-5 refills, and with the IPH lifetime guarantee on all moving parts and with a unique buy back policy, the downside to owning your own machine is very limited indeed. However, for those people who wish not to, they are available on free loan, and are serviced by a local operator who will restock, cash up and pay the site a commission, thus allowing the site all the benefits at no cost.

Hot Nut machines are also available on the same basis, either to compliment the Jelly Bean machines or as a stand alone point of sale. In this case the customer is served warm savoury nuts over the counter in handy sized cups, with the takings going in the till, the nuts being reordered and then delivered by a local operator as and when required.

With more and more pubs trying to get the maximum returns from their premises, whilst trying to offer the highest standards of service, these machines are a perfect way to help achieve this. So whether or not you run one pub or a whole estate, IPH are equipped to deal with your requirements and are dedicated to supplying cost effective quality machines and stock, backed up with helpful friendly service and advice.

*Stats MR LTDC Audit Dec 1996

TO CONTACT IPH TELEPHONE
0181 771 0011 (24 HOURS)

Maximising Machine Income

Claremont Automatics Limited

FOR ALL THE BEST COIN-OPERATED AMUSEMENT EQUIPMENT

✓ Personal Attention
✓ Experienced professionals
✓ Dependable service
✓ A company you can rely on!

Your local caring Independant operator
HEAD OFFICE: Chinnor, Oxon.
Tel: (01844) 353635 Fax: (01844)352750

BRANCHES AT:
Flackney, Leics.Tel:(0116)2403162. Dunmow, Essex.Tel:(01371)875131
Fleet, Hants.Tel:(01262)623845. Malksham, Wilts.Tel:(01225)790940

Are your coin machines in safe hands?
Do they continue to generate the maximum possible income?

There are plenty of people who will tell you a lot about amusement machines and entertainment systems - but there aren't many you can trust to know what they are talking about. And considering the contribution that your machine can make to your bottom line, the service and support they (and you) receive is critical.

Claremont Automatics was established in 1966. Since then we have remained specialists in our field, with no other activities to divert our attention. Now we employ over 150 people, servicing more than 4,000 machines at 2,000 venues in the South, South West, Midlands and East Anglia. We will work with you and for you to get the best from your coin-op equipment and provide hands on assistance in building your business.

At our five regional headquarters we have the most sophisticated computer systems in the industry to keep your machines right up to date with all the latest programmes. Our daily reporting scheme and computer monitoring system means that all the necessary information is available within 24 hours of collection so that trends can be identified and dealt with, very, very quickly. And our security systems are just as fast, minimising your risk and providing rapid solutions to security problems.

Claremont have made it a policy to control the size of the territories covered by our five regional offices so that our standards of service are never compromised. Collectors, sales liaison executives and engineers are all based close to you and are very accessible. Besides making for speed in responding to calls, this means that you will get to know and rely on Claremont people you are dealing with.

You will find that their first priority is to make sure that your coin-operated machines are making money for you and that you are totally satisfied with the standards of service and help you receive. You will also discover that they are a very efficient team, with years of experience and knowledge of the amusements and gaming industry.

Gaming and amusement machines, video machines, music systems and pool tables all have the potential to make a major contribution to your profits. Claremont customers find that cashing in on the opportunity is easy. We will install the right machine for your business and we'll monitor it's performance daily to keep it at its peak. Our teams of experts are at your service at all times, Making sure that Claremont systems are making money for you and helping your business to grow.

As a member of the Independent Operators Association, a nationwide group of proprietor-led companies, Claremont Automatics are linked with specialist machine operators who have trading areas that cover almost the whole of Mainland Britain. They are therefore able to compete with the major operators. while having all the advantages of personal service and individual attention that being independent brings.

The Publican's Handbook

much information as possible on their activities and methods. If you see a group of people who you believe may have targeted your machines, get descriptions and if possible a car registration number. The police are now beginning to take this type of organised crime extremely seriously.

In some cases customers will simply try it on. The most common approach is to claim that a machine has failed to pay out and demand money from bar staff. Our recommendation is to deal with this issue in the same way as you would when people claim that they've been underchanged. Just as a check on the till balance can be made, so an engineer is able to determine how much any player has really won. In all cases the bywords are communication with your operator, and vigilance.

WHAT ABOUT NON-GAMBLING MACHINES?

It may be that the location is big enough and has the right portfolio of customers to accommodate a video simulator – many of which are now available in mini-versions designed specifically for pubs. However, despite the appeal of hi-tech simulators, they come at a cost equivalent to five brand new, state-of-the-art AWPs. As a consequence, you have to be certain that they are right for your business. On video games it's possible for licensees to run a highest score or fastest time competition, thereby increasing repeat plays and attracting new custom. Furthermore, many of the manufacturers are including novelty features commonly known as 'cheats', whereby the experienced player can access an attention seeking feature. A current example can be found on TT Manx, where 'the player in the know' can swap his 750cc Kawasaki for a thoroughbred sheep conversant with the highways and byways of the Isle of Man!

With reference to pool, we encourage our customers to participate in leagues and to stage in-house competitions. We currently run 11 different pool promotions which are available to Rank Leisure Machine Services' customers. The objective is to assist in developing and sustaining trade, particularly on the traditionally quieter days.

AMUSEMENT MACHINES ARE JUST A PERIPHERAL PART OF THE BUSINESS, AREN'T THEY?

The latest figures produced by BACTA, the trade association for the domestic amusement machine industry, show that AWPs and club jackpot machines pay out an annual sum in prize money totalling £7.2 billion. Put into context, that is £19.7 million a day – the equivalent of a National Lottery roll-over jackpot 365 days a year.

Of the 240,000 AWPs and club jackpot machines in the UK, some 40 per cent are in licensed premises. Clearly, what we are dealing with is a significant element in the leisure industry, and one that plays an important part in the economic and commercial fabric of pubs and clubs. With the introduction of the £10 all-cash jackpot in June 1996, extensive research has shown that

THE LEADERS IN CIGARETTE VENDING

- Fast and efficient local service throughout the UK
- Flexibility - personalised package to suit you
- Excellent commission rates with pack receipts on every visit
- Modern, reliable machines to suit your premises
- Regular machine inspection and local technical support
- Best selling brands for your area
- Wholesale delivery service

Mayfair SERVICES

Freephone 0800 220 845

---

the on-trade takings have increased by 30 per cent where £10 all-cash jackpots have been combined with 25p play.

WHAT ARE THE LEGAL REQUIREMENTS OF SITING MACHINES?

Knowing your legal responsibilities is essential. The two main requirements relate to permits and Customs & Excise. Licensees require what is known as a Section 34 permit before they can site AWPs, and a Part III for club jackpot machines. The application and renewal procedure can be looked after by the operator, and most professional operators will do this as a matter of course. Permits are granted by the local magistrates and are not required for SWPs, pool, video, table football or pinball. Amusement Machine Licence Duty (AMLD) is a much more complex issue, and my advice is to get the most up-to-date information from your operator.

WHAT PRACTICAL MEASURES CAN I TAKE AS A LICENSEE TO IMPROVE MACHINE INCOME?

Advances in technology have made sound an important element of the entertainment value provided by an AWP, and manufacturers are investing considerable sums in sampled sound technology. Industry research has shown that sound represents 5 per cent of the total cost of developing a new AWP. Academic research has shown that players are encouraged by the noise and thrill of a machine paying out.

A compromise needs to be struck between the sound level generated by an AWP and the requirements of the public bar of a community pub. Too many licensees adopt a blanket ban on sound by requesting that speakers are disconnected altogether, when the volume can be adjusted by the operator's engineers.

Our experience clearly demonstrates that the best income figures are achieved on sites where the staff have a knowledge of their machines. As a company we encourage customers to appoint a machine champion - a member, or indeed members, of staff who take an interest in the products on site; people who know the features of a new machine, who ensure that the glasses are cleaned every day, and who will report even the smallest of faults. We can help in this process by providing demonstrations, printed player guides, and promotional material.

Other simple measures that can be taken include ensuring that staff give out as many coins in change as possible. Five £1 coins instead of a £5 note given in change at the bar often results in extra machine plays. The simple recommendation is, if not love your machines then certainly respect them for their tremendous income-generating potential.

Under Starter Orders For A Fun Night

THOROUGHBRED
PRODUCTIONS

Sara Fulda, Managing Director of Thoroughbred Productions, says "With the advent of large screen entertainment in many pubs and clubs, race nights are easy to organise. There is no longer any need to go to the expense and hassle of hiring projectionists to run the films, now customers can just hire videos and run the evening themselves. But one word of warning! As the picture is blown up to such large size, customers must be sure they have good quality videos otherwise the evening could be an embarrassing disaster. You can be confident that when you order a race night package from Thoroughbred you will have a successful evening's entertainment."

Thoroughbred Productions offers a race night for under £100 and as the name suggests their product is of the highest quality. The races are flat, jump and greyhound from the country's top courses with commentary by Peter Bromley and other professional commentators. The latest races are from 1996 race meetings and they add to their stable of races every year.

No other form of entertainment offers the added bonus of fundraising for local charity. With Thoroughbred's personalised race cards the horses can be sold to customers before the evening and that money combined with a percentage of the tote can raise a considerable amount of money.

Sara and her staff pride themselves on providing a quality service to go with their quality product. To send for their brochure or ask for furhter information, see their advertisement on the adjacent page and ring us on 0181 566 7788.

Thoroughbred Productions Ltd., Unit 3, Silicone Business Centre,
Wadsworth Road, Perivale, Middlesex UB6 7JZ.
Tel: 0181 566 7788 Facsimile: 0181 566 7789

Maximising Machine Income

Legal Notes

It is permitted to play dominoes and cribbage and other specially authorised games (whether for prizes or stakes) on licensed premises (other than restaurants) but subject to any restrictions which the Licensing Justices may impose to prevent play for high stakes, or in circumstances which constitute an inducement.

Gaming by means of machines with a limited payout – skill with prize machines (SWP) and amusement with prize machines (AWP) – may also be available on licensed premises subject to the grant of a permit from the Licensing Justices under Section 34 of the Gaming Act 1968. Usually a permit for up to two machines will be available. The licensing committee may require a plan of your premises indicating where the machines are to located. Any more than two machines will usually require a separate special application.

Any other gaming on licensed premises is unlawful.

For public dancing or music or any other public entertainment of a like kind, a **Public Entertainment Licence** issued by the appropriate local authority is required. There is an exception in the case of public entertainment by way of music and singing only which is provided solely by the reproduction of recorded sound, or by not more than two performers. A combination of recorded sound and live singer (as in the case of karaoke) will require the issue of a Public Entertainment Licence.

Public Entertainment Licences require annual renewal. If an entertainment is excessively noisy and disturbs local residents they may object at your next renewal. Be aware that these objections are taken seriously. Also watch against misbehaviour by patrons departing from your premises. This too can be grounds for objections to your Public Entertainment Licence, even though the behaviour is outside your premises.

RACE NIGHTS

Superb Pub & Club Entertainment

Boost Sales
Ideal Charity Fundraiser

Thoroughbred Productions
Unit 3, Silicon Business Centre, Wadsworth Road, Perivale, Middlesex UB6 7JZ
Tel 0181 556 7788

CHAPTER ELEVEN

SECURITY IN LICENSED OUTLETS

Brian Taylor

Crime of all sorts is, sadly, a very real problem for today's licensees and pub operators, and it is something that cannot be ignored.

Publicans and brewers carrying out refurbishments have their spending priorities, and are sometimes reluctant to spend money on sound practical security considerations.

This chapter looks at ways in which security measures can be

Example

Thousands of pounds had been spent on a refurbishment which was extremely attractive and turned the pub in question into the Place To Be.

But the back door was not steel-lined – unfortunate, as it allowed access to the cellar where the free-standing safe stood. The burglar alarm was one of those that could be de-activated by cutting the telephone wires.

Local thieves had been watching the refurbishment and soon noticed the lack of high-grade security.

The pub re-opened, attracting hundreds of free-spending customers into its delightful bars, and the takings for the opening weekend were placed in the safe.

During the night the thieves forced the sub-standard rear door, de-activated the alarm, moved the safe, sawed through its hinges, and helped themselves to the takings.

effective in pubs, ensuring that the premises, cash and stock are protected from criminals and providing safety and peace of mind for staff and management.

In addition advice is given on spotting and coping with drug dealing, how to prevent burglary, secure cash carrying, machine security, defusing potentially violent situations, and dealing with extortion.

The subject of doormen, registered or otherwise, is also discussed, together with details of pilot schemes being operated by police forces throughout the country.

STRATEGY

A clearly defined security strategy must be drawn up for each pub backed by commitment, determination and persistence from publicans, brewing companies and the police.

When analysing the need for security in licensed outlets we should first look at perceptions of security among both the general public and the criminal fraternity.

Banks and building societies, by the very nature of their businesses, are both overtly and covertly very security-conscious. Bullet-proof screens often separate customers from staff, and even when high-profile security has been relaxed to allow open-plan reception areas, the cash is transferred by air tubes and stored in a secure vault.

In contrast, most pubs have an open, welcoming air, with direct over the counter contact with customers and no evidence of security measures.

Pubs are attractive to criminals because they deal in cash, which in business hours is held in cash drawers behind the bar and stored on the premises at night. Gaming machines, juke boxes and cigarette machines also contain cash.

Before defining a strategy, account must be taken of the nature of the risk. Risk is defined as the probability of damage, injury or loss, not just a catalogue of actual crimes or incidents; and the risk assessment process must include realistic evaluation of the location of the premises, the design and construction of the building, any past incidents, and the value of the building and its contents.

Risk varies. It is higher at some times of the day than others. It may change if extensive alterations or additions to the pub are carried out or new and valuable equipment or stock is introduced. Good risk management tries to anticipate these variations by being pro-active.

A balance must be struck if security is not to interfere with the smooth running of the business. The difference between a pub and an industrial site is that conventional crime prevention measures - topping fencing with razor wire, say - are not always compatible with the relaxed and friendly atmosphere most pubs seek to create.

There is no single answer. Each preventative measure should support and reinforce each other in a balanced package. Some measures demand more effort than money and not all rely on electronic or physical protection. In an ideal world there would be funding for all crime prevention measures in

The Publican's Handbook

pubs, but security is not always the top priority and when cash is available there is a danger of concentrating resources and hardware on one risk to the exclusion of others – a situation which must be avoided.

The simplest way for a publican to assess the crime risk in his pub is to ask the following questions:

- ◆ If I was locked out, how easy would it be for me to get back in?
- ◆ When I am alone in the pub outside trading hours and someone knocks, can I see who it is?

Let us start at the beginning.

The front door

If there is a knock on the door and you can't see who it is, fit a wide-angle door viewer without delay.

There are many instances of publicans hearing a knock at the door outside business hours and being unable to see who it is, call out, only to receive the reply: 'It's the postman.'

Of course, everyone opens the door if they believe the postman is standing there waiting to deliver letters or a parcel. Only when the door is opened, the 'postman' turns out to be a criminal armed with a sawn-off shotgun. What happens next is ugly – and could easily have been avoided by the installation of a wide-angle door viewer.

Door viewers should be supported by door chains or doorstop devices, both of which are cheap to buy and simple to install and ensure that the publican and his staff are in control of any attempt at unauthorised entry into the pub outside normal business hours.

Another all too common method of entry arising from the publican's inability to see who is at the door when the pub is shut occurs in the momentary relaxation between the cleaners leaving and the pub opening.

The burglar alarms have been turned off while the cleaners were working and the publican is enjoying a cup of coffee and reading the newspaper, and there's a knock on the door. Because there is no door viewer, the publican assumes that one of the cleaners has forgotten something. He opens the door. There confronting him are the men with the baseball bats. Another crime which could have been prevented by installation of a door viewer.

So often, it's the simple devices which protect staff and management from criminals, together with a sound, well thought-out 'best practice' list of security measures.

Alarms

Most pubs are fitted with intruder alarms, but it is the style and standard of those alarms that causes concern.

All police forces adhere strictly to an Intruder Alarm Policy, and publicans are advised to seek out the terms and conditions of that policy with their intruder alarm installer or crime prevention officer.

Some publicans do not realise that the police will not respond to a bells-only intruder alarm not connected to a control room. If yours is such an alarm, get it replaced with a system which is fitted to a suitable specification. Publicans often look for the cheapest deal; but when you consider the building, cash, staff and stock you have to protect, you will see that it is worth spending a few pounds more on appropriate and effective alarms.

Intruder alarms must be designed to fit the specific needs of the pub, and not to suit the installers' standard package. There must be a combination of door and contact detectors, together with movement detectors which should be fitted so that some parts of the system can be de-activated when others are active. For instance, the alarms covering the public areas must be de-activated during normal business hours, but alarms covering the liquor store and safe should remain activated.

Many intruder alarm installers fit movement detectors, which are excellent in factories or offices where members of the public do not normally have access. But in pubs, unless they are 'anti-masking' detectors, which prevent 'customers' from de-activating them so they don't set off the alarm when they return after closing time as burglars, they are useless.

The living quarters should also be protected by alarms. The minimum requirement in these areas is a panic button at the bedside or other convenient place. The same applies to cash offices and areas where the publican or a member of staff counts and stores the cash takings.

Many of the older alarms are fitted with digital dialling systems which call the control room if the alarm goes off, and criminals have learnt simply to cut the telephone wires. Today's systems are fitted with BT Red Care, which rings the control room if there is any attempt to cut the wires. The difference in cost between the old and the new can be £1000 – but you have to remember that the saving in fitting a cheaper system is wasted if it doesn't work when it's needed, plus there is the cost of the stolen cash and stock.

Under no circumstances should an intruder alarm be fitted by an installer who is not approved by NACOSS, the National Supervisory Council which sets standards of equipment and service for the intruder alarm industry.

Safes

Safes are a must in all pubs, and if you have a vintage safe which has served the pub for a vast number of years, it is time to replace it.

There are many styles and shapes of safes, and whichever you choose the one thing to be sure of is that your safe should not be free standing.

Safes should be firmly fixed to the floor, either bolted or set in concrete. The room or cellar where the safe is housed should be protected by movement detector units, security cameras and a smoke cloak device, which fires a smoke cartridge when activated, quickly filling the area with a heavy cloud of smoke which completely disorientates the thief.

Inside the safe you can fit a smoke dye unit, which activates if the safe is tampered with, rendering the money useless to the thief. Critics say that money in cash bags is not affected. That may be so, but the thief himself will be covered in sticky dye.

Smoke cloak and dye cartridges are an excellent deterrent and the fact that they are fitted should be freely advertised in the pub. Similarly, time-lock safes are a great deterrent, especially if it is advertised in the pub that the safe cannot be opened by management or staff; and those who argue that restricted access to the safe can be inconvenient to the running of the pub ought to take into consideration how inconvenient it is to be forced to open the safe at gunpoint.

Lighting

Effective lighting in and around an pub is a must as part of an integrated security programme. Lighting does deter thieves both in car parks and at other vulnerable points such as cellar flaps, rear doors and windows.

Security lighting should in the main be movement activated, as this is both efficient and cost effective. Many publicans have found to their cost that regulars are soon deterred if the family car is stolen or broken into in a pub car park where there is no lighting or other security measures.

The same principle applies where areas used for storing stocks of kegs and bottles are raided by thieves because of the lack of security locks or lighting.

Remember: lighting is friendly to customers but a deterrent to thieves.

Anti-climb paint

As part of your security strategy, look at any drainpipes which could give access to flat roofs or windows leading into the pub or living accommodation. If you feel that thieves can easily gain access by climbing up the pipes a simple remedy is anti-climb paint, which can be bought from any good ironmonger.

Security cameras

Security cameras are a great deterrent to drugs users and dealers and extortionists, among others, and are arguably the best form of total security.

They are fast becoming a standard item of pub equipment, both inside and out, but can be a minefield to buy and install. Sales representatives may overquote the number of cameras you need, while in many cases failing to stress the need for adequate lighting as part of an integrated security programme, and you can end up with a system which is more expensive than it need be and not as effective as it should be.

Publicans with access to brewery security managers should take advantage of their expertise before deciding on the lighting and security cameras required for the pub. Security cameras are not cheap, but they are very effective when they work in conjunction with 24-hour video recording equipment.

Fast scan is a new generation of video surveillance whereby security pictures are transmitted by a telephone link to a control room, allowing staff to watch a burglary or other crime actually being committed.

Security cameras are also one of the best preventive measures against pilfering by staff members. Many instances have been recorded on video when members of staff left alone in the pub, mainly in late afternoon or the early evening, have plied their friends with 'free' drinks. In other cases customers are seen to be given change from receptacles other than the till - handbags, purses or pockets. These crimes have easily been detected using high-specification security cameras and video equipment.

Machine security

The contents of gaming and other machines can be vulnerable to theft during the day, and security is a key consideration when planning where to put them.

Machines should be placed so they are fully visible from behind the bar - awkward angles can be overcome with mirrors - or within the range of any security cameras inside the premises. As an added deterrent, alarms can be fitted to sound in the event of tampering and padlocks or security bars can be fitted to the cash box doors.

Machines should be regularly inspected for signs of damage and attempted pilfering.

Licensees should keep an eye on machines during opening hours. Individuals fiddling with the coin mechanism or groups forming around machines should be watched. A discreet way of doing this is to collect beer glasses and empty ashtrays regularly from the area.

Customers with frequent claims for non-payment should be monitored. If the machine supplier says the claims are invalid, the licensee will have to use his judgement and tact in deciding whether to pay future claims.

The identity of visiting supplier representatives should always be checked - bogus collectors and engineers who steal the machines or the money in them do exist.

The contents of gaming machines should be put overnight in the safe. The cash box should be left open to make it clear to any intruders that it is empty. To deter criminals looking for a potential target during the day, a notice can be stuck to the front of the machine advising that it is emptied every night.

Most gaming machine theft involves stealing the contents but the machines themselves can be targets too. To improve security machines can be bolted to the wall and covered at night with special cages.

Guard dogs

The presence of a dog in a pub always makes a thief think twice. The only problem with dogs is the health and safety regulations excluding them from the kitchen, cellar and bars.

There are no problems in a dog patrolling the back yard provided that notices are properly displayed giving a warning to trespassers. Dogs which are prone to attacking or biting people should always be chained in the yard and not allowed in public areas.

Dogs in general are a great asset in crime prevention providing that they are under proper control of the owner and do not become a health hazard within the perimeter of the pub by fouling public areas or being allowed into areas where food is prepared and served.

Carrying and storing cash

As discussed earlier, cash should be kept in a safe fitted with smoke cloak and time lock and supported by intruder alarm and security cameras: all of these work very well until the cash has to be taken to the bank.

Ideally only contracted cash carrying companies should be used to transport cash, but many publicans and breweries prefer that cash is deposited personally. Common sense and economic best practice must be the watchwords here, and the judgement whether or not to use a cash carrying service must depend on the following criteria:

- the area through which the cash is to be transported;
- the amount of cash likely to be built up over a given period including weekends;
- those days when the greatest amount of cash is taken;
- the safety and understanding of the staff being asked to transport the cash;
- the number of staff available to transport or deliver cash, which should never be one person only.

The usual well-publicised precautions such as varying routes and times also need to be implemented.

Many publicans favour the use of taxis, and I recommend that only licensed hackney carriages be used. Without wishing to get into any arguments with owner-driver taxis, there have been unfortunate instances when criminal attacks on publicans and staff have been traced back to persons who were not holders of a licensed hackney carriage licence.

Approved cash carrying bags with a wrist chain and dye cartridge are an excellent method of transporting cash. Several types of this specialist equipment are available, costing around £80 each and £25 per replacement dye cartridge.

Some publicans believe that using cash carrying bags marks them out as a target, and a carrier bag or sports bag is less conspicuous. In that case, simply carry the cash carrying bag inside the 'disguise' bag, but with the the wrist strap correctly attached so that in the event of a snatch the smoke dye cartridge will ignite.

I have heard many negative comments from publicans and staff about cash carrying bags, but for the safety and protection of users they are the only alternative to the takings being collected by a contracted cash carrying service.

Prostitution

For many years bars were frequently centres of prostitution. That is not the case these days, although some city centre pubs do attract this trade. In most cases it is easier to detect than the drugs trade, and easier to control.

Publicans must remember that their liquor licence can be revoked

Security in Licensed Outlets

if they allow prostitution on their premises. Even allowing touting for business can lead to a court appearance (although it is a misconception that publicans may not serve prostitutes who are 'off duty').

Tackling violence in pubs

There have been many studies over the years relating to assaults and violence affecting pub customers and staff. In this section the subject of defusing violent situations is discussed and the preventive methods now adopted in many licensed outlets are outlined.

During the 1970s and 1980s closed circuit television with recording facilities was not a common method of dealing with violence in pubs. However, the 1990s have seen an increase in the installation of CCTV, rewarded by a dramatic reduction in the incidence of violence in public houses.

People appear to be more aggressive in many aspects of life these days, and pub customers are no different. Violence can be sparked by the most minor incidents.

Pub management and staff cannot be physically screened off from the customers, so dealing with violence calls for a mixture of training and experience.

It is usually the same person or group of persons who cause violence and create difficulties for pub staff. One of the best preventative methods is joining the membership of a local pubwatch scheme. Problem customers are identified and discussed and can find themselves barred from all the member pubs – an extremely effective deterrent, and a message to all that anti-social behaviour will not be tolerated.

Meeting violence with violence is not the answer, and while staff may sometimes have to defend themselves, experience shows that a violent situation can be defused by a calm approach with the assistance of all the pub staff.

We all know of publicans who can 'handle themselves' in violent situations. The majority, though, prefer conventional methods of defusing situations – remaining calm, maintaining eye contact, and talking common sense.

Brewery management should develop and implement a company strategy regarding violence in pubs, and training programmes should be made available to free trade management and staff as well as managed house and tenanted staff. It is imperative that a combination of preventive devices such as security cameras and staff training are given high priority to ensure safety for staff and customers alike.

Extortion

Extortion is the securing of money, goods or favours by intimidation, violence or the misuse of authority, and sadly pubs, like other businesses, can be victims of it.

Criminal elements are most likely to target pubs in certain areas, especially where there is weak management and no sign of support for the publican from either the brewery or the police. The whole issue requires careful and skilful handling, not only to stop the loss of revenue but also to prevent violence and distress being caused to the management and staff.

The crime of extortion occurs every day in Britain, but few are willing to report it to the police. It can take various forms, from a small-time bully obtaining free drinks by threats to much more organised racketeers exacting large sums of money by terrorising the publican and staff, all of whom may know the violent capabilities of the perpetrator. If the extortionist's demands are not reported quickly, a cycle of terror begins which becomes harder and harder to break.

The cycle normally starts when a number of local criminals who know the pubs where they are least likely to meet resistance and who all have reputations for violence, enter the pub at once, demand a round of drinks, and refuse to pay, threatening either personal violence or damage to the property.

This will probably not happen at peak drinking times, but when the pub is least busy and there are only one or two bar staff on duty who perhaps lack the experience or training to cope. If they succeed at first, their demands escalate, and one of the typical indicators of an extortion problem is a worsening stock and cash shortage in a pub where such problems have not previously been recorded.

Despite the fear of personal injury or damage to property, and however well-grounded those fears may be, reporting approaches at the earliest possible opportunity is the only way to avoid months and years of suffering the financial loss of paying protection money and losing trade, and the misery and humiliation of having to endure the extortionist's threats.

Many police forces now have a wealth of expertise in dealing with extortion which, together with sophisticated technology, only needs the victim's co-operation to resolve these crimes.

Fitting security cameras is one of the best deterrents to extortion. There have been cases of extortionists demanding the videotape from the camera; police experts will often install covert camera equipment instead.

There is a new phenomenon used mainly by drug dealers to get their feet in the doors of youth venues, especially clubs and discos, and known as 'extortion in reverse'. Several cases have now been logged of publicans who maybe run a successful weekend disco in the lounge bar being approached by one or two smartly dressed men who ask permission to visit the disco and assess it, as they are thinking of operating similar ventures elsewhere. They even say they will pay for the privilege.

The publican, seeing no harm, agrees, and pockets the cash. Other visits follow, and on each occasion the publican is paid some cash. But in fact the visitors are dealers who have been busily setting up a drugs ring in the disco - which the publican can't report because, having accepted cash, he's implicated.

Once they've established that the publican is trapped the dealers stop paying him - but the dealing goes on. That's extortion in reverse, and the message is to learn from the folly of others and under no circumstances allow yourself to be conned into accepting payments.

Drugs

Busy, unsupervised pubs make the ideal place for drug dealers and their clients to operate unnoticed. But misuse of drugs on licensed premises, whether it be possession for one's own use or supply for another's, is a criminal offence and so is allowing one's premises to be used for the purposes of drug abuse.

It is therefore the responsibility of publicans and their staff to be observant and make every effort to spot people engaged in drug trafficking as soon as possible. If drug abusers or suppliers are allowed to become entrenched in a particular pub, it requires a great deal of effort to root them out. Any suspicions that persons either known or unknown are using licensed premises for the purposes of drug abuse must therefore be reported to brewery representatives at once.

Identifying them isn't always easy, but there are signs publicans and their staff should watch out for and, if spotted, never ignore.

- ◆ Usually, drug abusers and suppliers try to take over a small corner or private alcove in the bar. There won't necessarily be a large crowd of them, maybe only two or three – the supplier himself and a couple of minders or lookouts. They will usually act in a furtive way.
- ◆ A constant flow of strangers or persons who are not regular clientele will visit the pub where the dealer is operating. They will not buy a drink and will stay only long enough to make a purchase.
- ◆ Users of cannabis, who normally smoke the substance in hand-rolled joints, will leave sweet-smelling cigarette ends in ashtrays. The harder drug users who inject will leave used needles in bins in the toilets.

If there is any doubt in the publican's mind about how genuine certain customers are the advice of the police should be sought immediately. It is a misconception that a police investigation of drug abuse in the pub will cause massive disruption to trade. Generally speaking, and in the majority of such circumstances, this is definitely not the case. Usually, when the police receive information (which will always remain confidential) that certain licensed premises are being frequented by drug abusers or suppliers, a short, low-key undercover operation will be mounted.

Experienced plain clothes officers will soon spot the persons involved, and will quickly call uniformed colleagues to arrest them. The whole operation can be over in minutes, without any disruption to trade whatsoever.

Doormen

Since the early 1980s there has been a marked escalation in certain types of unsocial behaviour affecting the licensed trade. Drug abuse, the carrying – and use – of knives and other weapons, drunkenness and its consequent violence, protection racketeering, even political terrorism have all affected publicans and their businesses to varying degrees.

To protect their staff, customers and property, brewers and publicans have for many years employed doormen to monitor access and weed out customers who, in their judgement, would cause all sorts of problems.

In the past, doormen sometimes had as bad a reputation as the people they were supposed to be excluding. In time, the police, the local authorities, and the licensing justices got together and decided it was time to set standards for doormen.

Being a doorman has now become a legitimate profession. Proper training has to be given, and a certificate is issued to successful candidates, who are officially registered as doormen. The main aims of doorman training and registration schemes are:

♦ to regulate the employment of all people engaged in maintaining order in licensed premises;
♦ to insist, as a condition of the licence of all premises which employ doorstaff, on a commitment to certain standards on the part of those employed;
♦ to provide a framework within which licensees, police and local authorities can improve relationships and reduce crime, especially drug abuse and violent assault, and prevent door staff from being subverted by criminals.

Doorman registration schemes are generally administered by local authorities and implemented by making it a condition, through the Local Government (Miscellaneous Provision) Act 1982, that holders of public entertainment licences should not employ or engage in or about premises any person not registered with the local authority in any capacity concerned with the maintenance of order.

The use of unregistered doormen where a registration scheme was in force would be a breach of condition of the public entertainment licence rendering the holder liable to prosecution and revocation of licence.

Applications to become a registered doorman are considered by a local authority committee with regard to the suitability of the applicant, and taking into account any history of involvement in serious crime – for example assault, possession or supply of drugs, or sexual offences. However, a previous conviction, depending on the type and severity of the offence, is not an automatic bar to registration.

The police are involved throughout the procedure as a vetting body.

Having been accepted into the scheme, the applicant becomes a registered doorman or supervisor and is issued with a lapel tag bearing a registration number and a laminated ID card complete with photo, signature, and registration number. Registered doormen are required to wear the tag and carry the card while on duty.

As well as vetting, there is compulsory training given by police trainers including race relations advisors and the drugs squad, the fire brigade and the St John Ambulance Brigade. Subjects covered will include fire safety, licensing law, first aid, drugs awareness, power of arrest, use of reasonable force/restraint techniques and interpersonal skills, and training is followed by formal tests.

Registered doormen convicted of an offence or accused of inappropriate conduct such as a breach of code of practice or habitual association with criminals can be brought before the committee that originally appointed him, where his registration will be re-considered.

Properly trained and dedicated doormen are excellent representatives of the licensed trade. Because of the type of training they receive, they can give a genuine service to customers, advising, warning, assisting, and protecting.

CONCLUSION

Publicans may sometimes feel isolated, but the truth is that they are not alone. If they are unsure about any aspect of safety or security, they can and must turn to their brewery or to the police, where sound advice will be given.

Never act alone or think you can tackle a major security problem on your own. Help is readily available. Don't be negative about costs: security in a pub is as important as short-term profit, because without security tailored to the needs of your pub, profitability will soon decline.

Legal Notes

If a person is convicted of an offence committed on licensed premises and the court is satisfied that the person used or threatened violence, the court may issue an order prohibiting that person from entering those or any other named premises without the express consent of the licensee. The order can be from three months' to two years' duration as specified by the court. A breach of the order is punishable by a fine and/or imprisonment.

In addition to a licensee's ordinary rights to refuse entry to his premises, under the Act a licensee has the right to expel from his premises any person he suspects has entered his pub in breach of an exclusion order. The police must assist if requested.

A licensee has a legal duty not to permit drunken, violent, quarrelsome or disorderly conduct to take place on the premises, or to allow prostitutes to solicit or remain longer than is necessary to take reasonable refreshment. If a customer refuses to leave when asked to do so by a licensee, employee, or police officer in uniform, he may be prosecuted.

A licensee or member of his staff must not sell intoxicating liquor to a drunk.

As far as **door staff** are concerned, more and more licensing committees are insisting upon door security staff being registered with the local authority. You should make the appropriate enquiries at the town hall.

The only authority the police have to officially close licensed premises is under Section 188 of the **Licensing Act 1964** which provides the power to any two Justices of the Peace for the area to order every holder of a Justices' Licence for the premises in or near the place where riot occurs or is expected, to close for such time as may be ordered. It is an offence punishable by fine to ignore this order. However, wherever possible it is always preferable to co-operate with a request reasonably made by the police.

CHAPTER TWELVE

FIRE SAFETY

Glen Gorman

Fire is a peculiar monster, if you take a little time to think about it. One of the oldest forces harnessed by man and one of the most useful forces we can harness, yet it is taken more for granted than almost any other element in our lives. How often do we give a thought to the power fire has? Handled safely, fire will not give rise to any problems; but introduce a few combustibles and a little carelessness, and you summon up a monster worse than your worst nightmare.

Appreciating the power of fire is part of controlling it. Knowing what devastating effects it can have on property and lives is a step on your way to a better understanding of basic fire safety - not just knowing what measures to take, but understanding why you have to take them.

For instance, how long do you think it would take a fire to destroy the average living room furnished with everyday items - three-piece suite, coffee table, TV, video and so on - from time of ignition to blazing inferno? Ten minutes? Five?

In tests in fact, a fire started in an armchair by an unextinguished cigarette takes less than four minutes to rage totally out of control, with a heat so intense that furniture at the other end of the room will ignite even before the flame reaches it. Unconvinced? I can show you the video.

Make no mistake, fire is an extremely dangerous beast if let loose. But it is not often that victims of fire die from burning: the majority of fire-related fatalities are the result of smoke inhalation.

Smoke has many constituents including carbon monoxide and cyanide gas, depending on what is actually burning.

Carbon monoxide has an affinity for red blood corpuscles and will attach itself readily to them when you breathe it in, preventing the corpuscles from taking up oxygen from the air. It gives you a pleasant cherry-pink complexion - and it kills you. Cyanide gas attacks your nervous system: death can result from only short contact with very small amounts.

There are other deadly constituents of smoke: in fact most of the materials in your home will give off deadly gases, depending on their make-up, but by far the worst comes from what you are probably sitting on right now. Foam-filled furniture when subjected to heat or flames gives off fumes which are both flammable and poisonous. The situation has been improved by recent legislation governing newly manufactured furniture, but there is still a huge amount of pre-legislation furniture around.

> **Fire and smoke kill and do not discriminate. Young or old, male or female, day or night. In Blackpool in the late 1980s five people, some of them children, died in a hotel fire despite the best efforts of the fire brigade to save them. It was two o'clock in the afternoon.**

I hope that you now appreciate the destructive power of fire in your pub, which is probably also your home, and, armed with your understanding, will grasp the importance of fire safety. But before going into detail, there are certain generalities to be considered.

It is no good installing fire safety devices and instituting model fire safety procedures if no-one takes any notice of them. Take the humble self-closing fire-resistant door. Its purpose is to check the passage of fire and smoke, but it can only do this if it is closed. Consider this scenario. Five bedrooms, all fitted with perfectly good self-closing doors, open on to a common corridor leading to an escape stairway.

One bedroom has a fire; but the occupant has gone to the bathroom, leaving the door propped open. The smoke detector sets off the fire alarm and the other four occupants attempt to make their way to safety – only to be faced with a thick wall of choking smoke as soon as they leave their rooms. How do they make their escape? They don't. They die on the corridor from smoke inhalation – and all for a door left open.

There is no room for complacency with fire safety. Staff have to be properly trained by a competent person. Guests have to be adequately informed of fire routines. If you are responsible for fire precautions it is up to you to enforce them, because in the event of fire your guests', as well as your family's safety is in your hands. Should any contravention be found on inspection it could mean a hefty fine. Should death or injury occur as a result of laxity it will be on your conscience for the rest of your life.

STEPS YOU CAN TAKE NOW

There are several very simple common sense steps that you can take right now to improve fire safety in your pub.

- ◆ At night before going to bed, check you have unplugged any electrical appliances that don't need to be on.
- ◆ Don't empty ashtrays until morning – or if you, do make

Fire Safety

sure the butts go into a metal container.
- Don't run electrical flexes under carpets where you can't see if they're getting worn: they can set fire to the carpet.
- Fit correctly-rated fuses in plugs - 13 amps for any appliance incorporating a heating element.
- Make sure chip pans are never more than a third full of oil, or when you lower the food basket the oil will overflow and flame on the burner.
- Never leave a chip pan or frying pan unattended on the hob: it takes only minutes to reach ignition temperature. If you do have a chip pan fire, never try to put it out with water: water turned instantaneously into steam expands at a rate of 1700:1, so every cup of water you throw on to a blazing chip pan will come right back at you as 1700 cups of scalding steam, compounded by droplets of burning oil.
- When you go to bed, close all internal doors. What stands between you and the smoke if you've left them open? Close your doors and multiply your chances of survival.

There are many more equally simple measures - far too many to list here. Call in at your local fire station tomorrow: they will be glad to tell you more.

FIRE SAFETY LEGISLATION

If your pub provides sleeping accommodation for six or more staff and/or guests, and any of those are above first-floor level or below ground-floor level, then your premises falls within the scope of Section 1(2)a of the Fire Precautions Act 1971 and will have to have a fire certificate. If you are in any doubt contact your local fire safety department which will be more than happy to advise you - free. Remember, under Section 7(1) of the Act it is an offence to operate a premises without a fire certificate, and if you have a fire certificate it is your personal responsibility to ensure compliance with its requirements.

This is not merely bureaucracy: it could save your life. It is important to understand that your fire certificate is a legal document. It is not just a piece of paper but a booklet containing information about your premises, with the fire safety requirements that you must adhere to contained in writing and on a plan along with any other relevant documents issued by the fire safety department.

Any other documents issued to you - an inspection report, for example, are also legal documents.

You may not alter or add to your fire certificate, which must be kept on the premises to which it relates and be available for inspection at any time.

The fire certificate will detail certain measures with which you must comply. These will vary from premises to premises, depending on individual characteristics, so if you are comparing fire certificates with other publicans, do not be surprised if theirs differs from yours. If, on inspection, you are found to be in contravention of any of these requirements you will be advised on what to do and given time to put matters right. If you fail to comply you will be prosecuted and fined. If matters are judged so serious as to be a danger to life, the court may restrict the use of the premises or even close you down completely, using powers under Section 10 of the Act, until you have complied with the requirements of your fire certificate.

Some basic requirements

One requirement will always be to have a fire alarm system throughout the premises complying with BS5839 and fitted by a competent installer.

Each exit from the premises and each floor will have to have a break-glass call point to actuate the alarm (in public bar areas these can be fitted behind the bar).

Escape routes and rooms leading off them will have to have automatic smoke detectors. There are two common types: the ionisation type and the optical type. The former detects the invisible products of combustion and is thus very sensitive. False alarms can be frequent as the ionisation type can be set off by steam from kettles or bathrooms, aerosols, and even small insects.

The optical type detects larger particles of smoke and is less prone to false alarms. Both types are available as self-contained units for domestic use, but your fire certificate will require them to be linked into your general alarm system.

In the kitchen and other areas that can become smoky, a heat detector will be required. These go off either when a pre-set temperature is reached, or, where the area to be protected is naturally hot, ie the kitchen, they can detect anomalous or significant increases in temperature.

You will be required to test your alarm system and record the results in a log, which must be kept with your fire certificate and must be availabe for inspection. Most fire safety departments will also require a six-monthly test by a competent person other than yourself, who will supply a certificate of testing.

Escape routes and windowless areas will require emergency lighting installed to BS5226. This must also be tested and certified every six months.

Walls, doors and partitions that form part of the escape route must have a minimum of 30 minutes' fire resistance. Glazing in these areas must give the same fire resistance and be glazed shut. Doors opening on to escape routes must be self-closing and should never be propped open. New doors opening on to escape routes must be fitted with intumescent strips, which expand when heated to seal the gap between door and frame, and smoke seals which will operate when the fire is less hot but still producing smoke.

The escape route is the lifeline for your guests, any live-in staff, yourself, and your family. It must be kept clear of obstructions and combustible materials at all times of day and night.

If your pub is less than 11 metres tall or has fewer than four floors you will need only one escape route, but it must be treated as a sterile area – that is, there should never be any furniture, equipment or anything else there except fire safety equipment. Doors across the escape route must be free from any fastenings – in thick smoke you may not find the handle in time to save your life. Doors leading from the escape route to the open air may never be locked other than by an approved mechanism that works without the use of a key or card – a pushbar is common. These doors should never be blocked from the outside.

If your pub is taller than 11 metres or has four or more floors, then a second escape route must be provided to serve the upper floors – either an external fire escape or doors communicating with neighbouring properties.

All staff or guest bedrooms will need a comprehensive list of instructions on what to do in case of fire or when the fire alarm sounds. This should be prominently displayed – beside a mirror is a good spot, the back of the door not so good, especially if there are coathooks there.

You will need a number of portable fire extinguishers, which will be stipulated according to the floor area and nature of risks in your pub. These will mainly be water extinguishers, mounted on wall brackets, protected from vandalism and improper use, and tested annually by a competent service company. In the kitchen you will need at least one fire blanket and a CO_2 extinguisher. If you are in doubt about the proper use of extinguishers, ask at the fire station.

When the alarm sounds

All staff must be trained in what to do in case of fire or on hearing the fire alarm. Day staff need to be instructed every six months, night staff every three; and the dates of instruction need to be recorded in your log book. This can take various forms: fire drills; walking the escape routes; maybe discussing different possible scenarios. It should be the job of one responsible member of staff to ring 999 on hearing the alarm.

It is always good to have a fire action plan with one or two alternatives. Plan A, for instance, could relate to a fire where everyone could escape easily and unaided, whereas Plan B could outline action when residents are prevented from leaving their rooms by smoke in the corridors. Practice makes perfect, as they say, and if you design and learn these drills well, you may one day find yourself leading your staff, guests, and family to safety calmly and efficiently.

If there really is a fire, the first thing to do is to sound the alarm. Never assume someone else will do it. If the fire is obviously small, for instance, in a wastepaper basket, and you feel confident enough to tackle it safely, do so. Otherwise, close the door on it and institute the relevant fire action plan. Never put yourself at risk, and once the building is evacuaed no-one should re-enter it for any reason unless allowed to do so by the senior fire brigade officer present.

The person nominated to ring 999 should do so at once and never wait to investigate – the seriousness of the fire will already have been established by whoever sounded the alarm. The nominated person will be asked a number of questions by the 999 operator and should be prepared in advance to give them calmly and audibly. They may seem a waste of time in an emergency, but the more detailed information the operator can pass on, the more quickly the fire brigade can respond. In most cases two appliances will arrive within five minutes of the 999 call, and these early minutes can be vital in containing the spread of the fire. Do not be afraid that the call may turn out to be a false alarm – provided you are calling in good faith, the brigade would rather you called straight away rather than delay; and if false alarms are occurring because of a fault in your system you will be advised to call a maintenance engineer.

Never silence the alarms. If you do, people may assume the emergency is over and start heading back to their rooms and possible disaster. Never re-set the alarm panel: it can guide the fire crew to the seat of the fire.

Once the pub has been evacuated take a roll call. If anyone is missing inform the fire crew straight away and tell them where the missing person or persons were last seen and what room they should have been in.

How to save your own life

If you ever find yourself unable to get out of an upstairs room because of smoke in the corridor, there are steps you can take to improve your safety.

Make sure the door is properly closed and use any available sheets and towels to seal any gaps around it to keep the smoke out. Then open the window and shout for help, and if it is safe to do so wait near the window until help arrives.

However, it may be the case that the fire is so serious you are going to have to leave the room unaided by the window. In this case, stay calm. Drop out anything that will soften your landing – mattress and pillows, any bedding you haven't used to seal the door, and any available chair cushions.

Make sure the windowsill is free from sharp objects such as broken glass, and take a good look at the lie of the land below. Children can be lowered out to passers-by or dropped as gently as possible on to the cushioning below.

To rescue yourself, climb out of the window to full arm's length to reduce the distance you have to fall by as much as possible, point your feet downwards so they don't catch on anything, and let go. Be sure to bend your kness and roll as soon as you reach the ground.

This may all seem terribly dramatic and it is highly unlikely ever to occur, especially if you have been vigilant and meticulous where your fire safety precautions are concerned. But by knowing what to do you may one day save your own life.

CONCLUSION

What you have just read is by no means the ultimate compendium of fire safety in your pub, but more of a guide to what you might encounter, with a little insight into how dangerous fire can be.

There are other legal requirements that need to be taken into account - you need to be aware of your responsibilities under the Health & Safety At Work Act 1974 and the Licensing Act 1964, for example. If you want further detailed advice on fire safety contact your local fire safety department (they're in the phone book) or just pop along to the nearest fire station. There are also private safety companies all over the country - but expect to be billed for their services. The quality service you will receive from the fire brigade is mainly free - and very willingly given.

S.F.Leisure

206 Queens Promenade, Bispham, Blackpool FY2 9JS
For Hire and Sales Tel/Fax: 01253 595858

S.F.Leisure was formed in 1992 to meet the ever growing demands in the leisure industry for leisure products, initially for the purpose of hiring out these products.

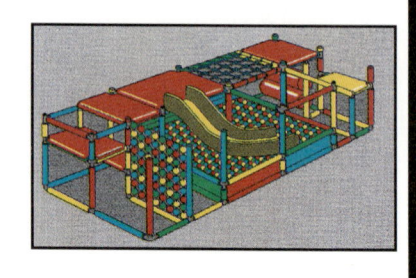

However, the business rapidly expanded and soon after the company began manufacturing a complete range of bouncy castles and adult inflatable games.

S.F. Leisure also design and build soft play areas and complete multi-level Play Centres and now due to demand from our customers, we have produced a complete range of outdoor equipment manufactured from pressure treated Hardwood and durable G.R.P. for slides and roofs.

All equipment is manufactured to the highest standards in our own factories and conform to the current British standards and legal requirements as set out by the Health and Safety.

CHAPTER THIRTEEN

THE FAMILY TRADE

Ted Bruning

Only a few years ago, catering for families with children was hardly an issue in the licensed trade. Those few pubs, or more commonly hotels, with separate dining rooms got a fair few families in, especially those with a boarding school nearby; some soft-hearted landlords allowed children to accompany their parents, even at risk of their licence; a hard core of opportunistic and unscrupulous landlords served teenagers with varying degrees of subterfuge; and the rest of us were left to fend for ourselves in the car park with a bag of crisps and a bottle of pop.

The pressure that led to the introduction of Children's Certificates built up slowly in the 1980s and 1990s and was collateral to the pub trade's advances in the eating-out market. Families on holiday or en route didn't necessarily like the offering available at Little Chef or Happy Eater. Parents who preferred the pub offering saw it as an injustice that the mere fact of having had children excluded them from their first choice of venue; and the family rooms where they could legally sit were often cheerless afterthoughts, cut off from the bar and everything that makes a pub a pub.

Hours reform in 1988, especially the extra hour on the Sunday midday session, added to the pressure. Going out for Sunday lunch became a majority occupation, but too many pubs could not legally cater for the new market and saw the bigger groups, (Beefeater, Roast Inns and the like) with their larger premises and limitless capital resources, running away with the business.

The time before Children's Certificates finally came in was one of adjustment. Police who used to prosecute if a door was left open between family room and bar began to turn a blind eye to well-run family pubs. Lawyers ruled it acceptable for children to dine in any area set aside for the purpose provided there was some token barrier - a change of level, or a low balustrade - dividing it from a bar. And play equipment sprouted

The Publican's Handbook

outside pubs the length and breadth of the land.

When Children's Certificates finally came in a couple of years ago, they proved a damp squib. The Home Office left it to local benches to decide what made a pub suitable for children; and the direst warnings of sceptics all came true. Too many benches ruled that a Children's Certificate would only be granted where there were separate children's toilets with low-level WCs, where there were no gaming machines, where all drinks were served in plastic glasses, where there were nappy-changing facilities in both ladies' and gents' toilets and so on. One bench even tried to rule that Children's Certificates should not apply to any part of the licensed premises where alcoholic beverages were for sale, which rather defeated the object.

This arbitrary approach has continued, despite warnings from both the Home Office and even the Magistrates' Association that the conditions attached to the award of a Children's Certificate should not materially alter the nature of the pub - should not, in the words of one cynic, create a licensed Macdonald's. As a result, fewer than 5 per cent of pubs have, at time of writing, bothered applying for a certificate. Those which have, have in the main been the big managed houses (especially those designed with children in mind, such as Allied Domecq's Wacky Warehouses) which can easily meet the most restrictive of magisterial criteria.

But the vast bulk of pubs have not turned their back on the family trade. In the years of waiting for Children's Certificates to be introduced, they were sub-legally discovering and meeting the challenges of the family trade with the tacit co-operation of police forces which were largely sympathetic and which had no appetite whatever for creating new and unjustifiable demands on their slender resources.

This unsatisfactory state of affairs has continued since the trade's disappointment at the form which Children's Certificates eventually took. It means that very many pubs are deriving an indispensable part of their business from a trade which is on paper illegal and which 15 years ago would have resulted in lost licences. Magistrates whose stipulations are being openly flouted by public and publican alike, with the more-or-less open approval of police chiefs who have other fish to fry, might reflect on this lesson in the limits of power.

But, however badly many magistrates have miscalculated, the trade should not dismiss their concerns lightly. Few justices, probably, are consciously aware of the legislative void of a century ago which permitted bad parents to carouse in bad pubs while their undernourished children slept in corners, or lay awake learning terrible lessons. But subconsciously, this is the picture which surely underpins their decisions. Publicans should bear in mind that in our culture there is a consensus that children and alcohol do not really mix, and that the Home Office has delegated to magistrates the impossible task of translating this vague consensus into hard and fast rules.

Basically, in practical terms, what this means is that happy families having lunch together in a well-run pub are fine; pale, pinched kids who ought to have been in bed an hour ago but are instead confined disconsolately to a corner under the giant TV screen, are not.

IS THE FAMILY TRADE FOR YOU?

There can be little doubt that the family trade has become essential to the pub trade as a whole – not just for the revenue it brings in, but because it corrects an impression, built up in the 1980s, of pubs in general as exclusive, largely male, and all too often unpleasant or even violent venues. Having said that, the family trade does not suit every outlet. If yours is a beer-house, no. There is a large minority opinion which says that pubs are places where grown-ups can escape the responsibilities of family life, where they can be themselves as they used to be before the kids came along. This is a valuable market, especially after 8pm. If children are likely to upset your regular clientele – and indeed if your regular clientele are likely to upset children – stick with the market you know.

If you are in a busy commercial centre next to an industrial estate and have a sharply defined business lunch trade and a younger destination-bound evening trade, probably no. It's unlikely that many families would have occasion to use your pub anyway, and it may well be that the presence of children would make your regulars feel uncomfortable.

But if you are in, or next to, a shopping centre where the competition is a cafeteria-style operation, probably yes, especially if you stay open all day and serve tea and coffee and the sort of light lunches popular with shoppers. If you have an appreciable tourist trade, emphatically yes. If you have a mixed local-tourist trade, emphatically yes. If you have a large local eating-out trade, emphatically yes. If you are a community pub with plenty of space and a diverse local population, then why not try it? You could build a whole new tea-time trade on the basis of cheap eating-out for families who, for one reason or another, don't want to cook that evening. How about, instead of the tired old happy hour, a promotionally priced family fun fry-up from 4-6.30pm?

Essentially, of course, this is a commercial question: the changes of the last 15-20 years have squeezed the ethics out of it. If, subject to the most basic strictures, you have a demand for family trade, then meet it. But do not take the decision lightly: catering properly for the family trade is not merely a question of letting families through the door; once they're in, you have to understand their needs.

And not only will you have to change the profile of your business to accommodate children; you will also have to alter your mindset to a degree. On the one hand, children running around freely are only a nuisance if you think they are; on the other, what seems to you like a well-behaved child sitting quietly with Mum and Dad is probably actually a little volcano who is bored, frustrated, barely restrained while in the pub and storing up a magnificent eruption for later.

FOOD FOR FAMILIES

Feeding the kids

Feeding children, as you will know if you are a parent, is very different from feeding adults. For instance, an overflowing plate of food might appeal to the acquisitive adult, but is just as likely to frighten a child and make him or her too anxious even to pick up a spoon. Child psychology is different from adult psychology in other ways too: for example, an adult kept waiting for a meal gets more eager for it, whereas a child kept waiting gets bored and becomes fractious, and by the time the food actually arrives the child is probably on too high a nervous plane to eat it.

Here are some practical tips for feeding children in your pub.

- **Get the menu right.** Most children like 'brown' food - burgers, sausages, fish fingers, chips, croquettes and other fried items - and 'soft' food - pasta in sauce, beans, fried eggs; and these foods form the basis of most children's menus. But many parents disapprove of this kind of food, and many older children don't care for it either. So in addition to special children's menus of brown and soft foods, offer half portions of the regular menu as well. Even if you don't sell a single one, you won't have lost a penny. (Incidentally, filled pancakes are the ideal children's food. Children perceive them as both brown and soft, while adults perceive them as cosmopolitan and grown-up. They also cost next to nothing and are easy to cook.)

- **Get the temperature right.** If you serve children food that is too hot, they will burn their mouths, but all your food has to emerge from the oven piping hot for reasons of hygiene. So serve it onto cold plates, and between dishing up and arriving at table it should have cooled sufficiently to avoid those burnt tongues. Avoid menu items which remain hot for a long time after serving, especially closed-in fruit pies.

- **Don't mix different items on the plate.** Some kids are picky: if there's sauce on their sausage, they won't eat it. So arrange to leave a little space between items; better still, use compartmentalised plates and sachet sauces.

- **Serve children quickly.** A few minutes after ordering, they will lose interest and become fractious, and when the food does arrive, they won't eat it. Given children's predilection for brown and soft foods, this is ideal microwave territory. And it's good if the children's fish fingers and chips arrive before the adults' gigot navarin: it means the adults have the chance to get the kids fed, or at least settled to their meals, and will be free to enjoy their own meals in comparative peace.

- **Provide free amusements.** A colouring-book and crayon set can cost under 50p and earn the undying gratitude (and repeat business) of the grown-ups by keeping the kids absorbed for minutes at a stretch.

◆ **Anticipate additional needs.** Providing a high chair for younger children is only half the battle. Why not earn a parent's undying gratitude (and repeat custom) by also offering plastic bibs and moist wipes? You could also keep a few jars of different baby-foods in stock: they cost very little and could be very useful for less well-prepared parents.

Drinks for kids

The traditional pub range of soft drinks is based on mixers and fruit-juices. These are second-best for children and teenagers, who are used to a whole world of brands which traditionally have no presence in the pub trade at all. The various guises of Coke and Pepsi have their followings, as do more traditional British brands such as Vimto and Irn-Bru. Then there are more exotic fruit carbonate brands, especially Lilt and Sprite, and heavily branded versions of old favourites, especially Fanta and Tango.

Sports drinks command the allegiance of health-conscious teenagers: important are Lucozade and Red Bull, but there is a host of other brands to choose from.

Then there are milk-based drinks. The post-mix shakes of the 1960s, which demanded special equipment and a lot of shelf-space, have been superseded by pre-mix brands such as Frijj, which you can buy in very small quantities to test the level of demand without too much outlay.

Most of these brand-names will be entirely new to most publicans: but rather than believing everything the reps tell you, try asking your own children what they prefer themselves; or if you have no children, try hanging inconspicuously around the nearest CTN at school chucking-out time and see what the kids are actually choosing to spend their own pocket money on.

Bag snacks

Exactly the same is true of bag snacks. Trends in the pub trade have been towards more adult snacks: cashews; dry-roast, honey-roast, and lightly curried peanuts; pork scratchings; Cheesy Moments; designer crisps such as Brannigans; hot nuts with special dispensers; jellybeans; Peperami; even (mercifully briefly) beef jerky.

Exactly the opposite is true if you really want to please an audience of children. They want the kind of cheap snacks – Nick Nacks, Monster Munches, Cheesy Wotsits and so on – which have never before had a pub trade presence. If you use a cash and carry, there should be a rep who will tell you what sells to kids in the CTN trade.

Sweets

It isn't just kids who have a sweet tooth: a bar of Cadbury's Dairy Milk goes down very well with a pint of Guinness. Children and adults alike will welcome a small display unit of

The Publican's Handbook

PLAY QUEST

Adventure Playgrounds today are enjoying unrivalled popularity. The wide range of equipment being offered in the current market would not have been imagined just a few years ago. The playground industry has changed beyond recognition, and the choice now available is staggering. Quality too has improved. Safety standards have been introduced which have been welcomed by everyone, and the resulting decline in injuries has been good news for us all. Styles too have changed. Perhaps the most noteworthy change is the return to the use of environmentally enhancing materials, such as natural timbers, bark or wood chip surfacing, grass covered mounding etc. Playground designers have come to realise that play can be a family event, that the playground should have warmth and a friendly appeal, should contain areas simply for relaxation, and will be far more inviting with the inclusion of flower beds, planters, and by the planting of trees. Fencing too has become part of the design, as has the inclusion of seating, tables waste bins etc. In short the days of the cold clinical often dangerous playground are coming to a close, thankfully to be replaced by far more appealing alternatives. We are pleased to be one of the companies instrumental in this change.

No doubt you are already well familiar with the Playquest rang of adventure playground equipment. Accompanying this catalogue is a list of some 500 or so sites at which our equipment has been installed in recent years. These include many holiday parks, beer gardens, schools, garden centres, local authority play parks etc. in fact you may be surprised to find our name popping up in all sorts of places. Our continued success is principally down to the fact that we as a company have continually remained in touch with a market which is constantly changing. We produce the type of equipment which people say they want to buy. Our many customers speak very highly in our favour, and for many reasons. If there is a problem we deal with it promptly and effectively, and we keep to our word.

As a result you will see Playquest playgrounds being commissioned nation-wide by clients who are well known family names. Included amongst these are such notables as Butlins Starcoast World, the Sealife Centres (at Portsmouth, Oban, Rhyl and Southend), First Leisure, Haven Holidays, Bridgemere Garden World, Marton's Brewery, Burtonwood Brewery, Toby Restaurants, Whitbred, Wellington Country Park, Paradise Wildlife Park, (we could continue but modesty forbids).

Playquest Adventure Playground Systems are an instant success wherever they are installed. They help to build up custom for a wide range of businesses, or simply provide a super environment in which children can safely play. It is therefore with this in mind, that we present "Playquest" to you. We hope to meet many of you in the coming year, so keep us in mind, we are only a phone call away.

PLAYQUEST U.K.
For more information or to request a catalogue, please call;
Phone / Fax: 0121 420 2071   Mobile: 0976 302186

The Family Trade

The Play Co

THE MARKET LEADERS IN CHILDREN'S ADVENTURE PLAY

- Sole suppliers to major breweries
- Full turnkey service - advice, design and installation to RoSPA guidelines

- Cost effective, exciting designs to choose from
- From the people who invented the modern play experience

CALL ON **01978 264 141**
OR FAX **01978 262 448**

THE PLAY CO., UNIT 2, WREXHAM TECHNOLOGY PARK, CLWYD LL13 7YP

Abbots Coffee Co.

Have some of the finest blends of ground coffees available.

For use with
Espresso - Filter Machines
Bulk Brewers and Cafetieres.

£71 + VAT per month buys a UNIC DIVA - Automatic 2 Group Cappuccino Machine

Call now on 01707 647390

Abbots Coffee Co., 2 Earls Lane, South Mimms, Herts EN6 3LT

---

selected confectionery lines located eye-catchingly near the till, and pub customers are not nearly as price-conscious as CTN customers: in fact, they often don't even look at the prices of individual lines, only of overall rounds.

PLAY EQUIPMENT

Children like to spend a lot of the time their parents spend in the pub outside it, making use of the climbing frame and other facilities you have thoughtfully provided for them. So what are the basic requirements?

Obviously, safety is the first consideration; and not just safety, but parental confidence in your standards of safety. Children might feel fine with the safety aspects of whatever provision you make: but anxious parents – and your insurers – need to be made to feel comfortable and secure. In fact it is a good idea to require children to be supervised by a responsible adult while playing outside.

Play equipment need not be too complicated: children will make up their own games, and equipment with finite possibilities may even limit their imaginative play. Plenty of space to run around and let off steam in is just as important as fancy equipment.

Three basic rules should be followed:

◆ **Rule one** is to fence the play area off completely from both the car park and the road, with a gate a toddler can't open.

- **Rule two** is to provide a soft landing under each item of play equipment, either rubberised flooring or properly maintained bark-chip – ie, bark-chip which is raked back into position every day and not allowed to scatter all over the countryside.
- **Rule three** is to separate toddlers from older children, who in their natural exuberance can cause distress and even injury without meaning the slightest harm. Fence the toddlers' play area off, and provide play equipment which is suitable for different age-groups: a 15ft slide is no good for toddlers, while a 3ft slide won't do much for an eight-year-old.

TOILETS

There is no real need for low-level urinals and WCs, although if you can provide them so much the better. But there are several points to watch nonetheless:

- Parents with small children are much more anxious about cleanliness than unaccompanied adults, so pay special attention to regular checking, recleaning, and replenishment.
- Turn down the thermostat! Children burn much more easily than adults, so make sure the hot water is not much more than lukewarm. (This will also save you money.)
- Sometimes, inevitably, dads will find themselves rescuing small girls from the ladies, or mums will have to venture into the gents after small boys. When this happens, it's your job to minimise any embarrassment that might arise.
- Nappy-changing facilities are, at their most basic, a high table or shelf big enough to accommodate a baby, with enough clearance at the foot end for the adult to stand. A hand-wash basin and towels, a hook for the nappy-bag, and a pedal bin for the dirty nappy are also essential; more deluxe establishments might run to a free supply of baby-wipes, and nappies in a coin-slot dispenser. These facilities, where provided, are almost always in the ladies' loo; this is a bit unfair, and if you can locate them in the gents as well, or in a neutral cubbyhole, or even in the disabled loo if you have one, so much the better.

BREAST-FEEDING

If you cater for the family trade, you will inevitably encounter a conflict between mothers who find it perfectly natural to breast-feed in public, and other, often older, customers who find it embarrassing or even revolting. Most mothers who breast-feed are very adept at doing so discreetly, and those who don't care for the sight can always look away. But to avoid upsetting anyone, it's best to have somewhere private available for the purpose – a facility which many nursing mothers will actually welcome: after all, just because they breast-feed doesn't mean they want to do so in public. Your own private lounge might be the best place,

The Family Trade

subject to the usual security considerations.

One point: never, ever try to banish breast-feeders to the ladies. Would you want to have to eat your dinner in a toilet? But not all mothers breast-feed: why not offer facilities for making up feeding bottles?

If all this seems too involved, and too expensive, don't lose heart. The family trade can be extremely lucrative, especially if good summers are to become the norm, and catering for it is really no more involved than catering for any other market. And there are few sights more gratifying on a fine day than to look into the bars and the garden and see them filled with well-cared for customers, young and old, having a splendid time.

Health and Safety Notes

Ensure that, in promoting the family trade, you have considered the relevant issues as part of the health and safety risk assessment.

The **children's play area** is a particular source of concern. Steps need to be taken to ensure the safety of the equipment and the area in which it is located. Issues to consider include regular checking of equipment, eg for damage caused by wear and tear, misuse or vandalism, and the avoidance of broken glass in the play area. If there are any particular safety-related conditions that apply, such as an age limit, this should be made clear. Guidance on outdoor play areas exists in British Standards and child safety organisations such as RoSPA can provide advice.

Certain items of play equipment, such as bouncy castles, necessitate a greater degree of control by the business, eg to ensure that the fixings remain sound and that it is used appropriately. The supplier of the bouncy castle should provide you with the necessary information on its safe use. Electrical risks associated with the compressor arrangement also need to be addressed.

Legal Notes

Much of the law relating to young persons is confusing and misunderstood. The basic rule is that (except in certain circumstances) **children under 14** are not allowed in the bar.

Difficulties arise with what is meant by a bar. It is defined in the Act as 'any place exclusively or mainly used for the sale and consumption of intoxicating liquor'. From this it can be seen that if there is a bar counter in a room where drink is sold and consumed, under-14s will be excluded. However, should the room contain an area set apart, as say a dining area separated by a rope or plants, and that area is used for a different purpose, it may not be a bar to which the legislation applies.

The exceptions to children being excluded from a bar are when the child is:

◆ the licensee's;
◆ a resident in the pub but not employed there;
◆ simply passing through the bar from one part of the pub to another (eg on the way to the toilet, if there is no other convenient way);
◆ there by virtue of a Children's Certificate.

Licensing Justices may grant a Children's Certificate allowing under-14s to remain in the bar if they are satisfied that the environment is suitable and meals and beverages other than intoxicating liquor are available. Many licensing committees have been criticised for being too stringent in their requirements for the granting of a Children's Certificate – it is essential to obtain the local policy document if an application is contemplated.

Although 14- to 18-year-olds are permitted in a bar at the licensee's discretion, it is not permissible:

1. to sell intoxicating liquor to under-18s or permit them to consume alcohol in the bar;
2. for a person under 18 to buy or attempt to buy intoxicating liquor or to consume it in the bar;
3. for anyone to buy or attempt to buy any intoxicating liquor for consumption by a person under 18 years in the bar.

Note, a licensee may not sell intoxicating liquor to any person under 18 for consumption away from the pub, or allow any other person to do so. There is an exception for a young person, aged 16 to 18, who may buy beer, porter, cider or perry to drink with a meal in an area set aside for service of meals. Where there is an area set apart for service of meals, in such an area young persons (over five years old) may consume intoxicating liquor with a meal provided the drinks have been bought by an adult.

CHAPTER FOURTEEN

ADDING VALUE

Paul Cooper

This chapter deals with ways to add value to your business in two areas; ways in which you can make all the areas of your pub work for you; and additional services you can offer.

It is essential that you make as much use as you can of your capital and fixed costs - the pub and its land. This will enable you to make the greatest profit. Small details can make a big difference in making your pub special and worth visiting, but there are many practical issues to consider when you are seeking to add value to your pub.

The ideas discussed here will not make money for all publicans, but will work in certain types of pub in certain locations. It is impossible to recommend which you should or should not deploy in your pub. It is up to you to decide which are appropriate, where your skills lie, what money you have available and what will give you the best returns on your money and time. It is unlikely that your pub will be suited to all of the ideas and even if it is, it is unlikely that there are enough hours in the day to do them all. However, you should endeavour to do as much as reasonably practicable to generate incremental income - as long as it leads to additional profit.

The point of all of the suggestions is additional income so I will concentrate on the considerations needed before you make a commitment.

FUNCTIONS ROOM

- Do you already have a functions room?
- Is there enough unused space to create one?
- Is there demand for one?
- Is there one at a nearby pub, and if there is, what niche does it fill?
- Is it posh, so you can offer a value for money alternative?
- Or is it basic, leaving the door for more upmarket events open to you?

If you already have one, you should consider whether it could or should be extended, and indeed whether to keep it at all – there may be a more profitable use for the space. If you don't have one, it is worth considering converting any unused space you may have – a disused first floor room, or an old barn or outhouse. But even if the space is lying idle and can be converted at a reasonable cost, you still have to evaluate demand for the room.

Assuming you have decided to enter the functions market, bear in mind your functions room's purpose and the facilities you will be providing. If the room is to be used solely for pool or major sporting events on big-screen TV, it is pointless lashing out on expensive, high-quality decor. But it is just as pointless fitting out a room intended for wedding receptions with lino floors, woodchip wallpaper and plastic chairs.

There are many potential uses for your functions room and each one needs careful consideration before committing to it.

A functions room could be the ideal place to put your pool tables, provided there is a market for pool and the clientele is one you want to cater for. You will need to consider the supervision of this room. Unless you are going to open a servery in the room and pay for the additional staff, you will not know exactly what is going on in there. You must also consider the difficulty of using the room for anything else if it means moving and storing the pool tables first.

If the room is relatively small, it may be possible to use it only for conferences and meetings (although a large room could also be used as a private meetings room or conference facility). A meetings room will only work if you have a catchment area which includes businesses and social/voluntary organisations. Research the facilities already offered in nearby pubs and hotels. Find out what they offer and how much they charge. You will probably be able to undercut the large hotels and offer an equivalent service.

Create a tariff of charges for the different facilities you can offer. This should include:

◆ A day delegate rate to include room hire, paper and a pencil for each person, mineral water, cordials, mints, morning coffee and biscuits, buffet lunch and afternoon tea and biscuits.

◆ An equipment hire service. Initially, the most cost-effective way to do this is to hire the equipment from a local company and pass the cost on to your customers. Equipment that may be requested includes a flip chart (don't forget to provide pens), overhead projector and screen, slide projector and screen and television and video.

◆ Cost scales for additional services, eg alternative lunch menus and room hire (remember 20 people in your functions room creates costs for you in staff, time and cleaning).

The conference market takes a lot of building up and continuous marketing. Can you generate repeat business by hosting regular events in your functions room? Are there local voluntary organisations, sports clubs, or societies that have regular meetings and could use your facilities? Alternatively, you could use the room for entertainment. If you have a large screen TV to show sporting events, why not make use of the functions room for this? This has the advantage of ensuring that vocal supporters will not upset other customers. You may be able to create a reputation for your pub for live bands, comedy nights or even less frequent events such as magicians or palm reading. If there is a local demand, arrange a monthly senior citizens' tea dance or Saturday night dinner dance.

An obvious use for a functions room is private parties. These are relatively easy to organise and can be very profitable. Again, you need to assess the facilities you can offer. Prepare a package containing information on different buffets and sit-down meals you can offer, room hire charges and any other services available, eg tie up with a good local DJ so you can offer the music for the party. (A cautionary note on 18th birthday parties – some of the guests will be under 18.)

Weddings can be a good source of income but they take a great deal of time and organisation. If you decide to cater for wedding receptions, you have to be prepared to commit the time needed to organise them. A wedding is one of the most important events in someone's life and if you make one mistake, no matter how small, it may ruin the whole day.

The easiest way to deal with enquiries for wedding receptions is to have information prepared and readily available. Think about all the services someone expects at a wedding reception – bar, wine, full three-course meal, buffet for the evening. To offer more than your competition, team up with other local businesses and offer a complete wedding service. If you can get an agreement between yourself, a photographer, a cakemaker, a car hire service, a wedding gownmaker and hirer, gentleman's suit hire etc, you could all offer the complete service each recommending the others. But remember, your reputation will be affected by the service offered by companies that you have recommended.

Another use for your functions room may be as an occasional restaurant, possibly to cater for Christmas meals and parties.

No matter what services you offer, the most important thing is to co-ordinate with the organiser of the event on every detail, in particular the required layout of the room. Do not assume anything, ask the questions. When you think all the arrangements are agreed, confirm them in writing, then telephone to check the arrangements a week before the event.

It should go without saying to keep a large, page-a-day diary specifically for your functions room and write every event in, whether or not it is confirmed. (You do not want an unexpected wedding party turning up.) Allocate the job of taking bookings to one person so there can be no confusion as to who is responsible for organising events and there can be no double bookings. Chase up provisional bookings for confirmation of the events. Do not assume that because a provisional booking has not been confirmed after two months the party will not turn up on the doorstep. Before taking a booking make sure that you can cope with it. There is no point in taking a booking for a meal for 80 if you can only seat 60, so make sure you know how many people you can accommodate for different formats – sit-down, finger buffet, horseshoe, theatre style.

Make sure you have all the equipment you need (don't forget you need enough for the function and the normal running of the pub) including cutlery and crockery. There is nothing worse than having to collect teaspoons from the first guests served with coffee before you can give the last guests theirs.

When it comes to calculating room hire charges remember to include all the additional costs that holding the function will incur. However, also remember that people in your functions room paying for drinks and food is income you would not have if they were not there – is it, perhaps, worth offering the room free if the group are having food and drinks?

Marketing your functions room is essential. It is unlikely that your bar customers will have seen the room, so no-one will know it's available unless you tell them. How you market the room will depend on what you are using it for. If you are hiring it out for meetings, private parties or weddings, put up a wall display in the pub with photos of the room laid out in different formats and brief information. You should also have a small brochure or leaflet available in the pub. The local tourist office may also carry the brochures for you, as this sort of use constitutes 'business tourism'.

If you are using the room for entertainment, put up posters, hand out leaflets, and contact the local papers and radio stations to get in their, often free, listings sections.

If you want to try to get clubs to use the room, write to them inviting them to come and have a look. Maybe offer a discount on drinks to all committee/club/society members attending meetings.

Word of mouth is still one of the best ways to advertise a functions room. If you have customers from local businesses, tell them you have a meeting room available and get staff to tell as many people as possible about the room.

One last thing to remember is to make sure the room is always clean and tidy and laid out in a basic format. You never know when someone will ask to see the room and first impressions always count.

GARDENS

If you have a garden or outside area, you should try to make the best possible use of it. The garden 'decor' is as important as that of the bar and will depend upon your trading patterns and customer profiles.

There is a huge range of furniture available. The type of furniture you choose should be determined by the type of pub you are running and the image you want to give. All in one wooden 'picnic-style' tables and benches are relatively cheap and long lasting and may be appropriate for large grassy areas. For patios there are many styles of

Anchor Fast

The Ultimate Big Bench Table For Pubs, Clubs & Hotels

PHONE 0115 922 7821 FOR COLOUR BROCHURE

seating available. Plastic tables and chairs are cheap but will not be appropriate for an upmarket wine bar, while cast-iron furniture is expensive but has a quality feel. You may decide that you want to build brick seating or incorporate it with flower beds which will ensure that it doesn't get stolen.

Planting can also have a huge influence on the appearance of an outside area. Even the smallest, most ill-placed piece of concrete can make a pleasant patio area with a bit of imagination. But do consider the maintenance of any planting before trying to re-create Kew Gardens: a well-planned garden of evergreens providing good ground cover will produce a good looking, maintenance free and indestructible environment. Flowers and bedding plants may look spectacular but need much more maintenance and care and may easily be damaged by customers. It is up to you to assess how green your fingers are, how much time you want to spend in the garden and how much destruction your customers are capable of.

Whatever you plant, make sure that it is not poisonous, especially if you have a family trade. Furthermore hanging baskets or window boxes on the front of the pub look fantastic when new, but remember that they need maintaining and watering. Nothing makes your pub look less cared for than dead plants hanging around the front door.

The type of custom you aim to attract and the size and nature of the garden will determine whether or not outdoor lighting is worthwhile. If you have a family trade in the evening and play equipment, good lighting will be essential to ensure the safety of the children.

Outdoor heating is a relatively new idea. It can extend the length of time that you can use your garden both later into the evening and further into the colder months. It is important that you fully understand the initial costs including getting a gas or electricity supply to the units, how many units you will need to be effective and the ongoing cost of running the units. Bear in mind that you are in effect trying to heat the whole town.

As mentioned previously, it may be possible to turn an outbuilding or barn into a functions room. Alternatively, it may be worth considering using the space as a children's room, family room or games room. Similarly, a large outside area could be used for other entertainment. You may be able to encourage additional custom by having a bouncy castle for children – or why not try a bucking bronco or pole jousting for big kids? If you are a more traditional operation, you could try boules, bowls, bat and trap or Aunt Sally.

Barbecues are now popular during summer months, and can attract a great number of people. You need to take into account the risks of a barbecue which include fire, storage of food at safe temperatures, cross-contamination of food and the possibility of customers burning themselves.

If your outside area is large, you might consider organising bigger events. A large car park could be used for Sunday morning car boot sales. A large garden could be used by a local group, eg Scouts or

Adding Value

Guides, for a fete. While the latter will not raise money for you, it will bring customers into your pub. Other ideas for a large garden could be a fun day or a fireworks display but these take some organising and have huge health and safety implications.

Whatever you do with your outside area is going to increase your work load. You are in effect extending your pub and creating greater sales opportunities. You must ensure that you consider all aspects of what you are doing and take into account issues such as theft of equipment, pub security and the health and safety of customers.

MULTIPLE USE

Multiple use of the pub will be most appropriate to those situated in small villages, towns or communities. It is a way of getting the greatest use out of your assets as well as providing a service to the community. If you have the space available, it may be possible to incorporate another business within the premises – perhaps an off-licence. This would not need any additional space as you offer the facility from the bar, providing that your justices' license permits off-sales.

An expansion of this idea would be to provide a local shop. If your pub is in a village with no shops or where a stand-alone shop is not viable, there is an opportunity for you to generate additional sales by opening a small shop within the premises. You may also consider operating a sub-post office facility within the pub.

First, though, consider whether you really want to run a shop/sub-post office? Do you have the expertise? Other considerations are:

- Is there enough local demand to make it worthwhile?
- Will the cost of conversion and equipment be returned?
- Will the post office accept your application to operate a post office facility?
- What additional hours will you need to work?
- Do the returns justify the extra effort needed?

Alternatively, you may be able to let spare space – for instance, a lounge bar or upstairs meetings room that you don't normally open at lunchtime – to visiting services. This will require little additional work on your part but will generate additional income.

Services that may be interested in this type of arrangement could include chiropody, citizens' advice bureau or an MP's surgery. This use doesn't just apply to spare trading space: there have been cases of pubs with surplus kitchen capacity producing meals on wheels under contract to the local services department. This is going to depend very much on your locality and the willingness of the service providers.

A longer term approach, which again will involve little ongoing work on your part, would be to lease any spare space you do not want to use to another party, eg let a disused outbuilding as a shop or studio or, if it's large enough, a micro-brewery. This will be subject to any restrictions laid down by your landlord, if you are a lessee or tenant, and planning restrictions.

OUTSIDE BARS

With an outside bar, you are renting your services to a private individual or group to operate a bar for a function.

To run an outside bar you need all the equipment required to run the bar in your pub. Pumps and coolers can be hired, although some breweries will provide you with them free of charge. You will need to buy extra glasses, fridges, optics, optic stands, ice buckets, etc. You will also require some kind of bar (a good sturdy trestle table will suffice) for venues such as marquees that do not have one already, and a way of providing ice.

When deciding whether or not you want to offer outside bars you must consider issues such as storage, transport, responsibility for running the bar and stock control. You will need a substantial amount of equipment to run an outside bar effectively and you must have somewhere to store it (it doesn't look very fetching in the middle of your lounge floor) as well as some way of transporting it. It is unlikely that a car will be large enough and so you will need to consider buying or hiring a van.

When you run an outside bar, you have to apply for an occasional licence for the event. This is tied to your full licence and you are personally responsible for the people at the function, in the same way as you are in your pub. You must therefore ensure that you have a responsible and trustworthy person to run the bar at the function and maintain stock control.

BREWING ON THE PREMISES

In the last decade more than 300 pubs have started brewing their own beer. A small brewery can be installed in any suitable outhouse or part of the main building for £12,000-20,000, but the local customs and excise office should be consulted before plans are laid.

Planning permission is also essential, even if no buildings are altered, because installing a brewery represents a change of use for which permission is required, and there is a possibility of brewing creating nuisances - especially smell and increased traffic - which residents have a right to object to.

The purpose of brewing on the premises is not usually primarily to trap the brewers' and wholesalers' percentage, which the costs involved can easily wipe out. Rather, it is a marketing device which attracts destination trade. Any publican contemplating brewing should take into account not only the additional time and effort that would be involved in the actual production of the beer, but also the time and effort needed for the marketing to make it all worthwhile.

Having said that, it can be an extremely worthwhile addition to a pub operation, especially if the brewery is visible - perhaps through a viewing panel - from the bar.

It is very much easier to make cider on the premises. It is legal to make, for sale, up to 7000 litres of cider of not more than 7.5 per cent abv a year without paying duty, which cuts out the paperwork and makes the business more profitable. The process is also considerably easier than brewing: you can either mill and press your own apples or buy the juice in. All you then need are enough fermentation vessels. You may not even need yeast, since most apples come with a ready supply of their own. The juice should not cost more than £1000, and the return should be £7500-10,000.

LETTING ROOMS

Many pubs have either spare bedrooms or an outbuilding that could be converted to letting rooms.

Before deciding whether to let them, ask frankly whether they are suitable. Rooms the size of a cupboard will not make good letting rooms. People expect to be able to get through the door and take more than two steps before they end up in bed. Is the room big enough to accommodate a wardrobe, bed, dressing table and sanitary ware? You will be able to charge more for rooms with en suite shower and loo, but all the rooms will need at least a hand-basin.

If you do not have the room to accommodate en suite bathrooms, you must provide sufficient toilets and bathrooms within easy reach.

If your letting rooms are above the pub, you must consider your own privacy. The last thing you will want is to come face to face with a stranger on your way to the loo in the middle of the night. Similarly there is the security issue. Guests will expect to come and go as they please and will therefore expect their own key to get in at night. You must ensure that guests cannot roam around the whole pub in the middle of the night helping themselves to your stock. You must also make sure that a guest who forgets to shut the door properly does not present a security risk.

Before going ahead with any alterations you will need planning permission. If you wish to be able to serve alcohol to your guests outside licensing hours, you will also need to make an application to the licensing justices.

You need to remember that fire regulations will apply to furnishings and doors in letting rooms. You should also bear in mind that it will be cheaper in the long run to buy better quality fixtures and fittings at the outset. They are going to get a great deal more wear and tear than in domestic accommodation - you can live with a dodgy wardrobe door but a paying guest will not, and they are not as careful with your furniture as they are with their own.

Next, consider the work required to operate the service. There is the time needed to service the rooms, wash laundry and serve breakfast. These all involve getting out of bed earlier in the morning and you must decide whether this is something you want to do.

If you have letting rooms and serve breakfast to guests, it may be worthwhile opening to non-residents for breakfast, depending on your location. Obviously if you are in the middle of nowhere with no passing trade, it won't be; but if you are on a busy road or in the centre of town, it might be. Even if business from non-residents is slow, you are not losing anything by offering the service.

In marketing your letting rooms, you need to be clear who you are trying to attract and how you can reach them. An advertising board outside the pub is essential. If you have local business people as customers, tell them about your rooms and give them a guided tour. If you are close to businesses that are likely to have visitors from out of town, try to get to talk to the person who books the accommodation in your area.

You are unlikely to reap benefits from advertising in the local press, after all the people most likely to see your advert live in the area. But if you are aiming your accommodation at specific customers, it may be worthwhile advertising in a related publication, eg if you offer fishing or there is good fishing nearby, advertise in a fishing magazine. An advert in Yellow Pages and a listing with Talking Pages are probably going to provide a good source of bookings.

Most tourist information offices will hold lists of local accommodation. You should try to get on this, even if you are asked to make a 'contribution'. It is also worth being included in other guides. Some of these provide free listings based on the standard of your accommodation, eg *Room At The Inn* published by CAMRA. Others require you to pay for inclusion, and you should be extremely wary of these – all too many are con tricks. You pay your money, but nothing ever gets published. If approached by a 'sales representative' for a paid entry guide, demand to see previous editions.

There are several organisations that offer a recognised grading system, eg AA and RAC. These schemes generally operate on the basis that the standard of your accommodation is assessed and then you pay to be accredited, have a listing in their guide and use the relevant logo.

Having your accommodation accredited by an organisation guarantees guests a certain standard of accommodation and service and therefore offers some peace of mind when they are booking.

SEASONALITY

The seasonality of your business will depend very much upon your location.

If you have a country pub, it is likely that good weather will bring the customers and the summer months will be your most profitable. However, in a town or city centre trade is likely to be much more evenly spread throughout the year, with a dip in January and the summer months. Wherever your pub is located, it is likely that Christmas and New Year will be your busiest time of the year and January will be your quietest.

You must be prepared to amend your staffing and purchasing habits as trade increases and decreases. Some pubs will see a 50 per cent drop in trade from one week to the next in September, an increase greater than this in December, a fall of over 50 per cent in January, increasing again in the summer. It is therefore essential to have flexible staffing arrangements in order to cope with this situation.

Adding Value

You must also be prepared in terms of stock levels. You must be realistic about trading levels while trying not to run out of anything: the tendency at Christmas is to fill every spare inch of the pub with stock to make sure you don't run out, but when January comes you will have great difficulty selling the excess and end up with wasted stock.

However, there are many fixed outgoings – loan repayments, vending machine hire, rent, business rates etc – which are not seasonal. It's up to you to make the most of opportunities to bump up cash flow in the quiet periods – for instance, Burns' Night falls in January, and St Valentine's Day falls in February. A winter ales festival may also give a cash boost on an otherwise dead weekend in January or February. Of course, this is also a good time for your annual holiday – the quiet trade means you can leave a responsible member of staff in charge, rather than going to the expense of hiring a relief manager.

SALES OPPORTUNITIES

There are many ways to increase trade that will cost you nothing. These are linked to your staff and their training. They are so simple and in some cases serve the double purpose of increasing your sales and offering a service to customers.

- If a customer has half-an-inch of beer left in his glass, offer another. If they were hovering over whether or not to have another, you are more than likely to sway them.
- When clearing glasses from a table (and if you have the time), offer to fetch customers another drink.
- Ask any customer who orders a short: 'Large one?' If they say no, fine; if they say yes (and they often do), you've chalked up a 100 per cent sales gain. Train staff to do the same.
- If you have a menu, it is pointless tucking one copy down the side of the till waiting for someone to ask for it. Make sure you have menus on all tables and the bar. Offer the menu whenever you can.
- Make sure that you and staff know your products and, in the case of food, what they contain. Promote products on sale, regardless of personal preference. Staff have been known to say to customers: 'I don't know how you could drink that.'

PROFESSIONAL PRESENTATION

It is important that the presentation of your pub is at all times professional. Gone are the days when it was acceptable to have the pub looking good only when you opened the doors – every customer who walks through the door expects the pub to look the same as when it has just opened, even ten minutes before closing. They do not know that three coach parties have just left, nor do they care.

This requires ongoing maintenance throughout the day. It may mean sweeping up cigarette butts at the end of busy periods or making sure that, if you have a sweet trolley, the last customer of the day does

The Publican's Handbook

not get a choice of two dried up gateaux.

Do not forget all the areas of the pub – garden and toilets (especially toilets) as well.

It is easy to open the pub and not actually go outside for days on end. Make a point of going outside and walking 100 yards down the road, then turning back imagining you are a customer. You will be amazed at what you notice – smudged chalk boards, old fag ends, crisp packets, dead hanging baskets, etc.

Point of sale and advertising material will be much more effective if it is presented professionally. This does not mean running up huge printing bills. Simple things like not sticking posters over the top of pictures and having a holder for leaflets rather than spreading them across the top of the cigarette machine do make a difference. Always ensure that your posters and point of sale are up to date and not damaged. There is little that looks worse than an out-of-date, nicotine-stained, dog-eared poster on the wall.

Remember to change your advertising regularly. Customers become blind to advertising material after about four weeks, and it becomes useless. I know one pub where the A board hasn't been changed for two years. Work out where in the pub most people will see material. Toilet doors, above the urinal in the gents, the back of WC cubicle doors and entrance lobbies are all good places. Once you have worked out where the most prominent positions are, stick to them. A pub completely plastered in posters and point of sale material looks cheap and tacky.

SESSION BY SESSION OPERATIONS

Throughout the day and week your pub will have different trading patterns. You should try to change your offer to the customer as the trading patterns change. Aim your offer at a particular time of the day and week for the customers that you are trying to attract.

Music plays an important part in this. You should change the style and volume of the music as your customers change. It is pointless playing full-volume heavy metal at lunchtime if you are trying to attract office workers and shoppers; conversely if you have a younger evening trade they won't stay for long if you're playing Mantovani. Remember the music is not there for you or your staff but for the customers – even if it is not to your taste.

If you have the facility, you should alter the lighting levels in the pub to create atmosphere.

You may even employ different staff to cater to different markets or simply give them different lunchtime and evening uniforms.

It may be possible to increase your sales and profit by changing your product offer. If you have a large and not too price-sensitive business custom wanting to sample different cask ales early in the evenings, why not buy a polypin of a special guest beer and serve it direct from the cask, charging a premium price, every Friday from 5pm?

On the food side, your lunchtime customers will probably want a snack on the hoof while your evening trade wants a full three-course meal.

Linked to the products you offer are the prices you charge. You may be able to generate additional custom by offering a Happy Hour at quiet times – but if your pub is really busy on Friday and Saturday nights and your customers are willing to pay, you can even put your prices up temporarily. This is easier if you have the right kind of electronic till which can be pre-programmed to switch to the higher prices automatically.

CONSISTENT IDENTITY

Whatever type of pub you decide to run, services you offer and customers you aim for, you must try to present a consistent message to your customers. If you are running a traditional pub, do not fit it out in chrome and glass or put up a neon sign outside. This will give confusing messages to customers. Decide what you are going to be and stick to it. Do not try to be all things to all people or you will end up being nothing to nobody.

Do not let one area of your business jeopardise main areas of your trade. If your clientele is predominantly senior citizens and your local bikers' club wants to hold their annual convention in your car park think about what effect this will have on your regular trade.

STAYING AHEAD OF THE COMPETITION

Once you have decided what type of pub you want, what services you will offer, what style of operation you are going to have, what products you are going to stock on the bar and what food you will offer, remember it is not set in tablets of stone for the next 25 years. You must constantly review what you are offering the customer. This is the only way you will stay ahead of your competition.

Constantly introduce new ideas. These could be small things like trying a new beer, changing the staff uniform or introducing a jellybean machine or more substantial changes like introducing a play area. Use your imagination, but listen to new ideas from staff and customers too.

Evaluate the chances of success of new ideas before you commit to them. If a new idea doesn't work then see if you can make changes to make it work and if you can't, learn from the mistake.

Finally, whatever you decide to do with your pub, make sure that it is what you really want to do. Ideas you are unable to fully commit yourself to will not work. Do everything wholeheartedly. Your biggest success will come if you can stamp your personality on your pub.

Most importantly, if you enjoy what you are doing, your customers will enjoy themselves and your pub will be a success. Good Luck!

The Publican's Handbook

Health and Safety Notes

In providing **accommodation** for either customers or staff, fire safety is a particular issue and advice on appropriate measures to take should be sought from the fire officer. In some instances a fire certificate will be required.

Fire is an issue to include in your health and safety risk assessment. In carrying out the assessment you will need to consider whether adequate precautions are in place and whether the necessary checks are being made to maintain those precautions.

Other issues to consider include **general maintenance** requirements and the checking of electrical appliances provided such as kettles, hairdryers and irons. The Health and Safety Executive has provided a booklet aimed specifically at electrical safety in hotels and tourist accommodation. This is available from your local environmental health officer or direct from HSE Books, reference IND(G) 164L.

If you provide accommodation for lodgers for whom it is their permanent place of residence, a 'house in multiple occupation' may be created. If so, specific housing legislation applies and advice should be obtained from the environmental health officer.

BREWING ON SITE

Requirements of the **Food Safety (General Food Hygiene) Regulations** discussed in Chapter 8 Catering apply.

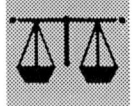

Legal Notes

The showing of videos requires the prior grant of a **Video Performance Limited Licence**.

A **Cinema Licence** may be needed for film shows and video jukeboxes. Application for **Cinematograph Exhibitions Licences** are made to the local authority. Under the **Cinemas Act 1985** exhibitions of moving pictures (other than TV or Cable TV) may not be given unless licensed. Terms and conditions may apply, including a condition requiring the premises to close on Sunday, Christmas Day or Good Friday.

There are exceptions in the case of occasional exhibitions (no more than six per annum) provided certain notices are given to the licensing authority, fire authority and police. An **Occasional Licence** is for the sale of intoxicating liquor at premises other than the applicant's. Application is to the magistrates' court.

The justices have a discretion to grant an Occasional Licence for a period not exceeding three weeks at any one time. There is no restriction on hours in the licence as specified even on Sundays, but an Occasional Licence is not available on Christmas Day or Good Friday.

The premises become licensed premises for the purpose of the Licensing Act 1964 and, therefore, restrictions regarding young persons apply.

The magistrates' court has a discretion to grant **Special Orders of Exemption** for special occasions (extensions) upon application by the holder of a Justices' On Licence adding such hours as specified in the order. There is a drinking-up time.

Sound Advice

It is a well known fact that music is good for business.

With PRS music, you can set the right atmosphere, attract new customers and increase turnover. PRS makes it simple to meet your licence obligations and offers advice.

Call PRS free on 0800 068 48 28
or Fax on 0171 306 4550 (Ref: SD)
Internet: http://prs.co.uk

PRS

PRS - our business is adding value to yours.

CHAPTER FIFTEEN

TELEVISION, MUSIC, SPORTS AND ENTERTAINMENT

Paul Cooper

This chapter will look at some of the many ways that you can offer entertainment for customers. This could be quiet background music, heavy rock bands, a magician entertaining at restaurant tables or showing a football match.

TELEVISION

Television, in particular to show sporting events, has become an important way of enhancing business in many pubs. Careful consideration must be given when deciding whether to have a television in your pub. A television offers an added facility for existing customers and may attract new customers. However, the way it is used makes an enormous statement about your pub. You need to consider what you are going to show on the television and whom it will attract. There are many types of sporting event and each will attract its own type of customer: football will attract a younger more rowdy crowd, whereas motor racing or cricket is likely to attract a more mature following. Will the screening of sport enhance the offer to your particular customer base or will it deter them from visiting? If a television is gong to alienate your existing customers, it is unlikely that it is going to be beneficial in the long term. This may not be true if you have a separate room that could be used for screening sports. Another major consideration must be whether a worthwhile return on your investment will be generated.

If a television will enhance your customer offer, then the next decision to be made is what type you are going to buy and where you are going to position it. The basic choice on what type of television to have is either standard or big

The Publican's Handbook

THE ART OF THE PROJECTED IMAGE

The EX2 Video Projector
State of the Art, Nicam Stereo, Proper 4x3-16x9 switchable aspect ratio. Specifically designed and built in the UK for the commercial and domestic markets.

The EX3 Video & Data Projector
Scans at 32KHz for Computer Data & Image Projection.

The EX4 Video, Data & Line Doubled Projector
32KHz Scanning with built in Line Doubler.

Scorpion 46" 52" 60" 67" Video, Data & Line Doubled Rear Projection Systems

Specialist Central Server AV Systems, LCD-DLP Projection systems, Message Generation, Playvision Multi Player Game Networks.

Satvision Plc, Northwest Teleport Centre, Stockport Road West, Stockport, Cheshire. SK6 2BP, UK Tel: 0800 317473.

The Licensed Trade's Ever Changing World

In today's technology led, swiftly changing world, the licensed trade needs to keep abreast of new products and developments, grasp the opportunities as they arise, and use the new technologies available today and in the future, to their best advantage.

Over the past few years it has been proved that the most cost effective form of entertainment for the wider audience has been the introduction of large screen projection systems. These systems when linked to the numerous terrestrial and satellite transmitted television channels deliver all types of sporting events to the public sector who frequent Britain's Pubs & Clubs.

Their has been many instances and events where the individual licensee or major brewer has doubled or trebled gross income on an ongoing basis in particular outlets where large screen projection is used.

The outlets which have been successful, are the outlets which promote and advertise the fact that they have the large screens and who promote, on an ongoing basis, the events which are to take place in the future.

We at Satvision are constantly striving to introduce new products in this everchanging market place, enabling licensee's to take advantage of these new technologies.

NEW PRODUCTS: Over the past year or so Satvision have launched the following new products;

THE EX2: A new video projector designed and manufactured in the UK specifically for the British Pub & Club Market. It is the lightest, brightest projector available in today's market. It offers unique features which are unavailable in any other product of it's type. Quadryl Nicam Digital Stereo, fastext and proper switchable widescreen aspect ratio to take advantage of the new digital widescreen television programming available in the near future.

THE EX3: As the EX2 but scans at 32khz to enable the projection of computer data direct from your PC.
The EX4: As the Ex3 but with a line doubler to enable the projection of the ultimate image.
THE SCORPION SYSTEMS: 67 - 60 - 52 - 46 inch Wide Screens. The new range of Scorpion systems are Rear Projection units, where the projector is installed within a mobile cabinet. This type of system counteracts problems of very brightly lit areas, pubs with low ceilings, or where a projection system needs to be available in more than one room in the Pub or Club. The Scorpion 67 uses the Ex series of projection systems enabling you to have the choice of Video, Computer Data and Line Doubling in one mobile unit.

PLAYVISION: The Game; The Worlds First Pay to Play, Interactive Multi-Player Games Network. A ten player five a side football game, each player operating an infa-red handset, each human player being a player on screen. The Game will enable the creation of local, regional, national and International football league Networks played out from our local pubs. Teams of five can play inter-pub leagues, or play other pubs inn other parts of the country or even play another country at the game, but each team will stay in their own home pub.

TRADENORTH LEASE & FINANCE; Tradenorth Leasing is a part of the satvision Group of companies. It is the finance arm of the group and offers competitive lease and finance packages to the purchaser of Satvision's range of products.

It is also used by a number of brewing and multi-site operator groups who, due to a budgetary requirements, do not have monies available at the right time to take advantage of a major event.

In this case Tradenorth steps in with a suitable finance arrangement, the system is installed, the outlet is able to take advantage of the event, payment is made sometime in the future when the budgets become available.

The Satvision group of companies is wholly committed to developing existing and new products aimed at enabling the licensee's of today, tomorrow and the future, to be more competitive, cost effective and profitable.

GIANT TV SCREEN

ASSOCIATED VIDEO
Est 13 yrs
Tel: 0151 346 9339
Freephone 0800 515690

TRIAL RENTAL OPTION
4 WEEKS FREE* RENTAL

The Best Deal
Top Quality Equipment
Best Quality Guarantee

Full UK Coverage
The Best Support Service

We will beat any price like for like
* subject to installation fee

GIANT SCREEN TV's
Maxi Eclipse 370 Projection TV's
(By far the best projector for pubs and clubs)

- Established 1980
- Super sound
- Professional Installation Teams
- No games, gimmicks or salesmen
- Latest Technology
- Biggest Bright Pictures
- Nationwide Service and installation
- Leases from £19.00 pw
- Flexible Rental Arrangements
- Over 2000 Installations Worldwide
- Exclusive Suppliers
- No "free" trials

Rent for 10 months and we give you the system
CALL THE EXPERTS
Brewery and trade enquires welcome
Tel: 0121 354 2393   Fax: 0121 355 0108
MAXIVIDEO ADVANCED SYSTEMS LTD

Misuse this card...

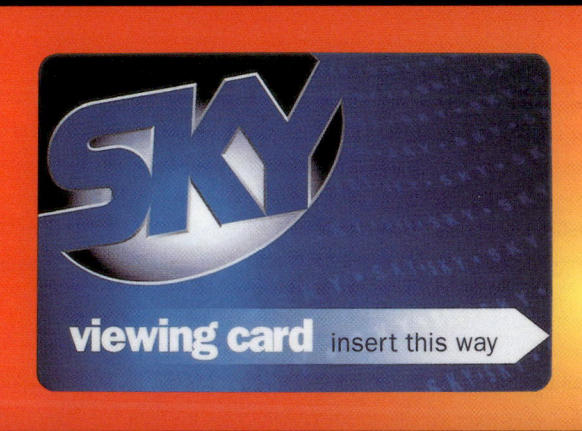

and a £5,000 fine and a criminal record could be on the cards.

If you manage commercial premises where Sky is shown, you must not use a card obtained under a Domestic Subscription Agreement.

There are no exceptions to this rule.

It is a criminal offence to show Sky dishonestly, including Pay Per View events, in any public or other non-domestic premises using a card obtained via a Domestic Subscription Agreement with intent to avoid the appropriate non-domestic payment*.

Individuals who commit this offence, when caught, face fines of up to £5,000, expensive court appearances, a criminal record and the associated problems that this could bring.

A small minority of establishments are still using domestic cards to show Sky. This must stop. Sky are committed to catching offenders so that honest subscribers win the extra business generated by key sports events.

Due to their success in catching offenders, Sky now has over 550 investigators making random visits to pubs and clubs nationwide. They will arrive unannounced during broadcasts and catch offenders unawares.

To check the terms of your agreement or obtain the correct viewing agreement please call 0990 741 147.

*The Copyright, Designs and Patents Act 1988 (Section 297). Under this Act, 'A person who dishonestly receives a programme included in a broadcasting or cable programme service provided from a place in the United Kingdom with the intent to avoid payment of any charge applicable to the reception of the programme commits an offence and is liable on summary conviction to a fine'. This fine is up to £5,000.

CREATE AN ATMOSPHERE

Seeing is Believing at Vision…

Vision is a company established to offer to you a 'state of the art' service in big screen entertainment.

This professional and innovative company has a wide range of experience in pubs, clubs and associated venues. Offering a nation wide delivery and installation service, with fully trained installation engineers and site surveyors.

Stockists of all leading names of video projectors, screens and big screen televisions, Vision's helpful sales team are able to advice and to discuss their seasonal offers (including trial periods, discounted prices, exclusive package deals etc) or to carry out a no obligation site survey to determine the most suitable product(s) to suit your requirements.

Based in Sutton Coldfield in the midlands for easy motorway access, Vision is happy to demonstrate the wide range of products available in one if their purpose built projection theatres.

A full twelve months on-site warranty is given on all equipment, with extended warranty packages available on request. All equipment is chosen carefully to ensure maximum reliability, quality and performance. Every system fitted comes with a complimentary promotional banner.

For creating image and atmosphere, big screen entertainment is the answer. It attracts new customers and encourages existing customers to stay longer and spend more, resulting increased bar takings and profits. When used to it's full potential not only can your customers enjoy the benefits from large audience viewing of sporting events, but they can also enjoy film nights, race nights, karaoke, not to mention pop videos and live music concerts.

Vision is enthusiastic about their products. Phone now for their latest offers and let them show you why.

Tel: 0121 3213393
Vision Projection Systems Ltd. The Royal Works,
Coleshill Street, Sutton Coldfield, West Midlands B72 1SJ

Television, Music, Sports and Entertainment

This is what you call REAL pulling power...

THE BIG SCREEN ENTERTAINMENT SYSTEM

Pull Down Your Screen..
Pull in The Punter's...
& **Pull** Those Pints.

- Live Sport
- Create Image & Atmosphere
- Encourage Customers to
- Film Nights
- Karaoke
- Quiz Nights

THE BIG SCREEN TRIAL...

Have your Big Screen Entertainment System installed today for the cost of a couple of pints a day

For our latest offers and package deals call now on
0121 321 3393

Vision Projection Systems Ltd
The Royal Works Coleshill Street
Sutton Coldfield West Midlands B72 1SJ

BIG SCREENS UP TO 27ft
BIG on installation nationwide
BIG experience in Pubs & Clubs
BIG value for money
BIG on-site warranty
BIG on personal service

For information call Video Monitor Services Ltd. on
0181 875 1144

Recognised and appointed supplier and installer of JVC, JBL, Thomson, Philips, Sharp and Sony.

VMS is a Trade Mark of Video Monitor Services Ltd.

SCREENTV

GIANT TV SCREEN

ASSOCIATED VIDEO
Est 13 yrs
Tel: 0151 346 9339
Freephone 0800 515690

TRIAL RENTAL OPTION
4 WEEKS FREE* RENTAL

The Best Deal
Top Quality Equipment
Best Quality Guarantee

Full UK Coverage

The Best Support Service

We will beat any price like for like

* subject to installation fee

screen. Your decision will obviously be influenced by the amount of space and money available. A standard television is more discreet and will have less impact on the appearance of your bar area. It will enable those who want to watch it to do so without becoming an annoyance to those who do not. The television will have even less impact if you turn off the volume. A big screen television needs a large amount of space and will dominate the room. Many of the screens available can be 'wound up' when they are not being used, which limits the impact on the room when the screen is not in use. If you have a separate room, eg a function room that can be used for the television then there is no impact on either regular customers or the appearance of the bar.

Satellite or terrestial programming

There are two types of programming available to you - satellite or terrestrial. If the sporting events that you wish to screen are shown exclusively on terrestrial television then you will need only buy a television licence. However, many major sporting events are now exclusive to satellite broadcasters. If the events you want to show fall into this category, you will need to purchase a satellite decoder and subscribe to satellite stations, in addition to purchasing a television licence (you need a television licence even if you do not have an aerial and cannot receive terrestrial channels). If you are subscribing to Sky television then you will need to apply for a card that is valid for licensed premises. These are different to those used in domestic premises and cost more.

MUSIC

Music makes a huge difference to the ambience of any pub and so you must carefully consider the style and volume of your music. Ensure that your music policy is what the customers want and not what you or your staff wants. It may be that your pub does not need music at certain times of the day or indeed at any time. If you have decided that your pub will benefit from music, then you should decide what music you should play at what times of the day and at what volume. If your customers at 9pm on Saturday nights are completely different to those at 2pm on Monday, the music should also be completely different.

The type and volume of the music that you play will determine the equipment that you need to buy. If you intend to only play background music, then you will need a much less powerful system than if you intend to play loud foreground music. The best way to choose and purchase a music system is to obtain a specification and quotation from two or three companies. They should be able to recommend exactly what equipment will be best for your needs.

The recordings that you play can be obtained in one of two ways. You can purchase CDs or cassettes from a local shop or you can rent them from a company who provides this service for pubs. Rented recordings will usually be categorised into styles of music ensuring there are

KARAOKE UK

THE NEW CONCEPT IN LIVE HI-TECH ENTERTAINMENT
The Lodge, Goyt Mill, Marple. Stockport SK6 7HX

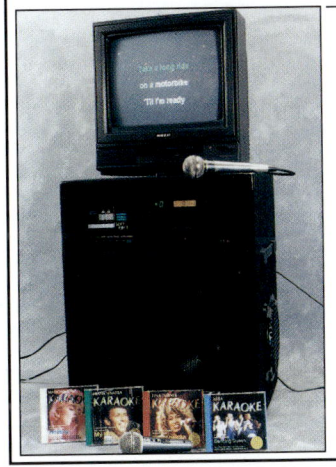

The Twister

- The best self-contained system available
- All in one CD/CDG player with skip-free shock resistant pick-up
- Built in cassette recorder and 200 watt amplifier
- Full mixing capabilities
- 19 step digital key control
- 2 Microphone inputs with digital echo
- Multiplex facility
- 6 speaker system

ALL WEIGHING LESS THAN 59LBS.

---

no songs inappropriate to your style of pub. Most of these services operate by the company sending you a number of recordings each month and you returning the same number to them. This can offer a cost-effective way of obtaining a constantly changing variety of music. However, there is usually a charge for lost recordings.

Another alternative would be to have a juke box. When considering a juke box, you need to take into account that you lose control of exactly what music is being played. If you have a varied customer base that requires varied styles of music, you cannot stop people playing music that may be inappropriate to other customers in the pub. In addition, a juke box may not be a reliable way of providing music as there will be times of silence when no customers have paid for music.

LIVE ENTERTAINMENT

Live entertainment can be a major attraction for customers. The most important thing is that the customers attracted are the ones that you want and they do not alienate regular trade. Different acts will attract different people. There are a multitude of different types of entertainment available including DJs, singers, comedians, karaoke and magicians. One way to find acts is by visiting other venues and approaching good performers for your pub. Alternatively, you can

The Publican's Handbook

KARAOKE UK

THE NEW CONCEPT IN LIVE HI-TECH ENTERTAINMENT
The Lodge, Goyt Mill, Marple. Stockport SK6 7HX

Well known in the licensing trade as leading suppliers of Karaoke equipment to the home and leisure industries have available, their 1997 catalogue, packed with a host of new products and 50 pages giving a selection of over 900 discs.

Introduced for the first time is "THE TWISTER", a complete mobile self contained CD+G unit with recording facilities for under £1000.

Video CD Karaoke is now replacing the large expensive 12" Laser format for which they have available a 51 disc autochanger and a discman style unit, playing standard audio, CD+graphics, Video Karaoke and feature films, with microphone inputs, echo and keychange. Ideal for public presentation or home use.

Their Rechargeable RADIO MICROPHONE avoids the expense of replacement batteries and is the most compact unit available.

Ten working systems, together with a range of accessories which includes lighting, large screen TV and disc storage are always on show at their studio in Stockport, where visitors are always made welcome.

Should you require a personalised alphabetical listing of your choice of songs or unable to find your favourite song, their computer will do the work for you.

A full range is also available via the internet at:

mailord@karaoke-uk.demon.co.uk

Or by telephone: 0161 449 0441

Television, Music, Sports and Entertainment

KARAOKE UK

THE NEW CONCEPT IN LIVE HI-TECH ENTERTAINMENT
The Lodge, Goyt Mill, Marple. Stockport SK6 7HX

LEADING SUPPLIERS OF KARAOKE EQUIPMENT
TO THE HOME AND LEISURE INDUSTRY

EQUIPMENT TO SUIT ALL NEEDS FROM HOME USERS TO PUBS, CLUBS AND PROFESSIONAL ARTISTS

MAIL ORDER SPECIALISTS

NEW — PORTABLE VIDEO & GRAPHIC PLAYER

NEW — AUTOMATIC VIDEO/CDG PLAYER 51 DISC AUTOCHANGER

CDG 3000 - GRAPHIC CD PLAYER FULL FUNCTIONS + AUDIO INPUT

PIONEER 100 CDG PLAYER 100 DISC AUTOCHANGER

DKK 200 - BIG ECHO - GRAPHIC CD PLAYER

SONY 200 DISC CDG 200 DISC AUTOCHANGER

MUSIC PARTNER KH300 COMPUTERISED KARAOKE PLAYER

CDG-X3 - GRAPHIC CD PLAYER WITH BUILT IN TAPE

CAMERA — ENHANCE YOUR PRESENTATION BY FEATURING THE SINGER ON YOUR TV

THE TWISTER COMPLETE CDG SYSTEM WITH RECORDING FACILITY

FEATURING:
GRAPHIC CD PLAYERS
LASER DISC PLAYERS
VIDEO CD PLAYERS
COMPTER KARAOKE
AMPLIFIERS
SPEAKERS
DISCS

253

The Publican's Handbook

contact local agents or performers whose numbers are listed in Yellow Pages. Once you become known for live entertainment, you will find that people approach you.

There are several ways to promote live entertainment both in-house and externally: posters, chalk boards and flyers inside and on the outside of the pub will tell both passersby and existing customers what is going on. A small advert in the local paper may also attract a larger following. In many areas there is a 'what's on' guide, and inclusion in this would probably be worthwhile. Most local papers and some radio stations have listings of what is going on locally and, in most cases, these are free.

LICENSING FOR ENTERTAINMENT

If you decide to provide music or live entertainment, you must ensure that you are properly licensed. For live entertainment, you may need a public entertainment licence, depending on what sort of entertainment you are having. Consult your local authority, who issue the licenses, as to whether or not you need one. You will need to comply with certain regulations before they will issue it and the cost of the licence varies between authorities. They will also issue you with a fire limit that you must not exceed.

If you are playing music of any kind you will need to obtain licences from both the Performing Rights Society (0171 580 5544) and Phonographic Performance Ltd (0171 437 0311). The cost of these licences will vary depending on what equipment you have and what music you provide.

QUIZ NIGHTS

Quiz nights are a way of providing entertainment at minimal cost. They are relatively easy to arrange and require only a small effort on your part. One way to get the questions is to buy a number of quiz books and pick the questions yourself. Another is to buy the question sheets from a company who provide them specifically for pub quizzes. If you decide to find your own questions, then it is worth making sure that they cover a range of subjects (even in a pop quiz do not make all the questions about the 70s). The questions should also vary in difficulty: if people cannot answer any questions they are unlikely to come to the quiz again and if they are too easy you will have a large number of winners. The easiest way to provide prizes is to charge for taking part and use this money for prizes. It may be worthwhile, in the long run, subsidising the prize fund until the quiz becomes established.

SPORTS AND BAR GAMES

Sports and bar games can provide an additional feature to your pub. As with all things, the first consideration must be whether these are in keeping with the type of pub that you are running.

Within the pub you should consider darts (although space may be a limitation), dominoes and traditional games such as shove ha'penny, table skittle or quoits. You could also consider modern

Television, Music, Sports and Entertainment

Sound Advice

...Don't just take it from us!

"Music has boosted
my bar profits by 200%"

Bob Crossley
John Bull
West London

"If I stopped the music
my takings would drop by half"

Thomas Holmes
Finnegans Wake
Bristol

"We made this pub a music pub
and we've never looked back!"

Terry & Pam Kent
Springhead
Hull

For a licence call free on
0800 068 48 28

PRS

The Publican's Handbook

Music brings business to life

Music is good for business!

It is a well known fact that music is good for business - in a pub or club background music can create a good atmosphere and helps customers relax.

Live music, discos or theme nights are the best ways of attracting people to your pub and a good band can guarantee a good time.

> This means increases takings over the bar.

The money generated by a music event more than covers the cost of DJ's or musicians and the necessary licence fees for public performance of music.

What is the right type of music?

The music you use should be appropriate for your business and your customers.

People respond best to hearing well known, recognisable pop or light classical music that they are familiar with, Research shows that popular music, tailored to suit the existing or desired clientele can encourage customers to stay longer, buy more and can also influence purchasing choice.

Fortunately, a PRS licence means you are free to offer practically all popular copyright music that you will need, from country to classical, folk to rock and jazz to current chart hits.

> So you can play the music your customers want to hear.

Who are PRS?

The Performing Right Society (PRS) is a non profit making, membership organisation which collects licence fees from music users and distributes the money as royalties to those who create the music - songwriters, lyricists and composers.

Is a licence require by law?

Yes, the Copyright, Design & Patents Act 1988, states that you must obtain the permission of all the writers and composers whose music you intend to use - a near enough impossible task.

> PRS make things easier for the music user so they can fulfil all their obligations through one point of contact.

We can also give you advice about other licences you may need.

What does the licence cover?

A PRS licence will cover you to use most types of music from around the world - whether it is a recording you have bought or rented, a radio programme, satellite TV or a live performance by a band or solo artist. In fact - any type of musical performance.

You need a PRS licence even if you have the following:

- TV licence
- PPL Licence
- Entertainment Licence

Television, Music, Sports and Entertainment

Who is responsible for the Licence?

You, the owner or manager of the premises - musicians do not hold a PRS licence.

How much will it cost?

For a pub with background music using a tape or CD player it could cost as little as £2.21 per week.

For live music the rate starts from £5.25 per event.

Contact us today and we will arrange for one of our representatives to call and assess your premises and provide you with a full costing.

Where does the money go?

PRS makes no profit for itself. After deducting operating costs, all of the licence fees collected are distributed as royalties to the writer and publishers of music throughout the world.

Some of our members rely on income from PRS for a living.

However, in 1995, 61% of members received less than £250 throughout the year.

How do I contact PRS?

If you would like to use music in your business you can apply for a licence by calling FREE on 0800 068 48 28.

You can Fax on 0171 306 4550 (Quoting Ref:SD)

Or alternatively you can find us on the Internet at http://prs.co.uk

If you are a customer who already holds a licence from PRS and you have and enquiry about your account please contact you local Account Office on the following numbers.

Scotland & Northern Ireland
Edinburgh - 0131 226 5320

North of England
Warrington - 01925 234456

Midlands & East Anglia
Peterborough - 01733 312 712

Wales & West England
Bristol - 0117 930 0036

London & South of England
London - 0171 580 5544

Please note that if you play recordings of music (CD's, tapes, records, jukebox) you may need a licence from Phonographic Performance Ltd (PPL)

They can be contacted at;
Granton House
14/22 Ganton Street
London W1V 1LB
Tel: 0171 437 0311

PRS

Our business is adding value to yours.

games such as Connect 4 or Jenga. One way of making a feature of the games may be to have a games night. If you have the space, it may be worthwhile considering a skittle alley. You need to be sure that there will be enough demand to make it a worthwhile investment. If you are thinking of having a pool table, you should consider whether the type of customers attracted by pool are right for your pub (a pool table will give a negative message to some people). All these ideas give you the opportunity to start teams and become involved in local leagues. This could boost trade on nights that would otherwise be quiet.

Similarly, it may be possible to become involved with a local sports team. This may be cricket, rugby, football or whatever is played in your area. You could sponsor the team or hold a fundraising night for them. The overall aim is to get the team to 'adopt' the pub as their own. It may be worthwhile providing a few nibbles for the team on a night after their practice to ensure they spend their money in your pub.

This chapter has only covered the main types of entertainment that can be used in pubs. There are many others and new ideas are always emerging (Internet cafés were not heard of a few years ago). Be on the look out for something that can give your customers more than your competition offers. Ideas may not necessarily come just from other pubs, but can be from high-street retailers or leisure outlets for example. What ever you decide to do, stick with it. There is little point in trying something once and giving up if it is not an instant success. If it is a good idea and you feel that it should work then give it a couple of months.

APPENDIX ONE

LICENSING JUSTICES

Licensing Justices are Justices of the Peace elected from amongst themselves in their particular Petty Sessional Division. They sit as a licensing committee and consider licensing applications at their licensing sessions. Intoxicating liquor must not be sold by retail without a justices' licence.

Licensing committees must hold not less than five meetings in the 12 months beginning with February in every year. Each Petty Sessional Division fixes its own meeting dates in good time prior to the February meeting, which must be held in the first 14 days of the month and is known as the General Annual Licensing Meeting (sometimes referred to as Brewster Sessions). Other meetings throughout the year are known as Transfer Sessions.

Application to the Licensing Justices must be submitted in accordance with strict rules set out in the Schedules to the Licensing Act 1964. In addition, most licensing committees issue their own *Policy Guidelines* which are available upon request from the office of the Clerk to the Licensing Justices. It is essential for any prospective applicant to obtain a copy of the local policy document. A few courts make an administration charge for this document.

Licensing Justices generally have a discretion to grant or refuse applications made to them for new licences. They also deal with most other licensing applications including, for example, applications to transfer or renew existing licences, or for approval of alterations to licensed premises, or for the grant of additional hours by approving Special Hours Certificates or Extended Hours Order. They also hear applications for revocation of Justices' Licences.

In considering applications, the Licensing Justices may grant a Justices' Licence to anyone (who is not disqualified) as they think may be fit and proper to hold a Justices' Licence.

259

PERMITTED HOURS

The usual permitted hours are:

- 11am to 11pm Mondays to Saturdays inclusive;
- noon to 10.30pm Sundays and Good Fridays;
- noon to 3pm and 7pm to 10.30pm Christmas Day.

There is a 20-minute drinking-up period at the conclusion of permitted hours. Where a Supper Hour Certificate applies in an area set apart the permitted hours are:

- 11am to midnight Mondays to Saturdays inclusive;
- noon to 11.30pm Sundays and Good Fridays and Christmas Day.

There is a 30-minute drinking-up period.

Extended Hours Order (Section 70 of the Licensing Act 1964)

Where there is a Supper Hour Certificate and music or any other entertainment is provided for diners, an Extended Hours Order may be granted allowing service up to 1am. There is a 30-minute drinking-up time which is allowed.

Special Order of Exemption (Section 77 of the Licensing Act 1964)

This may be granted for special occasions (eg wedding receptions) upon application. Note, this is not granted by Licensing Justices but a magistrates' court (or by the police in London).

DIFFERENT TYPES OF LICENSES

Justices may limit the manner in which a licensed premises may operate by imposing the following restrictions:

- beer, cider and wine only;
- beer and cider only;
- cider only;
- wine only (Section 1 of the Licensing Act 1964).

APPENDIX TWO

DISABILITY DISCRIMINATION

It is now an offence under the Disability Discrimination Act 1995 not to offer people with disabilities the same facilities and service available to others without justification.

While there have been no prosecutions yet and so no-one knows what constitutes justification, two things are certain. First, the pub trade has been slow to adopt either the physical alterations or the changes in mental attitude necessary to offer an adequate welcome to people with disabilities. And second, once the alterations are in place, important financial benefits will follow:

- ◆ Proper facilities for people with disabilities will attract, not only those customers themselves, but also their able-bodied friends, and are, therefore, a potential traffic-builder of considerable importance.
- ◆ Lunchtime specials for organised parties of people with disabilities from day-centres etc create the potential for large sales at otherwise slack times.
- ◆ Facilities suitable for people with disabilities will also attract two other customer groups: the elderly infirm; and patients released from hospitals with legs in plaster or other temporarily disabling conditions. These customers will also bring able-bodied companions. Community pubs which have installed facilities for people with disabilities find there is another important benefit: their reputation as a place of welcome for the whole community is enhanced.

The most obvious facilities for people with disabilities are wheelchair ramps and specially adapted lavatories. However, wheelchair users want to use all the pub's services so all areas and services should be accessible to them.

- ◆ Doors should be wide enough and free-swinging. Double

The Publican's Handbook

doors are ideal for external access.
- Aisles between seat-backs should be wide enough for wheelchairs.
- The bar and food servery should be low enough for wheelchair-users to use: they want to buy their round too. A shallow well behind the bar will save the staff's backs!
- The toilet should include a handbasin at suitable height with elbow taps.
- An ordinary toilet mounted on a concrete plinth is much, much cheaper than the tall-pedestal toilet needed by wheelchair-users, and just as effective.
- Make both of the toilet arms moveable: not all wheelchair-users are right-handed!
- If you have a tampon machine in the ladies' loo and a condom machine in the gents', install them in the disabled toilet as well: people with disabilities have the same needs as anyone else.
- Keep the access to the disabled toilet clear, and don't use the toilet itself as a cleaner's cupboard. People with disabilities want to feel wanted, not just 'catered for' as if they were some sort of after thought.

Remember too that wheelchair-users are not the only people with disabilities. Staff should be able to serve customers with varying degrees of hearing impairment: if you have a member of staff who can sign, so much the better; if not, at least train the staff not to keep saying 'eh?' and 'you what?' Smoke alarms should have a built-in strobe light to help the hearing impaired.

Braille menus for sight-impaired customers can normally be made up locally for a nominal charge. Emergency lighting should have extra-strength bulbs.

Staff should be prepared to serve half-pints in pint glasses to customers with Parkinson's or other tremors or spasms without crass jokes about long pulls. Staff should not gawp at customers with facial injuries or deformities; if staff set the tone, other customers will soon follow.

Essentially, offering a welcome to customers with disabilities is no more than an extension of the kind of mentality a successful publican will possess anyway: a mentality which considers what people want and need in order to have a good time, and a willingness to provide it.

Advice on making alterations is available from the local council's Social Services Department. However, publicans who wish to get on with it are advised not to wait for grants which may or may not be available and which usually come with strings. Alterations need not cost more than £1,000, and can cost much less if the publican is a handyman able to install ramps etc himself.

A pub with facilities for people with disabilities is not the same thing as a pub for people with disabilities: it is a pub for everyone.

APPENDIX THREE

USEFUL PHONE NUMBERS & ADDRESSES

Academy of Food & Wine Service
Burgoyne House
8 Lower Teddington Road
Kingston
Surrey KT1 4ER
Tel: 0181 943 1011
Fax: 0181 977 5519

ACAS
Clifton House
83-117 Euston Road
London NW1 2RB
Tel: 0171 396 5100

Alliance of Independent Retailers
Alliance House
14 Pierpoint Street
Worcester
Worc WR1 1TA
Tel: 01905 612733
Fax: 01905 21501

Association of Licensed Free Traders
Dane House
55 London Road
St Albans
Herts AL1 1LJ
Tel: 01727 841644
Fax: 01727 852208

Association of Licensed Multiple Retailers
11 Fairway Drive
Greenford
Middx UB6 8PW
Tel: 0181 813 2800
Fax: 0181 575 8678

Brewers & Licensed Retailers Association
42 Portman Square
London W1H 0B
Tel: 0171 486 4831
Fax: 0171 935 3991

British Hospitality Association
Queens House
55-56 Lincolns Inn Fields
London WC2A 3BH
Tel: 0171 404 7744
Fax: 0171 404 7799

British Institute of Innkeeping
Wessex House
80 Park Street
Camberley
Surrey GU15 3PL
Tel: 01276 684449
Fax: 01276 23045

The Publican's Handbook

Business Link
Tel: 0800 50020

CAMRA
230 Hatfield Road
St Albans
Herts AL1 4LW
Tel: 01727 867201
Fax: 01727 867670

Catering Equipment Suppliers
Association
Carlyle House
235-237 Vauxhall Bridge Road
London SW1V 1EJ
Tel: 0171 233 7724
Fax: 0171 828 0667

Chartered Institute of Environmental
Health
Chadwick Court, 15 Hatfields
London SE1 8DJ
Tel: 0171 928 6006
Fax: 0171 827 5865

City & Guilds
1 Guiltspur Street
London EC1A 9DD
Tel: 0171 294 2468
Fax: 0171 294 2400

Confederation of Tourism, Hotel, &
Catering Management
204 Barnett Wood Lane
Ashtead
Surrey KT21 2DB
Tel: 01372 278 572

Cookery & Food Association
1 Victoria Parade
331 Sandycombe Road
Richmond
Surrey TW9 3NB
Tel: 0181 948 3870
Fax: 0181 332 6326

Paul Cooper
67 Front Street
Slip End
Luton LU1 4BP
Tel: 01582 424484

English Tourist Board
Thames Tower
Blacks Road
London W6 9EL
Tel: 0181 846 9000
Fax: 0181 563 0302

Federation of Licensed Victuallers
Associations
126 Bradford Road
Brighouse
West Yorks HD6 4AU
Tel: 01484 710534
Fax: 01484 718647

Federation of Retail Licensed Trade
91 University Street
Belfast
Northern Ireland BT7 1HP
Tel/Fax: 01232 327578

Fleurets
18 Bloomsbury Squre
London WC1A 2NS
Tel: 0171 636 8992
Fax: 0171 636 7490

Health & Safety Executive
Information Services
Broad Lane
Sheffield
South Yorks S3 7HQ
Tel: 0541 545500
Fax: 0114 289 2333

The Hospitality
Training Foundation
International House
3rd Floor
High Street
Ealing
London W5 3DB
Tel: 0181 579 2400
Fax: 0181 540 6217

Licensed Victuallers Trade
Association
(London & South-East)
The Royal Six Bells
22 High Street
Colliers Wood

Useful Phone Numbers & Addresses

London SW19 2BH
Tel: 0181 540 1275
Fax: 0181 540 2715

Licensed Victuallers Trade
Association (Midlands)
Larkfield
Ashlawn Road
Rugby CV22 5QE
Tel: 01788 553353
Fax: 01788 535626

Licensed Victuallers Trade
Association (West)
Lord Haldon Hotel
Dunchideock
Exeter EX6 7YF
Tel: 01392 832483
Fax: 01392 833765

Licensed Victuallers Wales
2 Derwendeg Station Road
Govilon
Abergavenny
Gwent NP7 9RG
Tel: 01873 830415

Office of Fair Trading
Field House
15-25 Breams Buildings
London EC4A 1PR
Tel: 0171 242 2858

Tony O'Reilly
317 Conniburrow Boulevard
Milton Keynes
MK14 7AF
Tel: 0402 293 360

Pannane & Partners
123 Deansgate
Manchester M3 2BU
Tel: 0161 832 3000
Fax: 0161 834 2067

Performing Right Society
29-33 Berners Street
London W1P 4AA
Tel: 0171 580 5544
Fax: 0171 306 4050

Royal Society for the Prevention of
Accidents
Edgbaston Park
353 Bristol Road
Birmingham
Midlands B5 7ST
Tel: 0121 248 2000
Fax: 0121 248 2001

Scottish Licensed Trade Association
10 Walker Street
Edinburgh
Scotland EH3 7LA
Tel: 0131 225 5169
Fax: 0131 220 4057

Scottish Tourist Board
23 Ravelston Terrace
Edinburgh
Scotland EH4 3EU
Tel: 0131 332 2433
Fax: 0131 343 1513

Wales Tourist Board
Brunel House
2 Fitzalan Road
Cardiff
Wales CF2 4AY
Tel: 01222 640456
Fax: 01222 640048

APPENDIX FOUR

CHECKLIST OF ESSENTIAL CONTACTS

Solicitor: _____

Accountant: _____

Financial Adviser: _____

Bank Manager: _____

VAT Inspector: _____

Local Council Environmental Health Dept: _____

Local Council Planning Dept: _____

Local Council Trading Standards Dept: _____

Police Licensing Officer: _____

Police Crime Prevention Officer: _____

Fire Safety Officer: _____

Licensing Justices Clerk: _____

INDEX

accomodation 213, 237-8, 242
accountants 10, 22, 182, 188
accounts 10, 11-12, 182, 184
added value 229
   brewing on site 236-7, 242
   consistency 241
   function rooms 229-32
   gardens 232-5
   letting rooms 237-8
   multiple use 235
   outside bars 236
   professional presentation 239-40
   sales opportunities 239
   seasonality 238-9
   stay ahead of competition 241
   trading patterns 240-1
Advanced Leadership and Motivation Certificate, BII 71
advertising 91, 94-5, 238, 240, 254
   see also publicity
advertorials 91
agents 7-10, 12, 184
alarms
   fire 214, 215
   intruder 200-1
alcohol-free drinks 53
alcopops 30
ales
   bottled 106
   India Pale Ales 106-7
   keg 103
   real 37, 102-3, 111, 112, 116-20
Alsace wines 138

American whiskies 149
American wines 139-40
Amusement Machine Licence Duty (AMLD) 195
amusement machines 189
   changing regularly 190-1
   importance 194-5
   legal requirements 195, 197
   maximising income 189-90, 195-6
   non-gambling 194
   operators 189-90
   rental prices 190
   security 191-4, 203
Apprenticeships, Modern 74
Argentinian wines 140
asbestos 126
Australian wines 140, 144
awards 96
AWPs *see* amusement machines

back fittings 29, 36, 37
bag snacks 26, 36, 223
banks 19, 20, 183, 184
bar stools 37-42
barbecues 167-73, 176, 234
Barcardi 152
barley wine 110
bars
   backs and counter tops 29-30
   children in 227-8
   design 26, 29
   displaying products 30-7

267

Index

equipment 37-44
  health and safety 48-52
  legally required notices 52-3
  outside 236
BCAs (bottle-conditioned ales) 106
bed and breakfast 237-8
beer 102
  at the bar 112-20
  bottled 103-8
  brewing on site 236, 242
  canned 106
  cellar management 110-12
  keg ales 103, 110
  measures 116, 128
  nitrokeg 103, 110
  real ales 37, 102-3, 111, 112, 116-20
  styles 106-10
Beer Orders 1990 6, 18, 112
Bergerac wines 135
betting shops 190
beverages, hot 36
BII *see* British Institute of Innkeeping
bitters 106, 116
blackboards 37
blended whisky 149
book-keeping 186-7
Bordeaux wines 134-5
bottled drinks 30-2, 103-8
breast-feeding 226-7
breweries 101
  and free houses 20
  and leases 6, 7, 18
  and tenancies 3, 6, 7
  and training 156
Brewery manual 7
brewing on site 236-7, 242
British Institute of Innkeeping (BII) 62
  advanced qualifications 65-7
  Certificate of Induction Examination 62-5
  Qualifying Examination 65
brown 110
Budweiser 110
building surveyors 13
Bulgarian wines 139
Burgundy wines 134
Business Development Certificate, BII 71
business plans 20, 184

Californian wines 140
cameras, security 202-3, 205, 206
CAMRA (Campaign for Real Ale) 101
canned beers 106
carbon dioxide 103, 111-2, 126
card games 99
cash 184-5, 201-2, 204
cash and carries 186
cashflow 20, 184
cask breathers 111-2
cask-conditioned ales *see* real ales
Caterer & Hotelkeeper 7
catering 155, 241
  barbecues 166-73, 176, 234
  children 222-3
  creativity 160
  dining areas 157
  free nibbles 166
  fresh versus convenience 160-1
  health and safety 48, 170-80
  lunches and dinners 157-60
  microwaves 161
  planning 156
  promotions 161-2
  staff 157, 176-7, 188
  Sundays 166
  supper hour certificates 181
  training 66, 72, 155-6
  vegetarians and vegans 162-6
Catering Management Certificate, BII 66
CCTV 205
cellar management 110-12, 121-6
Certificate of Induction Examination, BII 62-5
Champagne 134, 144
chemicals 126, 175, 177
children *see* family trade
Children's Certificates 219-20, 228
Chilean wines 140
chillers, eye-level 30
Christmas trade 238, 239
Christmas tree lights 32
cider 120-1, 236-7
cigarettes 25-6
Cinema Licence 242
cloudy pints 111
Cognac 152
computers 187
confectionery 26, 223-5
conferences 230

268

Index

contracts of employment 76-7
Contributions Agency 187
Control of Substances Hazardous to Health Regulations (COSHH) 1994 89, 126, 177
convenience foods 160-1
Côte du Rhone wines 135
counter tops 29
credit cards 183
cribbage 99
customer areas 52
Customs & Excise 183, 186, 195

daily routine 2-3
Dalton's Weekly 7
dark rum 152
darts 254
deliveries and collections 126, 185
dessert wines 147
dining areas 157
dinners 160
Disability Discrimination Act 1995 77, 78
discounts 186, 188
discrimination 77, 78, 85
dismissals, staff 85-7
dogs 203-4
dominoes 99, 254
doormen 207-9, 209-10
doors 200, 215
draught lagers 103
drinks 101-2
  for children 223
  display 30-6
  see also beer; wine etc.
drugs 206, 207

EHOs (environmental health officers) 87, 174, 177
Electricity at Work Regulations 1989 89
Electronic Data Capture (EDC) 191
employees *see* staff
Employers Liability (Compulsory Insurance) Regulations 1969 89
Employment Rights Act 1996 76, 79
entertainment, live 98, 231, 251-4
Environmental Protection Act 1990 99
EPOS till system 185

equal opportunities 78-9
extinguishers, fire 215
extensions 243
extortion 205-7

family trade 219-21
  breast-feeding 226-7
  children in the bar 227-8
  food and drinks 222-5
  play equipment 225-6, 227
  suitability for 221-2
  toilets 226
finance 20-2, 182-3
  maximising profits 187-8
  for purchase of pub 18-20, 183-4
  records and book-keeping 186-7
  stock and cash control 184-5
  suppliers 185-6
Financial Management Certificate, BII 66-7
fire certificates 213
Fire Precautions Act 1971 213
fire safety 211-12, 216-17
  basic requirements 214-15
  improving 212-13
  legislation 213-14, 217, 237
  letting rooms 213, 237, 242
  saving yourself 216
  when the alarm sounds 215-16
First Aid at Work Regulations 1992 89
fonts, branded 30
food
  safety 48, 53, 174, 177, 180
  see also catering
Food Premises (Registrations) Regulations 1991 180
Food Safety Act 1990 177
Food Safety (General Food Hygiene) Regulations 1995 48, 53, 174, 242
Food Safety (Temperature Control) Regulations 1995 48, 176
fortified wines 144-7
free houses 6-7, 7-10, 10-11, 12-13, 19-20
French brandy 152
French wines 133-8
fresh foods 160-1
fridges 30, 32

269

Index

frozen foods 160-1
function rooms 229-32

games 254-8
gaming 99-100, 197
Gaming Act 1968 197
gardens 173, 232-5
Gas Safety (Installation and Use) Regulations 1994 89
German wines 138
gin 152
Girobank 183
glassware 42
    beer and cider 120, 128
    collection 30
glasswashers 42-4
grain whisky 149
gravity dispense 37, 120
green beer 114
guard dogs 203-4
guest ales 101, 112-16
guide books 96, 238

hand pumps (pulls) 29-30, 112, 116
health and safety
    catering 48, 174-80
    cellars 121-6
    customer areas 52
    play areas 227
    risk assessement 48-52
    staff 87-90
    see also fire safety
Health and Safety at Work Act 1974 88
Health and Safety (Consultation with Employees) Regulations 1996 90
Health and Safety (Information for Employees) Regulations 1989 89-90
Health and Safety (Young Persons) Regulations 1997 90
heat detectors 214
hours of work 79-80
Hungarian wines 139
hygiene 48, 53, 174-7

ice 48, 153
ice beers 103
impulse purchases 36

India Pale Ales (IPA) 107-10
Inland Revenue 183, 186-7, 188
insurance 183
interviews, staff 77-8
Irish whiskeys 149
Italian wines 138-9

job descriptions 77
journalists 92-3
juke boxes 251

keg ales 103

lagers 103, 106, 110
    bottled 30, 103
leases 6, 10-11, 12-13, 18-19, 183
Licencee, The 7
licences 23
    entertainment 197, 254
Licensing Act 1964 210, 243
Liebfraumilch 138
lighting 202, 234, 240
limited companies 182
liqueurs 152-3
live entertainment 98, 231, 251-4
loans 18-19, 20, 184
Local Government (Miscellaneous Provisions) Acts 174, 208
lotteries 99
low-alcohol drinks 53
lunches 157-60, 166

machines *see* amusement machines
Malaga (wine) 147
malt whisky 148-9, 152
managed houses 3, 7, 10, 12
Management of Health and Safety at Work Regulations 1992 88, 90
managers 2-3
Manual Handling Operations Regulations 1992 89, 121
market research 13-18, 156
Marsala 147
matches 26
measures
    beer and cider 116, 128
    spirits 154
    wines 147-8, 154
media *see* publicity
meetings rooms 230

Index

menus 156, 222
microwaves 161
milds 106
milk-based drinks 223
minerals 32
mixed gas beer 103
Montilla 145-6
mortgage brokers 12, 20-2
Muscadet 135-8
music 98, 240, 250-1

National Insurance 90, 183, 187
National Licensee's Certificate (NLC) 62-5
new products display 36-7
New Zealand wines 140-4
news releases 92-6
nibbles, free 166
nitrokeg beer 103
noise 99, 177-80
Northern ales 116
Northern bitters 116
nuisances 99, 177-80
NVQs (National Vocational Qualifications) 72-5, 155

Occasional Licence 242-3
odours, cooking 180
Offices, Shops and Railway Premises Act 1963 90
Offices, Shops and Railway Premises (Lift and Hoists) Regulations 1968 121
Optics 32-6
outside bars 236

paint, anti-climb 202
papers, local 92, 98
part-time staff 85
partnerships 182-3
PAYE 90, 183, 186-7
payouts (machines) 189-90
Performing Rights Society 254
Personal Protective Equipment at Work Regulations 1992 89
Phonographic Performance Ltd 254
Pilsners 110
plants 234
play areas 225-6, 227
Point of Sale (PoS) 32, 240
pool 194, 230, 258

port 146-7
porters 107
post offices 183
PR (public relations) *see* publicity
price lists 128
Price Marketing (Food and Drink on Premises) Order 1979 128
prices 241
private parties 231
profit and loss accounts 10, 184
profits 187-8
promotions *see* publicity
prostitution 204-5
Provision and Use of Work Equipment Regulations 1992 89
PubCos 6, 7
Public Entertainment Licences 52, 197, 254
Publican 7
publicity 91, 232, 238
    catering promotions 161-2
    contacting the media 92-6
    news value 91-2
    planning and targeting 92
    pro-active 96-8
    see also advertising
pubs
    appropriateness 13-18
    assessing 10-12
    business plans and advice 20-2
    financing cost 18-20, 183-4
    finding 10-12
    other considerations 22-4
    the right price 12-13
    trading information 11-12
    types 3-7
pumps 29-30, 112, 116, 120

Qualifying Examination, BII 65
quiz nights 254

radio, local 92, 98
raffles 99
rates, business 188
real ales 37, 102-3, 111, 112, 116-20
refuse 180
Reporting of Injuries, Diseases and Dangerous Occurences Regulations (RIDDOR) 1995 88-9

Index

rinse aid 42, 44
Rioja 139
risk assessment
    fire 242
    health and safety 48-52, 88, 90
    security 199-200
Romanian wines 139
rooms, letting 213, 237-8, 242
rum 152

safes 201-2
safety *see* fire safety; health and safety
Safety Representatives and Safety Committee Regulations 1977 90
salaries, staff 79, 187, 188
satellite television 250
Section 34 permits 195, 197
security 198-200, 209, 210
    alarms 200-1
    amusement machines 191-4, 203
    anti-climb paint 202
    cameras 202-3, 205, 206
    cash 204
    doormen 207-9, 209-10
    drugs 206, 207
    extortion 205-7
    front door 200
    guard dogs 203-4
    letting rooms 237
    lighting 202
    prostitution 204-5
    safes 201-2
    stock 184-5
    tackling violence 205
servery *see* bars
Sherry 144-6
shops, pubs with 235
single-malt whisky 148
smells, cooking 180
smoke detectors 214
snacks, bag 26, 36, 223
soft drinks 32, 223
sole traders 182
solicitors 22, 182, 188
South African wines 144
Spanish wines 139
sparkling wines 144
Special Orders of Exemption 243
speciality beers 107-10, 110
spirits 148, 152
    display 32-6
    liqueurs and speciality 152-3
    measures 154
    presentation 153
    whiskies 148-52
sports 254-8
sports drinks 223
staff 2, 61-2, 240
    catering 157, 176-7
    contracts of employment 76-7
    dismissals 85-7
    equal opportunities 78-9
    health and safety 48, 87-90, 174-80
    illegal workers 79
    part-time 85
    recruitment 77-8
    and take-overs 80-5
    training 215, 239
    wages 79, 187, 188
    working hours 79-80
stock control 184-5, 187, 239
stocktakers 10, 22, 185
stout 106
Sunday lunches 166
Supper Hour Certificates 181
suppliers 185-6
surveyors 13
SVQs (Scottish Vocational Qualifications) 72, 155
sweets 26, 223-5
SWPs *see* amusement machines

T-bars 30
table wines 135, 147
tax 186, 187
television 231, 245-50
tenancies 3-6, 7, 10, 12, 18
tenancy brokers 7, 10
tied loans 20, 101
tills 185
tobacco products 25-6
toilets 174, 226
Town and Country Planning 23
trading patterns 240-1
training 60-1
    BII qualifications 62-7
    catering 155-6
    necessary knowledge 61-2
    NVQs 72-5
    staff 239

Index

working part-time 1-2
Transfer of Undertakings (Protection of Employment) Regulations 80-5
turnover 11
TV 231, 245-50

valuers 10, 12, 18
VAT 11, 183, 186
vatted malt whisky 149
vegetarians and vegans 162-6
video games 194
Video Performance Limited Licence 242
violence, tackling 205
vodka 152

wages, staff 79, 187, 188
water softeners 44
weddings 231
wet sales 101-2, 188
  see also beer; wines etc.

whiskies 148
  retailing 149-152
  types 148-9
white rum 152
Wine Retail Certificate, BII 71
wines 133-4
  the Americas 139-40
  Australia, New Zealand and South Africa 140-4
  Central and Eastern Europe 139
  display 36
  fortified 144-7
  French 133-8
  German 138
  Italian 138-9
  measures 147-8, 154
  serving 147
  Spanish 139
  sparkling 144
Workplace Health Safety and Welfare Regulations 1992 89

273

INDEX OF ADVERTISERS

Abbots Coffee Co 181 225
Active Solutions Ltd 165
Adnams Brewers 128
Air Products Plc 127
Anchor Fast Products 233
Associated Video 246 249
Bar Equipment & Refrigeration 27
Bass Brewers vi, 122–3
BB Supply Centre Ltd 117-19
Berentzen 154
Berrymans 125
BHMA 97
BOC Gases Europe 31, 33–35
British Sky Broadcasting 247
BT Payphones 28
Carlsberg Tetley 113-15
Chadburns Ltd 38-9
Cinders Barbeques Ltd 158
Claremont Automatics 193
Coatings Solutions 59
Dairy Farm Products 165
Daltons Weekly 14-5
DiverseyLever OBC
Durex Vending Services 39
Everards Brewery 21
Frederic Robinson Ltd 108-9
Fujitsu General UK Co Ltd 40-1, 43
German Wine Information Service 136-7
Gordons Gin 150-1
Guy Simmonds 64
Hardy & Hansons 100, 109
Honeywell 45-7

Hoshizaki IFC, 49-51
HP Food Services 170-2
Inn Accounting Services 81-2
Inn Pro 70
Inn Relief Services 83-4
IPH Group 192
Jaymart Rubber & Plastics Ltd x, xviii, xix
Jeffrey Green Russell 15-7
Karaoke UK 251-3
King Production 167-9
KP Foods Ltd 178-9
Leisure Business Services 73-4
Maxivideo Advanced Services 246
Mayfair Services 195
Mayfair Taverns xx
Mermaid Industries Ltd 104
Mirus Group Ltd 124
Morland Plc 67-9
Natco's 159
Original Leisure 63-4
Pete's Wicked 104
The Play Company 225
Playquest UK 224
PRS 244, 255-7
The Publican Newspaper, ii
Pubmaster 4-5
Read World of Wine 141-3
SF Leisure 218
Satelliet 58
Satvision Insatcom Ltd 246
Savills License Retail 8-9
Scandafloor Ltd 45

Index of Advertisers

Seafish Authority 163-5
Servaclean Bar Systems 54-7
Shackleford Sales Ltd 105
Swaffham Discount Carpets 39
Tavern Ltd 129-31
Thoroughbred Productions 196-7

United Distillers 132
Viscount Catering 158
Vision Projection Systems Ltd 248-9
VMS Ltd 249
Westminster College 59, 64, 97